Microsoft® Office Excel® 2016: Part 1 (Desktop/ Office 365™)

Microsoft® Office Excel® 2016: Part 1 (Desktop/Office 365™)

Part Number: 091055
Course Edition: 3.1

Acknowledgements

PROJECT TEAM

Author	Media Designer	Content Editor
Jason Nufryk	Brian Sullivan	Michelle Farney

Logical Operations wishes to thank the Logical Operations Instructor Community, and in particular Mickey Curry, Dawn Hunter, Gary Leenhouts, Carol Marion, and Elizabeth Robinson, for their instructional and technical expertise during the creation of this course.

Notices

DISCLAIMER

TRADEMARK NOTICES

Microsoft® Office Excel® 2016: Part 1 (Desktop/ Office 365™)

About This Course

Organizations the world over rely on information to make sound decisions regarding all manner of affairs. But with the amount of available data growing on a daily basis, the ability to make sense of all of that data is becoming more and more challenging. Fortunately, this is where the power of Microsoft® Office Excel® 2016 can help. Excel can help you organize, calculate, analyze, revise, update, and present your data in ways that will help the decision makers in your organization steer you in the right direction. It will also make these tasks much easier for you to accomplish, and in much less time, than if you used traditional pen-and-paper methods or non-specialized software. This course aims to provide you with a foundation for Excel knowledge and skills, which you can build upon to eventually become an expert in data manipulation.

This course covers Microsoft Office Specialist exam objectives to help students prepare for the Excel 2016 Exam and the Excel 2016 Expert Exam.

Course Description

Target Student

This course is intended for students who wish to gain the foundational understanding of Microsoft Office Excel 2016 that is necessary to create and work with electronic spreadsheets.

Course Prerequisites

To ensure success, students will need to be familiar with using personal computers and should have experience using a keyboard and mouse. Students should also be comfortable working in the Windows® 10 environment and be able to use Windows 10 to manage information on their computers. Specific tasks the students should be able to perform include: opening and closing applications, navigating basic file structures, and managing files and folders. To obtain this level of skill and knowledge, you can take either one of the following Logical Operations courses:

- *Using Microsoft® Windows® 10*
- *Microsoft® Windows® 10: Transition from Windows® 7*

Course Objectives

Upon successful completion of this course, you will be able to create and develop Excel worksheets and workbooks in order to work with and analyze the data that is critical to the success of your organization.

You will:

- Get started with Microsoft Office Excel 2016.
- Perform calculations.

- Modify a worksheet.
- Format a worksheet.
- Print workbooks.
- Manage workbooks.

The CHOICE Home Screen

Logon and access information for your CHOICE environment will be provided with your class experience. The CHOICE platform is your entry point to the CHOICE learning experience, of which this course manual is only one part.

On the CHOICE Home screen, you can access the CHOICE Course screens for your specific courses. Visit the CHOICE Course screen both during and after class to make use of the world of support and instructional resources that make up the CHOICE experience.

Each CHOICE Course screen will give you access to the following resources:

- **Classroom:** A link to your training provider's classroom environment.
- **eBook:** An interactive electronic version of the printed book for your course.
- **Files:** Any course files available to download.
- **Checklists:** Step-by-step procedures and general guidelines you can use as a reference during and after class.
- **LearnTOs:** Brief animated videos that enhance and extend the classroom learning experience.
- **Assessment:** A course assessment for your self-assessment of the course content.
- Social media resources that enable you to collaborate with others in the learning community using professional communications sites such as LinkedIn or microblogging tools such as Twitter.

Depending on the nature of your course and the components chosen by your learning provider, the CHOICE Course screen may also include access to elements such as:

- LogicalLABS, a virtual technical environment for your course.
- Various partner resources related to the courseware.
- Related certifications or credentials.
- A link to your training provider's website.
- Notices from the CHOICE administrator.
- Newsletters and other communications from your learning provider.
- Mentoring services.

Visit your CHOICE Home screen often to connect, communicate, and extend your learning experience!

How to Use This Book

As You Learn

This book is divided into lessons and topics, covering a subject or a set of related subjects. In most cases, lessons are arranged in order of increasing proficiency.

The results-oriented topics include relevant and supporting information you need to master the content. Each topic has various types of activities designed to enable you to solidify your understanding of the informational material presented in the course. Information is provided for reference and reflection to facilitate understanding and practice.

Data files for various activities as well as other supporting files for the course are available by download from the CHOICE Course screen. In addition to sample data for the course exercises, the course files may contain media components to enhance your learning and additional reference materials for use both during and after the course.

Checklists of procedures and guidelines can be used during class and as after-class references when you're back on the job and need to refresh your understanding.

At the back of the book, you will find a glossary of the definitions of the terms and concepts used throughout the course. You will also find an index to assist in locating information within the instructional components of the book.

As You Review

Any method of instruction is only as effective as the time and effort you, the student, are willing to invest in it. In addition, some of the information that you learn in class may not be important to you immediately, but it may become important later. For this reason, we encourage you to spend some time reviewing the content of the course after your time in the classroom.

As a Reference

The organization and layout of this book make it an easy-to-use resource for future reference. Taking advantage of the glossary, index, and table of contents, you can use this book as a first source of definitions, background information, and summaries.

Course Icons

Watch throughout the material for the following visual cues.

Icon	Description
	A **Note** provides additional information, guidance, or hints about a topic or task.
	A **Caution** note makes you aware of places where you need to be particularly careful with your actions, settings, or decisions so that you can be sure to get the desired results of an activity or task.
	LearnTO notes show you where an associated LearnTO is particularly relevant to the content. Access LearnTOs from your CHOICE Course screen.
	Checklists provide job aids you can use after class as a reference to perform skills back on the job. Access checklists from your CHOICE Course screen.
	Social notes remind you to check your CHOICE Course screen for opportunities to interact with the CHOICE community using social media.

1 | Getting Started with Microsoft Office Excel 2016

Lesson Time: 1 hour, 30 minutes

Lesson Introduction

You want to use Microsoft® Office Excel® 2016 to store and analyze data for your organization, but you're new to Excel and it's hard to know where to begin. In order to take advantage of everything Excel has to offer, you must first understand the "lay of the land." How do you interact with Excel? What, exactly, can it do? How do you get Excel to do these things for you? It is precisely these types of questions this lesson aims to answer.

Like many Microsoft Office applications, Excel has a standard layout that provides you with access to all of the commands, work areas, options, and settings you will need to begin developing and using electronic worksheets in your day-to-day life. Taking the time to become familiar with Excel's layout, its various parts, its commands, and its terminology is a critical first step toward your goal of storing and analyzing organizational data.

Lesson Objectives

In this lesson, you will:

- Navigate the Excel user interface.

- Use Excel commands.

- Create and save a basic workbook.

- Enter cell data.

- Use Excel Help.

TOPIC A

Navigate the Excel User Interface

Before you can effectively use Excel 2016 to store and manage your data, you need to become familiar with the application's environment. Specifically, you need to be able to locate and identify key components of Excel on its user interface. In this topic, you'll examine Excel's interface, including its various commands and options, so that you can quickly and efficiently work with your data in the ways you see fit.

Microsoft Office Excel 2016

Microsoft Office Excel 2016 is an application that is part of the Microsoft Office 2016 suite of user productivity software. Excel is a powerful electronic spreadsheet program that allows you to store, present, manipulate, and analyze a number of different types of data. Excel's functionality enables you to work with and analyze massive amounts of raw data in order to obtain actionable organizational intelligence. This intelligence will help you make sound decisions to improve any number of business and organizational operations.

Figure 1-1: Microsoft Office Excel 2016.

 Note: Excel Online App

In addition to the Excel 2016 desktop application, you also have access to the Excel Online app through your Office 365™ subscription. Throughout this course, you will see notes that identify any significant differences between the desktop application and the online app.

Office Online Apps

When you purchase an Office 365 subscription, you also have access to the Office Online apps, which include Excel, Microsoft® Word, Microsoft® PowerPoint®, Microsoft® Outlook®, and a variety of other apps. You can use any web browser to access Office 365 by navigating to **login.microsoftonline.com** and signing in with your Office 365 user account and password. These online apps are scaled-down versions of the Office 2016 desktop applications and provide basic features and some of the same functionality that exists in the desktop applications. The advantage of using the Office Online apps is the ability to access, edit, share, and store your online files across a variety of devices.

Spreadsheets, Worksheets, and Workbooks

A *spreadsheet* is simply a paper or an electronic document, arranged in tabular form, that is used to store, manipulate, and analyze data. A *worksheet* is an electronic spreadsheet that is used for entering, storing, and analyzing data in Excel. Think of worksheets as individual pages within Excel that display and allow you to work with your data.

A *workbook* is an Excel file that serves as a container to store related Excel worksheets. If you apply the individual page analogy to the workbook as well, the worksheets are the individual pages, whereas the workbook is the binding that holds the pages together. The default number of worksheets in a new Excel 2016 workbook is one. You can add or remove worksheets to suit your needs and you can name, rename, and rearrange the order of worksheets in a workbook. The number of worksheets that a workbook can contain is limited by your computer's available memory.

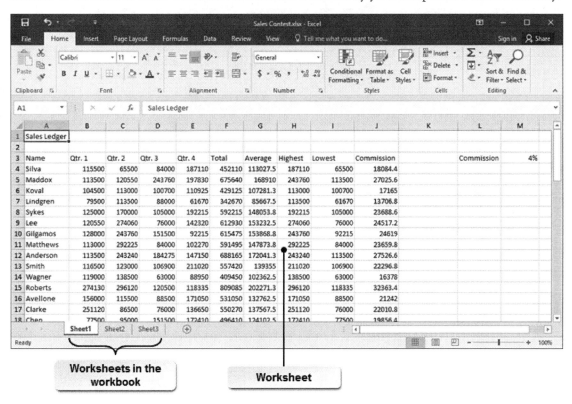

Figure 1–2: Excel workbooks act like binders for related worksheets.

Cells and Ranges

An Excel worksheet is arranged in a tabular format, meaning it consists of a series of columns and rows that intersect to form cells. A *cell* is a singular container that you can use to input and store data. Each individual rectangle that you see on an Excel worksheet is a separate cell.

In Excel, a *range* is a group of cells that typically contains related data. A range can consist of an entire row or column, a group of cells in a row or column, or a group of cells that covers multiple rows and columns. You can use ranges to organize your worksheets by related sets of data.

Cell

	A	B	C	D	E	F
1	**Employee Name**	**Region**	**Qtr. 1**	**Qtr. 2**	**Qtr. 3**	**Qtr. 4**
2	Silva	Northeast	$115,500	$65,500	$84,000	$187,110
3	Maddox	Northeast	$113,500	$120,550	$243,760	$197,830
4	Koval	Southwest	$104,500	$113,000	$100,700	$110,925
5	Lindgren	South	$79,500	$113,500	$88,000	$61,670
6	Sykes	North	$125,000	$170,000	$105,000	$192,215

	A	B	C	D	E	F
1	**Employee Name**	**Region**	**Qtr. 1**	**Qtr. 2**	**Qtr. 3**	**Qtr. 4**
2	Silva	Northeast	$115,500	$65,500	$84,000	$187,110
3	Maddox	Northeast	$113,500	$120,550	$243,760	$197,830
4	Koval	Southwest	$104,500	$113,000	$100,700	$110,925
5	Lindgren	South	$79,500	$113,500	$88,000	$61,670
6	Sykes	North	$125,000	$170,000	$105,000	$192,215

Range

Figure 1-3: Cells and a range on an Excel worksheet.

Cell Regions

You may also come across the term *region* in reference to worksheet cells. A region is simply a group of contiguous, populated cells. A region is different from a range because a range can, technically, contain blank cells, rows, or columns; a region does not.

Cell and Range References

In Excel, cells are identified by using *cell references*. Think of a cell reference as the name of a cell, used to differentiate it from among the other cells on a worksheet. A cell reference consists of a letter and a number. The letter refers to the *column headers* in Excel, whereas the number refers to the *row headers*. So, the cell on a worksheet that is located at the intersection of column C and row 5 has the cell reference C5.

Column headers are displayed along the top of an Excel worksheet and are used to differentiate individual columns. Column headers begin with the letter A for the first column, and run through the course of the entire alphabet. After Z, column headers continue with AA through AZ. After AZ comes BA through BZ, and so on. Row headers are displayed along the left side of an Excel worksheet and are used to differentiate individual rows. Row headers begin at 1 and increase sequentially.

 Note: In Excel 2016, a worksheet can contain up to 16,384 columns and 1,048,576 rows. The last possible cell reference in an Excel worksheet is XFD1048576.

You will use *range references* to identify particular ranges of data in your worksheets. A range reference consists of two cell references separated by a colon. The first cell reference identifies the top-leftmost cell in a range; the second cell reference identifies the bottom-rightmost cell in a range. So, for example, the range of cells that includes the first five rows in columns A through D is A1:D5.

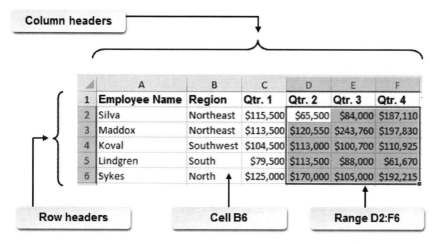

Figure 1-4: Use column and row headers to define cell and range references.

The Excel UI

The Excel user interface (UI) contains all of the workspaces and commands that you will use to create and work with workbooks and worksheets. The general areas along the top and bottom of the Excel UI contain elements that display information about the current workbook and provide you with access to some of the more commonly used commands and tools.

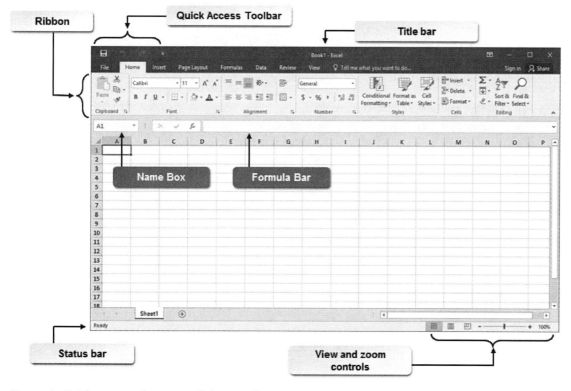

Figure 1-5: The outer elements of the Excel UI.

The following table describes the functions of the outer elements of the Excel UI.

Excel UI Element	Description
Title bar	Displays the workbook file name.

Excel UI Element	Description
Quick Access Toolbar	Provides you with easy access to commonly used Excel commands, such as **Save**, **Undo**, and **Redo**. You can customize the **Quick Access Toolbar** to suit your needs.
Ribbon	Provides you with access to the most commonly used commands for working with Excel workbooks and worksheets. The ribbon is organized into a series of tabs, each containing groups of related commands. You can customize the ribbon to suit your needs.
Formula Bar	Displays the contents of the currently selected cell in a worksheet. You can also use the **Formula Bar** to edit cell contents.
Name Box	Displays the cell reference for the currently selected cell, or the cell reference of the active cell in the currently selected range. The **Name Box** can also display custom range names and can be used to navigate to a particular cell.
Status bar	Displays the status of various conditions pertinent to Excel, such as the mode of the active cell, and whether or not **Caps Lock** or **Number Lock** is enabled. You can customize what information is displayed on the status bar.
View and zoom controls	Provide you with quick access to commands that change the current workbook view and change the magnification level of the displayed worksheet.

> **Note: Excel Online App**
>
> From the list of elements in the previous table, three elements are not included in the Excel Online app: the **Quick Access Toolbar**, the view and zoom controls, and the **Name Box** for defining and navigating to named ranges.

The inner part of the Excel UI displays your workbook and worksheet contents and some common navigation controls to help you locate and work with data.

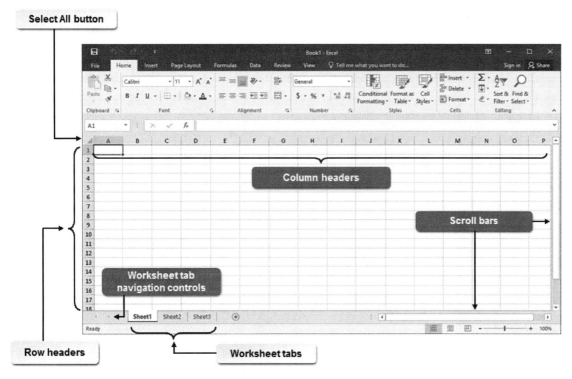

Figure 1-6: The inner elements of the Excel UI.

The following table describes the various elements of the inner portion of the Excel UI.

Excel UI Element	Description
Column headers	Identify each separate column with a unique letter or letter combination.
Row headers	Identify each separate row with a unique number.
Select All button	Selects all cells in the worksheet.
Scroll bars	Navigate vertically and horizontally across worksheets.
Worksheet tab navigation controls	Navigate among the various worksheets within a workbook.
Worksheet tabs	Open a particular worksheet within a workbook. You can also use worksheet tabs to name, rename, and arrange worksheets, and you can apply certain formatting options to the tabs.
New sheet button	Adds a blank worksheet to the workbook.

Each workbook file that you open simultaneously appears within its own instance of the Excel user interface, and each window displays the same commands and workspaces. You can open as many simultaneous instances of workbooks as your computer's memory can support.

Note: Excel Online App

With the exception of the **Select All** button, all of the other elements in the inner portion of the Excel user interface are also included in Excel Online. If you want to select all of the data in an online worksheet, select the first cell, press **Ctrl+Spacebar** and then press **Shift+Spacebar**.

Note: If you would like more information about the Excel 2016 user interface, access the LearnTO **Navigate the Microsoft Excel 2016 Interface** presentation from the **LearnTO** tile on the CHOICE Course screen.

Excel Window Commands

You can resize the Excel UI to better fit your computer screen and modify the general display setting for the ribbon by using the Excel window commands in the top-right corner of the UI. You can also close the Excel 2016 application from here.

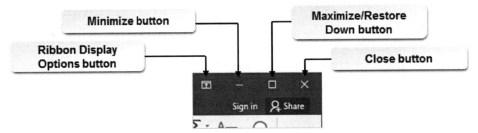

Figure 1–7: The Excel window commands.

The following table describes the functions of the Excel window commands.

Command	Enables You To
Minimize button	Hide the entire Excel 2016 UI. The application remains open, however, and the **Excel 2016** icon still appears on the Windows® taskbar.
Maximize/Restore Down button	Reduce the size of the Excel UI from full screen to a smaller sized window, or maximize a smaller window back to full screen. When the window is reduced in size, you can drag the bottom-right corner of the UI to resize the Excel window to suit your needs.
Close button	Close the currently selected workbook. If there is only one Excel workbook file open when you select the **Close** button, the entire application closes, too.
Ribbon Display Options button	Change how Excel displays the ribbon in the UI. You have the following three options: • **Auto-hide Ribbon**: This option hides the ribbon entirely until you select the top of the Excel UI. Once displayed, the ribbon remains visible until you select something outside of it. • **Show Tabs**: This option hides the ribbon groups and commands, but leaves the ribbon tabs visible. The command groups and commands appear when you select a ribbon tab and disappear again when you select an item outside the ribbon. • **Show Tabs and Commands**: This is the default ribbon display option, which leaves the entire ribbon on screen at all times.

The Backstage View

The *Backstage view* appears when you select the **File** tab on the ribbon. Along the left pane in the **Backstage** view, Excel displays a series of commands and tabs that enable you to save and access Excel workbooks, as well as work with your Excel files and configure Excel application options. Common tasks you may perform in the **Backstage** view include previewing and printing workbooks, saving and accessing Excel files, applying security options, and sharing workbooks with colleagues. You can exit the **Backstage** view by selecting the **Back** button ⬅ at the top of the left pane.

Note: In earlier versions of Excel, it was easier to distinguish the commands from the tabs in the **Backstage** view. In Excel 2016, however, tabs and commands have the same appearance.

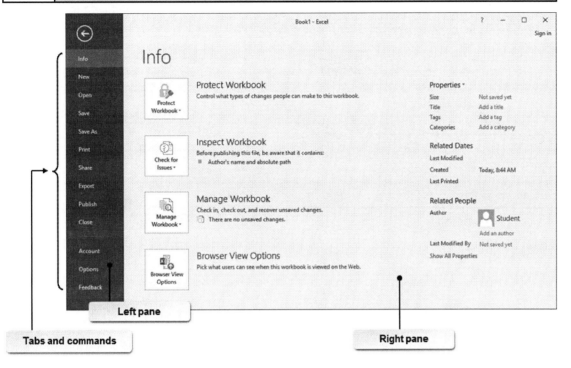

Figure 1-8: The Excel 2016 Backstage view.

The following table describes the various elements of the Excel **Backstage** view.

Backstage View Element	Description
Left pane	Displays the file commands and the various **Backstage** view tabs.
File commands	Enable you to open, close, and save your Excel workbook files.
Tabs	Provide you with access to commands for working with your Excel workbooks and various options for configuring the Excel environment.
Right pane	Displays various commands and options for working with your Excel workbook files depending on the tab you select in the left pane.

 Note: Excel Online App

The structure of the **Backstage** view in Excel Online is the same as described in the previous table; however, the significant difference is the absence of the **Save** and **Close** commands. When you work in any of the Office Online apps, your files are stored in your OneDrive® account and automatically updated and saved whenever you make a change. When you close the browser window, the file is closed. OneDrive is discussed more throughout the course.

 Access the Checklist tile on your CHOICE Course screen for reference information and job aids on How to Open Workbooks.

Mouse Navigation

As with many Microsoft Office applications, Excel 2016 provides you with a number of options for performing the same task. This is no different for navigating your worksheets and workbooks. One of the most basic methods you will use to navigate your workbooks and worksheets is to use the mouse.

 Note: This content assumes the use of a desktop computer, a laptop computer, or a touchscreen device with a mouse attached. As touchscreen devices are becoming commonplace, you may find yourself using Excel 2016 on a touchscreen device without a mouse. Consult your device's operation manual for common equivalents to mouse-click commands.

The following table describes some of the most commonly used mouse navigation techniques within Excel 2016.

Navigation Option	Mouse Command
Select a particular cell.	Select the desired cell.
Select a range of cells.	Click and drag to select the desired range of cells.
Select an entire column or row.	Select the desired column or row header.
Move the worksheet display up or down by a single row.	Select one of the vertical scroll arrows.
Move the worksheet display left or right by a single column.	Select one of the horizontal scroll arrows.
Move the worksheet display by more than one row or column at a time.	Click and drag the vertical or horizontal scroll bars to the desired view.
Move the worksheet display one screen at a time.	On the vertical scroll bar, select the area between the scroll bar and the desired direction's scroll arrow.
Display a different worksheet.	Select the desired worksheet tab along the bottom of the *workbook window*.

Mouse Cursor Icons

In Excel, your mouse cursor will change its icon based on the current context and/or location. As you navigate or manipulate a worksheet with the mouse, pay attention to the mouse cursor icon so you can be certain about the action you're about to perform.

 Note: Some concepts in this table, such as AutoFit and AutoFill, will be discussed later in the course.

The following table describes some of most common mouse cursor icons in Excel.

Icon	Cursor Context/Location	Description
▷	Placed on ribbon tabs or commands, **Backstage** tabs or commands, **Quick Access Toolbar** commands, scroll bars, sheet tabs and navigation commands, and view and zoom controls.	Select an element to perform the associated action.

Icon	Cursor Context/Location	Description
	Placed at any edge of a cell or range of cells.	Drag a cell or range of cells to move the data inside to another cell or range.
	Placed over a cell in a worksheet.	Select an individual cell, or drag to select a range of cells.
	Placed between worksheet column headers.	Resize the column to the left of the cursor, or double-click to AutoFit the column to the left of the cursor.
	Placed between worksheet row headers.	Resize the row above the cursor, or double-click to AutoFit the column above the cursor.
I	Placed inside an active cell, the **Formula Bar**, or various text boxes.	Select inside a text box or the **Formula Bar** to begin typing data into it. Or, double-click an active cell to do likewise.
+	Placed at the bottom-right corner of a cell or range of cells.	Drag vertically or horizontally to copy or AutoFill data into adjacent cells.

Keyboard Navigation

Excel 2016 also provides you with a number of options for navigating your workbooks and worksheets using keyboard commands.

 Note: This content assumes the use of a desktop computer, a laptop computer, or the use of a touchscreen device with an attached keyboard. If you are using Excel 2016 on an exclusively touchscreen device, consult your device's operation manual or support material to determine if these keyboard navigation options will work or if there are equivalent commands.

The following table describes some of the most commonly used keyboard navigation techniques in Excel 2016.

Navigation Option	Keyboard Command
Move one cell up, down, left, or right from the currently selected cell.	Press the **Up**, **Down**, **Left**, or **Right** arrow key.
Move to the cell in column A of the current row.	Press the **Home** key.
Move to the first or last column or row of data.	Press and hold down the **Ctrl** key, and then press the **Up**, **Down**, **Left**, or **Right** arrow key.
Scroll up or down by one screen.	Press the **Page Up** or the **Page Down** key.

Navigation Option	Keyboard Command
Scroll left or right by one screen.	Press **Alt+Page Up** or **Alt+Page Down**.
Move one cell to the right.	Press the **Tab** key. This will also enter any data you have typed into the cell.
Move one cell to the left.	Press **Shift+Tab**.
Move one cell down.	Press the **Enter** key. This will also enter any data you have typed into the cell. To enter data without navigating away from the cell, press **Ctrl+Enter**.
Move one cell up.	Press **Shift+Enter**.
Move to cell A1.	Press **Ctrl+Home**.
Navigate left or right through the worksheets in a workbook.	Press **Ctrl+Page Up** or **Ctrl+Page Down**.

> **Note: Excel Online App**
>
> It's important to remember that you are working in a browser window, so while many of the common keyboard shortcuts are available, there will be instances when the keyboard shortcut behaves differently than you expect. You can find a complete list of Excel Online keyboard shortcuts by opening Excel Online Help and then searching for "keyboard shortcuts."

Basic Data Entry

When you select a cell in Excel, it becomes the *active cell*, and it is only into the active cell that you can initially enter data. An active cell is displayed with a solid green border around it. When you select a range of cells, only one cell within the range is the active cell; that is the cell that is displayed without a shaded background. You can use the **Tab** and the **Enter** keys to navigate among cells within a selected range while maintaining the range as your selection. In addition to dragging to select a range with your mouse, you can press and hold down the **Shift** key to select a contiguous range of cells, or you can press and hold down the **Ctrl** key to select a non-contiguous group of cells.

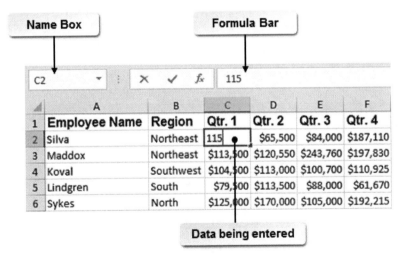

Figure 1-9: Entering cell data. Notice that the Name Box displays the active cell, and the Formula Bar reflects the cell's current contents.

The following table describes the two main methods you can use to enter data into the cells in your worksheets.

Data Entry Method	Description
Directly into the active cell	The most basic method of entering data into a cell is to select the cell, type the data, and then press either the **Tab** or the **Enter** key. Pressing **Tab** will enter the data and navigate one cell to the right. Pressing **Enter** will enter the data and navigate to the first open cell in the next row down.
	If there is already data in the cell, using this method will overwrite the previous data.
Using **Edit** mode	You can use **Edit** mode to either enter new data in an empty cell or edit existing data. Using **Edit** mode is more useful for editing existing data; otherwise, **Edit** mode is simply an extra step if you're just adding new data.
	To use **Edit** mode, either double-click the desired cell, select the desired cell and then place the insertion point in the **Formula Bar**, or select the desired cell and then press **F2**. Once in **Edit** mode, you can place the insertion point wherever you like, in the cell or the **Formula Bar**, and edit the existing data as you normally would in a word-processing application. Once you've edited the data, regardless of where the insertion point is, you can press either **Tab** or **Enter** to enter the data and navigate to the desired next cell.

Note: To enter data in a cell and keep that cell as the active cell, press **Ctrl+Enter** to enter the data. Also, you can use the **Up**, **Down**, **Left**, or **Right** arrow key to enter data and then navigate one cell in the desired direction.

Cell Modes

When interacting with the cells in your worksheets, an active cell can be in one of three modes: **Ready**, **Enter**, or **Edit**. Excel displays the status of the selected cell on the left side of the status bar.

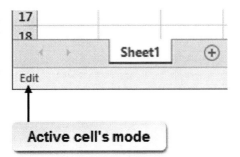

Active cell's mode

- **Ready** mode tells you a cell is selected and that it is waiting for you to interact with it.
- **Enter** mode activates once you start typing data into a cell.
- **Edit** mode activates as described in the previous table.

Note: Excel Online App

When you open a workbook in Excel Online, it opens in **Reading** view. To make any changes to the worksheet content, you must activate **Editing** view by selecting **Edit Workbook**→**Edit in Excel Online**.

Access the Checklist tile on your CHOICE Course screen for reference information and job aids on How to Navigate the Excel Environment.

ACTIVITY 1-1

Navigating the Excel User Interface

Data File

C:\091055Data\Getting Started with Microsoft Office Excel 2016\Develetech Holiday Schedule.xlsx

Before You Begin

You are logged in to your computer and the Windows 10 desktop screen is displayed, but Excel 2016 is not open.

Windows 10 is set to display file extensions.

Scenario

Develetech Industries is a mid-size home electronics manufacturer located in the fictitious city and state of Greene City, Richland (RL). Develetech has continued to grow and now has stores throughout the United States, as well as stores in select cities in Canada and Mexico. Recent industry rumors indicate that expansion into Europe is on the horizon.

You have recently joined Develetech as a sales manager. Your responsibilities include using Excel to analyze sales trends and other company data. You have used other spreadsheet applications to work with data in the past, but not Excel. You realize you'll need to get up to speed on how Excel works, and fast. You decide to start by locating the critical user interface elements you'll work with most often. As part of the onboarding and orientation process, your HR representative provided you with the company paid holiday schedule for the current year as an Excel workbook file. Because you need to plan your paid time off anyway, you decide to open that file in Excel to explore the user interface.

 Note: Activities may vary slightly if the software vendor has issued digital updates. Your instructor will notify you of any changes.

1. Open Excel 2016.

    a) From the Windows 10 taskbar, select the **Excel 2016** icon.

    b) If Excel does not appear full screen, select the **Maximize** button. ☐

2. Open the **Develetech Holiday Schedule.xlsx** file.

    a) From the Excel screen, in the left pane, select **Open Other Workbooks**.

    b) From the **Open** screen, select **Browse**.

    c) In the **Open** dialog box, navigate to the **C:\091055Data\Getting Started with Microsoft Office Excel 2016** folder.

    d) Select the **Develetech Holiday Schedule.xlsx** workbook file, and then select **Open**.

3. Navigate the ribbon.

    a) Select several of the ribbon tabs other than the **File** tab.

    b) Verify that the displayed commands change for each tab.

4. Explore the **Backstage** view.

    a) Select the **File** tab.

    b) In the left pane, select **New**, then **Open**, and then **Print**.

    c) Verify that the commands and options in the right pane change for the various tabs.

    d) Select the **Back** button ⊙ to exit the **Backstage** view.

5. **Navigate the worksheet with the mouse.**

    a) Ensure that cell **A1** is selected. Verify that it is displayed with a solid green border and that **A1** appears in the **Name Box**.

    b) Verify that **Day** appears in the **Formula Bar**.

    c) Select cell **C10**. Verify that it is now the active cell, that **C10** appears in the **Name Box**, and that **Christmas** appears in the **Formula Bar**.

    d) Click and drag from cell **A1** to cell **A10**. Confirm that the range **A1:A10** is selected and that cell **A1** is the active cell.

    e) Verify that **A1** appears in the **Name Box** and that **Day** appears in the **Formula Bar**.

    f) Press **Enter**.

    g) Verify that cell **A2** is now the active cell, that **A2** appears in the **Name Box**, and that **Wed** appears in the **Formula Bar**.

    h) Press the **Enter** key until cell **A10** is the active cell.

    i) Select cell **A2**.

    j) Press and hold down the **Shift** key, and then select cell **C2**.

    k) Verify that the range **A2:C2** is selected and that cell **A2** is the active cell within the range.

    l) Press and hold down the **Ctrl** key, and then select the range **A10:C10**.

    m) Verify that the ranges **A2:C2** and **A10:C10** are both selected.

	A	B	C
1	Day	Date	Holiday
2	Wed	1-Jan	New Year's Day
3	Mon	19-Jan	Martin Luther King, Jr. Day
4	Mon	16-Feb	Presidents Day
5	Mon	25-May	Memorial Day
6	Fri	3-Jul	Independence Day Observed
7	Mon	7-Sep	Labor Day
8	Thu	27-Nov	Thanksgiving
9	Thu	24-Dec	Christmas Eve
10	Fri	25-Dec	Christmas

6. **Use the keyboard to navigate the worksheet.**

    a) Select cell **A1**.

    b) Use the **Down** arrow and **Right** arrow keys to navigate to cell **C10**.

    c) Use the **Up** arrow and **Left** arrow keys to navigate back to cell **A1**.

    d) Press the **Enter** key to navigate to cell **A2**. Press and hold down **Shift** and press **Enter** to navigate back to cell **A1**.

    e) Press **Tab** to navigate to cell **B1**. Press and hold down **Shift** and press **Tab** to navigate back to cell **A1**.

7. **Leave the workbook open.**

TOPIC B

Use Excel Commands

You've navigated your way around the Excel environment and entered basic cell data. Having taken these few important first steps, you're ready to begin taking advantage of the wide array of functionality Excel 2016 has to offer. But, in order to do so, you'll need to be familiar with where to look to find the commands you need.

The Ribbon

The *ribbon*, a common interface element shared by all Microsoft Office 2016 applications, is a component of the Excel 2016 UI. The ribbon is a graphical user interface that contains all of the most commonly used commands you will need to create, modify, and work with your Excel workbooks. It was designed as a way to provide quick access to frequently used commands without the need to extensively navigate menus and submenus. The ribbon is displayed along the top of the Excel UI and is organized into a series of tabs that contain command groups. These command groups contain sets of functionally related commands that you will use to enter, format, revise, and work with your workbook data.

> **Note:** This course uses a streamlined notation for ribbon commands. They'll appear as "**[Ribbon Tab]→[Group]→[Button or Control]**" as in "Select **Home→Clipboard→Paste**." If the group name isn't needed for navigation or there isn't a group, it's omitted, as in "Select **File→Open**." For selections that open menus and submenus, this notation convention will continue until you are directed to select the final command or option, as in "Select **Home→Cells→Format→Hide & Unhide→Hide Rows**."

> **Note:** Some Excel 2016 command buttons are split, meaning there are actually two separate buttons you can select independently. This is often the case with commands that have multiple options/variations accessible by selecting a drop-down arrow. The **Paste** command button in the **Clipboard** group on the **Home** tab is an example of this. For these commands, you will be directed to either select just the button, as in "Select **Home→Clipboard→Paste**," or you will be directed to select the drop-down arrow if necessary, as in "Select **Home→Clipboard→Paste drop-down arrow→Paste Special**."

Some ribbon groups also display a *dialog box launcher*. These downward-facing arrows in the bottom-right corner of some command groups open dialog boxes that provide you with access to even more commands and options related to the functionality of the particular group's commands.

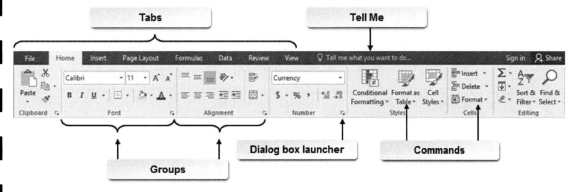

Figure 1-10: The Excel 2016 ribbon.

The ribbon is a customizable element of the Excel UI. You can add tabs, groups, and individual commands to suit your particular needs and work habits. You can also hide the ribbon to create more workable space within the *application window*.

The following table provides a description of the various ribbon elements.

Ribbon Element	Description
Tabs	Organizes the ribbon at the highest level according to task functions such as inserting objects, working with formulas, and configuring the view of your worksheets.
Groups	Contain functionally related sets of commands that you will use to perform most Excel tasks.
Commands	Execute the desired action or configure the desired settings and options.
Dialog box launchers	Open dialog boxes containing further commands or options related to the functionality of the group's commands.
Tell Me	Allows you to perform a keyword search for Excel commands.

The following table describes the types of commands each of the ribbon tabs displays.

Ribbon Tab	Contains Commands For
File	Working with your Excel files and configuring system-wide and application settings and options. Selecting the **File** tab accesses the **Backstage** view, providing you with access to these commands and settings.
Home	Executing some of the most common Excel tasks. The **Home** tab displays commands for basic text formatting and editing; applying various styles and formatting to your data; and sorting, filtering, and searching your data.
Insert	Inserting a variety of objects, such as charts, tables, and graphics, into your workbooks; creating and editing hyperlinks; adding headers and footers to worksheets; and inserting equations and symbols.
Page Layout	Applying themes and effects to worksheets; configuring the overall layout of your worksheets; and arranging worksheet objects.
Formulas	Inserting and working with formulas and functions; naming cells and ranges; troubleshooting workbook data, functions, and formulas; and setting calculation options.
Data	Importing data from other sources; performing various data analysis tasks; and organizing worksheet data into a hierarchical structure.
Review	Reviewing, proofing, adding comments to, and sharing your workbooks.
View	Configuring workbook views, viewing multiple workbooks simultaneously, and setting the magnification level.

Note: Excel Online App

Unlike the ribbon in the desktop application, the online app ribbon does not have the **Page Layout** and **Formulas** tabs and their related commands. To use the advanced workbook formatting, layout, review, and data features, you can use the **OPEN IN EXCEL** button to open the workbook in the desktop application.

Note: If you'd like a virtual tour of the ribbon, view the LearnTO **Navigate the Office 2016 Ribbon** presentation from the **LearnTO** tile on the CHOICE Course screen.

Tell Me

Excel 2016's *Tell Me* feature, located after the rightmost ribbon tab, provides you with the ability to quickly search for a particular command. While it's helpful to become acquainted with the ribbon, there are times when you may not be able to find exactly what you're looking for. By typing text into **Tell Me**, Excel will return several of the most relevant search results in a drop-down menu; each keystroke will update the results on-the-fly, so the more information you provide in your search, the more likely **Tell Me** is to show you what you're looking for.

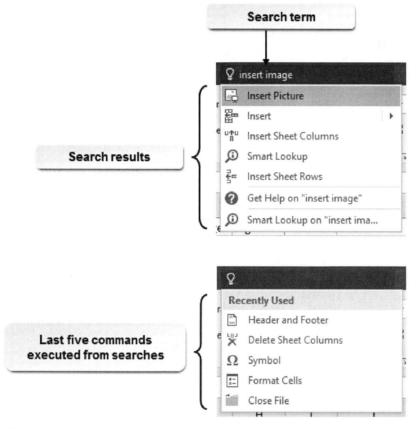

Figure 1-11: Using Tell Me to search for a command, as well as displaying Recently Used search results.

Even if you don't know the exact name of the command you're looking for, **Tell Me** can still return useful results when you use relevant search terms. For example, searching for "insert image" will return the actual command **Insert Picture**. Additionally, when you place your insertion point in the **Tell Me** text box, a **Recently Used** section of the drop-down menu will automatically display the last five commands you searched for and executed. This can help you save time if you need to repeatedly search for the same few commands.

ScreenTips and KeyTips

Excel 2016 provides two features that can help you identify and access various elements of the UI: ScreenTips and KeyTips. *ScreenTips* appear when you place the mouse pointer over commands and some other elements of the UI. ScreenTips appear in a small pop-up window, and provide information such as a command's name, a description of what the command or screen element does, and the keyboard shortcut that performs the same function.

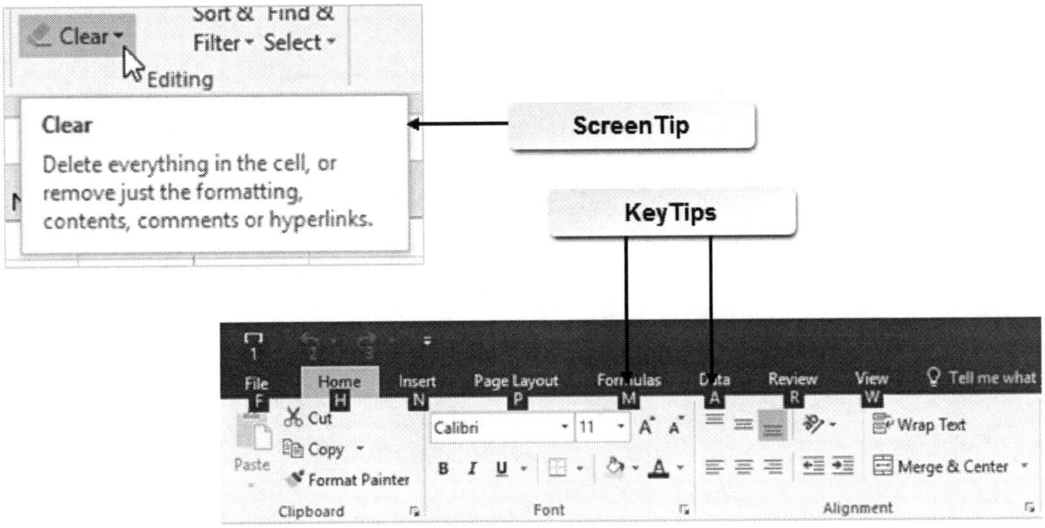

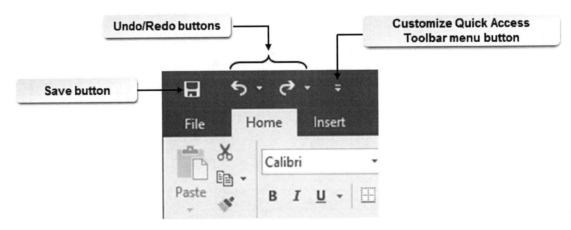

Figure 1-12: A ScreenTip and KeyTips in Excel 2016.

KeyTips differ from ScreenTips in that they allow you to actually interact with particular commands on screen. KeyTips appear along the ribbon and the **Quick Access Toolbar** when you press the **Alt** key. KeyTips appear as either a single alphanumeric character or a sequence of them. To access the particular tab or engage the particular command associated with a KeyTip, simply press the corresponding key or sequence of keys on the keyboard. It is important to note that KeyTips do not function the same as keyboard shortcuts. If a KeyTip is displayed as a sequence of characters, you press the corresponding keys one at a time, not at the same time as you would with a keyboard shortcut such as **Shift+Enter**. To turn off KeyTips, simply press the **Alt** key again or select any screen element with the mouse pointer.

The Quick Access Toolbar

The *Quick Access Toolbar* is another element of the Excel UI that provides you with easy access to commonly used commands. The **Quick Access Toolbar** appears above the ribbon in the top-left corner of the Excel UI. By default, the **Save**, **Undo**, and **Redo** commands appear on the **Quick Access Toolbar**. Like the ribbon, the **Quick Access Toolbar** can be customized.

Figure 1-13: The Quick Access Toolbar.

The Mini Toolbar and Context Menus

Excel 2016 provides you with two other options for easily accessing certain commands: the *Mini toolbar* and *context menus*. The **Mini** toolbar is displayed when you right-click the active cell on a worksheet. It is a small, rectangular pop-up window that contains a set of common text editing and formatting commands that you can use to work with the data in the active cell.

In Excel 2016, there are actually multiple versions of the **Mini** toolbar: the main version that is displayed when you right-click an active cell, and variations of the main **Mini** toolbar that are displayed when you right-click various other objects on worksheets, such as images and charts.

Context menus also appear when you select or right-click particular objects or data within worksheets. Context menus display a list of commands and options that pertain to working with the specific type of content you have selected.

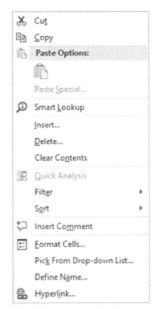
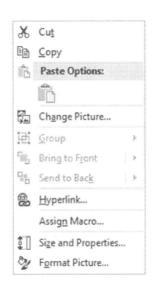

Mini toolbars

Context menus

Figure 1-14: Variations on the Mini toolbar and context menus in Excel 2016.

Note: Excel Online App

In Excel Online, the **Mini** toolbar is unavailable; however, the context menus can be accessed by right-clicking a cell. While the list of commands is not as robust as those show in the aforementioned figure, basic commands such as **Cut**, **Copy**, **Paste**, and **Number Format** are available.

Access the Checklist tile on your CHOICE Course screen for reference information and job aids on How to Use Excel Commands.

ACTIVITY 1-2
Using Excel Commands

Before You Begin
The **Develetech Holiday Schedule.xlsx** file is open.

Scenario
You are now familiar with the overall general layout of the Excel 2016 environment. You'd like to focus on discovering where some of the commonly used commands are. You decide to use ScreenTips to help you begin to identify some of the commands you've been wondering about. The **Tell Me** feature will also help you find some of the commands you haven't yet located on the ribbon. You also want to look over one or two of the dialog boxes to see what commands are available there.

Additionally, you've just received an email message from the HR department informing you of an error on the holiday schedule, which you'll need to correct. The holiday schedule workbook is already open, which works out well as you also want to add a few entries to the worksheet to help you plan your vacation time.

1. **Use ScreenTips to identify common commands.**
   a) Ensure that the **Home** tab is selected.
   b) In the **Font** group, point the mouse pointer at several of the commands to view their ScreenTips.
   c) Do the same for several commands in each of the other groups.
   d) Select the **Insert** tab.
   e) View the ScreenTips for several commands in each of the command groups.

2. **Examine the commands in a dialog box.**
   a) Select the **Home** tab.
   b) In the **Font** group, select the dialog box launcher.

   c) Verify that the **Format Cells** dialog box is opened.
   d) Select the various tabs and review some of the available commands.
   e) Select the **Close** button ✕ to close the **Format Cells** dialog box.

3. **Find another dialog box with Tell Me.**
   a) On the ribbon, to the right of the **View** tab, select the **Tell Me** search box.
   b) Type *symbol*

c) From the list of commands, select **Symbol** to open the **Symbol** dialog box.

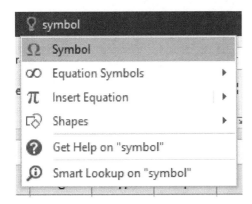

d) Close the **Symbol** dialog box.

4. Add data to a cell.

a) Select cell **C11**.
b) Type *And day after* and press **Enter**.
c) In cell **C12**, type *Consider NY's Eve* and press **Enter**.

5. Replace existing data in a cell.

a) Select cell **A2**.
b) Type *Thu* and press **Enter**.
c) Verify that the cell content has changed.

6. Save and close the file.

a) On the **Quick Access Toolbar**, select the **Save** button.
b) On the ribbon, select the **File** tab.
c) Select **Close**.
d) Leave Excel open.

TOPIC C

Create and Save a Basic Workbook

Although knowing how to open and work within existing workbooks is an important skill set, you will, undoubtedly, need to create your own Excel workbooks to suit your particular needs. It's likely you will be called upon to work with data for a number of different purposes and regarding a number of different subjects. You may also need to present similar information to multiple audiences. As such, you'll find yourself creating a variety of different workbooks that you will need to save as separate items, as well as saving multiple versions of the same workbooks. Microsoft Excel 2016 makes it easy to accomplish these tasks.

The New Tab

The **Backstage** view's **New** tab provides you with a variety of options for creating new Excel workbooks. You can create a new blank workbook to start from scratch, or you can decide to start with an existing Excel workbook template, and then make changes to suit your needs.

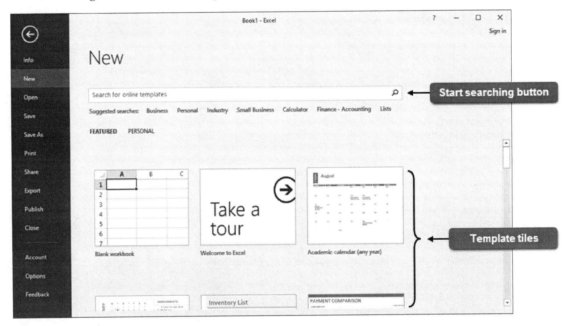

Figure 1-15: The New tab in the Backstage view.

The following table describes the various elements of the **New** screen in the Excel 2016 **Backstage** view.

New Screen Element	Is Used To
Search for online templates field	Enter search criteria to look for available Excel workbook templates from **Office.com**.
Start searching button	Execute a search based on the search term(s) entered in the **Search for online templates** field.
Suggested searches section	Search for **Office.com** templates in a variety of commonly searched categories. These categorized searches are also broken down into sub-categories for more precise searching.
Blank workbook tile	Create a new, blank workbook.

New Screen Element	Is Used To
Template tiles	Create new Excel workbooks based on the selected template.

> **Note: Excel Online App**
>
> In the online app, if the template you are searching for is not listed, you can go directly to **office.com** and select **Templates** at the top of the page. The Office templates are organized by category and when you find the template you want to use, simply select it and then select **Open in Excel Online**.

Excel 2016 File Formats

The default file format for Excel 2016 workbook files is the XLSX format. This is an XML-based file format that allows Excel to compress files when you close them, making them up to 75 percent smaller than files saved in the previous Excel file format, XLS. When you open an XLSX workbook file, Excel automatically decompresses it. The XLSX file format also provides other benefits over the previous file format, such as easier recovery of damaged files, increased security and protection functionality, and greater compatibility with other applications.

Microsoft Excel 2016 also supports a host of other file types that enable you to open workbook files from previous versions of Excel and share files in a variety of formats with other users. The following table provides a partial list of the file types available in Excel 2016.

File Type and Extension	Description
Excel Workbook (.xlsx)	The default file type in Excel 2016.
Excel Macro-Enabled Workbook (.xlsm)	Allows you to save workbook files containing Visual Basic® for Applications macrocode.
Excel Binary Workbook (.xlsb)	Compressed, binary-based file format that reduces file size and improves performance in complex, calculation-dense workbooks. This file type may not be compatible with some applications that work only with XML-based files.
Excel 97-2003 Workbook (.xls)	The previous default Excel file format. The XLS format is a binary file format, which isn't as compatible with other computer applications as the newer, XML-based file format.
Excel Template (.xltx)	The default file type for Excel templates. This format is used to save workbooks as templates so that you can create new workbooks based on the template contents, layout, and format.
Excel Macro-Enabled Template (.xltm)	The default file format for Excel macro-enabled templates.
Excel 97-2003 Template (.xlt)	The default template file format in prior versions of Excel.
PDF (.pdf)	Allows you to save workbooks in the Portable Document Format (PDF).

> **Note: Excel Online App**
>
> You can open most of these file formats in Excel Online with the notable exception of the Excel Macro-Enabled Template type. In addition, Excel Online supports the OpenDocument Spreadsheet format (.ods). It's important to note that when you open files in the older Excel 97-2003 formats, the file will open in Excel 2016.

The Save and Save As Commands

Excel provides you with two options for saving your new and existing workbook files: the **Save** command and the **Save As** command. You use the **Save** command to save changes to an existing workbook without changing the file name or the file location. You use the **Save As** command to save new workbook files or to make changes to existing files, such as the file name and location. Both the **Save** and **Save As** commands are accessible in the left pane in the **Backstage** view. The **Quick Access Toolbar** also provides access to the **Save** command by default.

 Note: If you select **Save** to save a new workbook file, Excel 2016 automatically displays the **Save As** screen, as you must specify a location and a file type when saving new files.

Figure 1-16: The Save and Save As commands in the Backstage view.

The Save As Screen

The **Save As** screen contains the commands and options you will use to select a location to save your workbook files, either on your computer, on an attached storage device, or in a remote location such as a network share or an online file storage service.

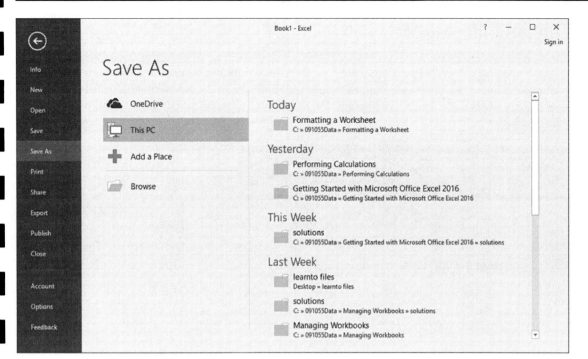

Figure 1-17: The Save As screen with the This PC option selected.

The following table describes the four main options on the **Save As** screen.

Save As Option	Description
OneDrive	This option provides you with direct access to your Microsoft OneDrive® account, if you have one. OneDrive is a file storage and sharing service that enables you to store files online (or "in the cloud") for easy access from any location that has Internet access. You must have a Microsoft account to access this service, but it is free to sign up.
This PC	This option acts as a shortcut to display a list of locations that you've recently saved your workbooks to. The shortcuts are divided into various sections based on time, such as **Today** and **Yesterday**. **This PC** also shows where your currently opened workbook is saved, under the **Current Folder** section. Selecting one of the shortcuts opens a **Save As** dialog box to that location. In this dialog box, you can name your file and select the appropriate file type.
Add a Place	You can use this option to add other options for workbook file storage, such as network servers and Microsoft SharePoint® sites.
Browse	This option immediately opens the **Save As** dialog box to your local **Documents** folder, or to the current workbook's location if it's already been saved. You can use this option to quickly browse to a specific location where you want to save your workbook.

Note: Excel Online App

As you work in Excel Online, your workbooks are automatically updated and saved to OneDrive; therefore, you will not see a **Save** command. The **Save As** command is available to save the file with a different name but not in a different location. To save the file on your local computer, you can use the **Download a Copy** command. Keep in mind that this command is only creating a copy while the original file remains in OneDrive.

Compatibility Mode

When you open a workbook file in Excel 2016 that was created by using Excel 2003 (or an earlier version), Excel opens the file in *Compatibility mode* and the **Title bar** displays the file name with the text *[Compatibility Mode]* next to it. You can open and work with files in Compatibility mode to preserve the original file format, allowing you to subsequently open the file in previous versions of Excel. Keep in mind that some Excel 2016 features are not available in all versions of Excel.

Figure 1-18: The Title bar of a workbook file open in Compatibility mode.

The Convert Option

When you open a workbook in Excel 2016 that was created in a 97-2003 version of Excel, and you no longer need to keep the workbook in the previous file format, you can convert the workbook into the current XLSX format. Using the *Convert option* provides you with access to all of the features and functionality available in Excel 2016. Often, converting a file to the newer file format will also reduce the size of your workbook file.

Compatibility Mode

Some new features are disabled to prevent problems when working with previous versions of Office. Converting this file will enable these features, but may result in layout changes.

Figure 1-19: The Convert option.

When you convert a workbook, Excel replaces the old file with a copy of the workbook in the XLSX or the XLSM file format. The previous version of the file is no longer available for you to work with. You can access the **Convert** option from the **Info** tab in the **Backstage** view of any workbook that is open in Compatibility mode.

The Compatibility Checker

The *Compatibility Checker* allows you to test the compatibility of objects and data in an Excel 2016 workbook when you intend to save it in an earlier Excel file format. This is typical when you need to share a file you created in a newer version of Excel with a user who has an older version of Excel installed on their machine. Selecting the **Check Compatibility** command opens the **Microsoft Excel - Compatibility Checker** dialog box, in which you can view a list of features in your Excel 2016 file that are not supported in earlier versions of Excel. You can access the **Check Compatibility** command by selecting **File→Info→Check for Issues**. Excel will also run the Compatibility Checker automatically when you attempt to save a current Excel workbook file in the previous file format.

Unchecking the **Check compatibility when saving this workbook** check box allows you to save in previous versions without the Compatibility Checker running automatically. However, be careful when you uncheck this feature; you will lose certain functionality when you save back to previous versions.

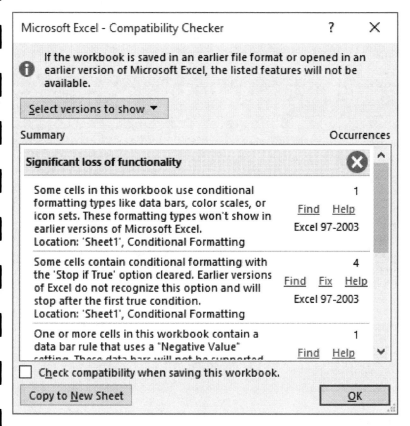

Figure 1-20: The Microsoft Excel - Compatibility Checker dialog box.

There are two levels of compatibility issues the Compatibility Checker can detect: minor loss of fidelity and significant loss of functionality. With minor compatibility issues, you can likely save the workbook in an earlier file format with limited loss of functionality. Common changes when saving back to an earlier file format include the removal of table and text formatting not supported in earlier versions.

When you encounter significant compatibility issues, it is recommended that you not save your file in the earlier file format. Doing so may cause you to lose data, experience formula or calculation failures, or experience other serious issues.

 Access the Checklist tile on your CHOICE Course screen for reference information and job aids on How to Create and Save a Basic Workbook.

ACTIVITY 1–3
Creating and Saving a Basic Workbook

Before You Begin
Excel 2016 is open.

Scenario
Now that you're more familiar with the Excel UI and some of its basic commands, you feel comfortable enough to create your first new workbook. A colleague has emailed you some basic sales data for two new products, and you expect more data soon. You decide to create a new workbook, enter the data, and then save the workbook so you can add more data to it as it comes in. Another colleague has asked for a copy of the file, but she works in Excel 2003. So you'll also have to save a copy of the file in an earlier format.

1. Create a new blank workbook.
   a) Select **File→New**.
   b) From the **New** screen, select **Blank workbook**.

2. Add column labels for the data.
   a) Ensure cell **A1** is selected, type *Product* and press **Tab**.
   b) Ensure cell **B1** is selected, type *Quantity* and press **Tab**.
   c) Ensure cell **C1** is selected, type *Price* and press **Enter**.

3. In the **Product** column, enter the product names.
   a) Ensure cell **A2** is selected, type *Laptop* and press **Enter**.
   b) In cell **A3**, type *Monitor* and press **Enter**.

4. In the **Quantity** column, enter the quantity data.
   a) Select cell **B2**, type *1550* and press **Enter**.
   b) In cell **B3**, type *3125* and press **Enter**.

5. In the **Price** column, enter the price data.
   a) Select cell **C2**, type *685* and press **Enter**.
   b) In cell **C3**, type *289* and press **Enter**.

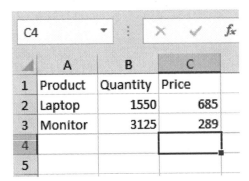

6. Save the workbook in the default Excel 2016 file format.

   a) Select **File→Save As**.

   b) From the **Save As** screen, select **Browse**.

   c) In the **Save As** dialog box, navigate to **C:\091055\Getting Started with Microsoft Office Excel 2016**.

   d) In the **File name** field, type *My New Products*

   e) From the **Save as type** drop-down menu, ensure that **Excel Workbook (*.xlsx)** is selected.

   f) Select **Save**.

   g) Ensure that the file name now appears in the **Title bar** with the *.xlsx* file extension.

7. Save a copy of the workbook file in a previous file format.

   a) Select **File→Save As**.

   b) From the **Save As** screen, ensure that **This PC** is selected.

   c) In the **Current Folder** section, select the **Getting Started with Microsoft Office Excel 2016** folder location.

   d) In the **Save As** dialog box, ensure that the **C:\091055Data\Getting Started with Microsoft Office Excel 2016** folder is selected.

   e) From the **Save as type** drop-down menu, select **Excel 97-2003 Workbook (*.xls)**.

   f) Select **Save**.

   g) Ensure that the file name now appears in the **Title bar** with the *.xls* file extension.

8. Select **File→Close** to close the workbook file but leave Excel 2016 open.

Microsoft OneDrive

Microsoft OneDrive provides online file storage, management, and sharing services that you can use to store, share, and collaborate on your Excel workbook files as well as other types of files. There are two versions of OneDrive: personal and business. Anyone can create a personal OneDrive account, but your organization would provide you with the credentials for a business account. With a OneDrive for Business account, you have up to 1 terabyte (TB) of free OneDrive storage. However, if you have a personal Microsoft account (with an @outlook.com email address), the maximum free storage space is 5 GB. You can certainly purchase additional space if you want to.

Managing your files in OneDrive is very similar to managing files in File Explorer. The major difference is that you must upload the files to OneDrive, which enables you to access and work with your files from nearly any location using different devices. From within the OneDrive browser window, select **Upload→Files** or **Upload→Folder** and then navigate to the file or folder you want to upload. If you are working in Excel 2016, another way to "upload" a file to OneDrive is to select **File→Save As** and then select **OneDrive** to be the **Save As** location.

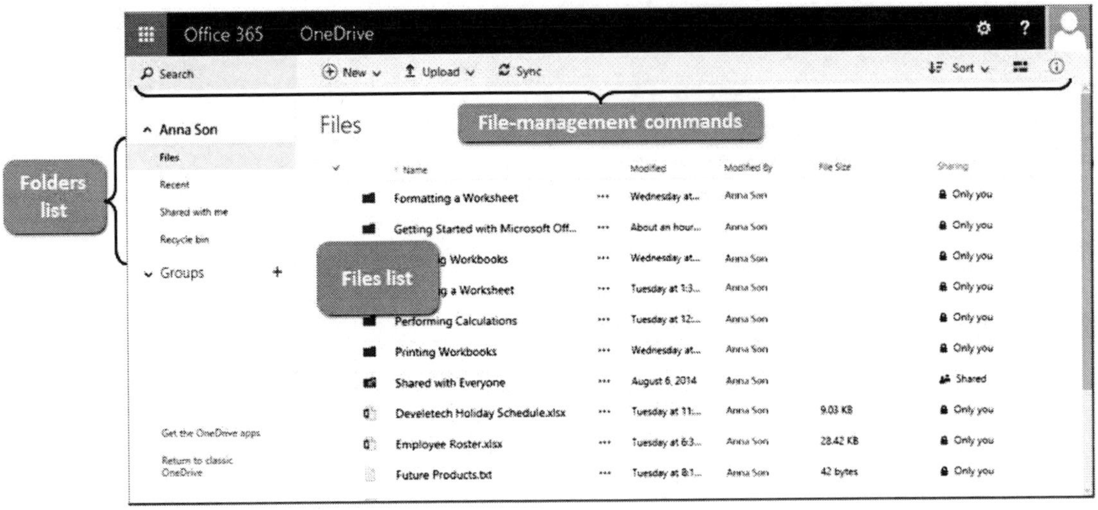

Figure 1-21: A sample OneDrive for Business page.

ACTIVITY 1-4

Signing in to Office 365 and OneDrive (Optional Instructor Demo)

Data File

C:\091055Data\Getting Started with Microsoft Office Excel 2016\Develetech Holiday Schedule.xlsx

Before You Begin

You have an Office 365 login user name and password.

Scenario

Develetech now uses the Office 2016 applications through their cloud-based Office 365 subscription. While you are becoming comfortable working in the desktop versions of Office, the features of the Office 365 apps are new and unfamiliar. You're especially interested in the collaboration and mobility capabilities of these online apps. After signing in to Office 365, you'll check out the file storage app called OneDrive.

1. From the Windows **Start** screen, open Microsoft Edge and go to the Office 365 login screen and sign in to Office 365.

   a) Select the **Microsoft Edge** tile.
   b) In the **Address** box at the top of the screen, enter *https://login.microsoftonline.com*

2. Enter your credentials to sign in.

   a) In the **User ID** box, enter your user ID, including the @ symbol and the domain name.
   b) In the **Password** box, enter your password.
   c) Select **Sign in**.
      When Office 365 opens, your Outlook mail appears in the Office 365 Outlook app.

3. Open OneDrive.

   a) In the upper-left corner of the window, select the **App Launcher** icon
   b) From the menu, select the **OneDrive** tile.

c) Observe the elements of the OneDrive user interface.

The Office 365 header at the top of the screen displays both the App Launcher and OneDrive to indicate that you are working in the online apps. At the right end of the header bar, there are buttons to access **Notifications**, **Settings**, **Help**, and your account settings, from left to right, respectively. Immediately below the Office 365 header are context-specific commands. In OneDrive, these commands are used to perform basic file management tasks, such as creating new Office files as well as uploading, syncing, sorting, and viewing files.

 Note: If you have a OneDrive personal account, the text "Office 365" might not appear next to the **App Launcher** icon even though you are accessing it through Office 365.

4. **From the student data files to OneDrive, upload the Develetech Holiday Schedule.**

a) From the command bar, select **Upload→Files**.
b) In the **Open** dialog box, navigate to the **C:\091055Data\Getting Started with Microsoft Office Excel 2016** folder.
c) Select the **Develetech Holiday Schedule.xlsx** workbook file, and then select **Open**.
d) Observe the **Files** list.

The uploaded workbook file appears in the **Files** list.

 Note: You can select **Upload→Folder** to upload multiple files in an entire folder at one time. According to Microsoft, you can use the drag-and-drop method to upload files, but only if you're using Microsoft® Internet Explorer® 11.

e) Select the check mark column to the left of the file name.

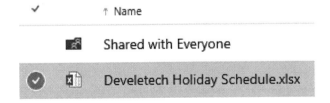

f) Observe the file management commands.

When a file is selected, file management commands become available. You can use these commands to delete, move, share, or otherwise manage your OneDrive files. You can access additional commands by selecting the **More commands** button. ⬚ From the **Open** command, you can open the selected file in its associated application—either the online or the desktop app.

5. Open **Develetech Holiday Schedule** in Excel Online.

a) From the command line, select **Open**.

b) Select **Open in Excel Online**.

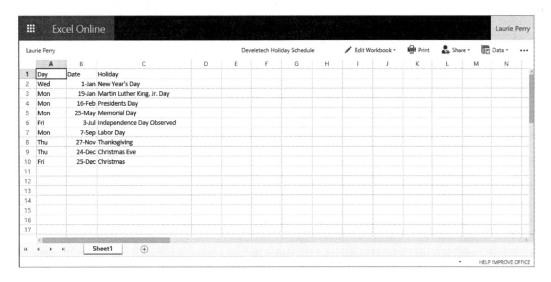

The workbook opens in the Excel Online app on a separate browser tab.

Excel Online

As part of the Office set of apps, Excel Online is included in your Office 365 subscription. You can access this scaled-down version of Excel through your web browser with an Internet connection. You can use Excel Online to view and work with files you have saved in OneDrive, or workbook files that other users have shared with you via OneDrive.

From your Office 365 Home page, select the **App Launcher** icon ⬚ and then select the **Excel** tile to open Excel Online. Another way to access Excel Online is from within OneDrive. From the **Files** list, select an Excel file and then select **Open→Open in Excel Online**.

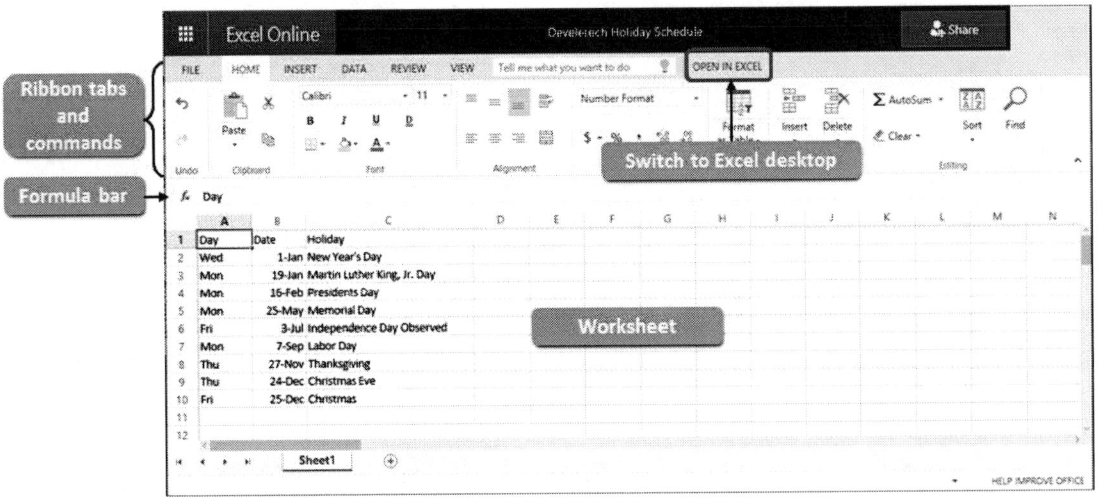

Figure 1-22: The Excel Online user interface.

You will immediately notice that Excel Online is a simplified version of the Excel desktop application. There are two views in Excel Online: **Reading** view and **Editing** view. Some considerations for working in Excel Online are:

- By default, workbook files open in **Reading** view.
- You must be in **Editing** view to make changes to the file. To do so, select **Edit Workbook→Edit in Excel Online**.
- In **Editing** view, you will see the familiar Office ribbon tabs and commands; however, they are scaled down from the full Office ribbon in Excel 2016.
- Any changes you make to the file are automatically saved. There is no Save command in Backstage view.
- Use the **OPEN IN EXCEL** button to open the current file in the desktop version provided Excel 2016 is installed on the computer you are using.

ACTIVITY 1-5
Navigating in Excel Online (Optional Instructor Demo)

Before You Begin
You are signed in to Office 365, and the Develetech Holiday Schedule file is open in Excel Online.

Scenario
Before you can take full advantage of the collaboration features, you need to familiarize yourself with the Excel Online user interface.

---

1. Edit the workbook in Excel Online.

   a) In the command bar, select **Edit Workbook→Edit in Excel Online**.

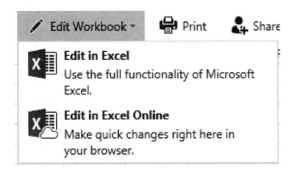

   b) Observe the available ribbon tabs and commands.

   While many of the tabs are the same as those on the familiar Excel 2016 ribbon, there are some differences. At first glance, the **Page Layout** and **Formulas** tabs are not included, and the buttons that do exist appear larger and slightly simplified. Additionally, there are no dialog box launchers in the Excel Online ribbon.

   c) Select cell D1 and enter *Days*
   d) In the range D2 through D10, enter *1*
   e) In cell C11, enter *Total Days*

2. Observe the available tools on the Excel Online ribbon tabs.

   a) Verify that cell C11 is selected and then select **HOME→Font→Bold**.

   b) Select the **INSERT** tab.
   There are buttons to insert functions, tables, charts, links, and comments. However, the **Shapes** and **SmartArt** buttons are absent.

   c) Select the **DATA** tab.

To set up and perform advanced data calculations on your worksheet data, you will need to work in Excel 2016.

d) Select the **REVIEW** tab.

You are limited to adding and working with comments in Excel Online. In Excel 2016, the **Review** tab contains commands to password protect sheets or the entire workbook. It's important to note you cannot even open password protected workbooks in Excel Online.

3. Save the edited workbook file.

a) Select **File** to access the Backstage view.

b) In the left pane, select **Save As**.

c) Select **Where's the Save Button?**

If Excel Online is new to you, this might be the biggest difference from Excel 2016. As the message explains, your workbook is saved automatically.

d) Click **OK**.

4. Observe the remaining commands and tabs in the Backstage view.

a) Select **Info**.

You must open the workbook in Excel 2016 to view the workbook properties and have access to the full functionality of Microsoft Excel.

b) In the left pane, select **New**.

You can create a new blank workbook or select from a list of available templates. However, you are unable to search for online templates like you can in Excel 2016.

c) In the left pane, select **Open**.

You are only able to choose from **Recent Documents** or select the **OneDrive** link to access more files. There's no option to open files stored anywhere else.

d) Observe the other File tab options: **Print**, **Share**, **About**, and **Help**.
The settings found on these tabs provide the information and settings you'd expect.

e) Select the **Back** button  to return to the workbook.

5. Open the **Develetech Holiday Schedule** in Excel 2016.

a) In the Excel Online command bar, select the **OPEN IN EXCEL** button.
If the workbook opens in Excel 2016 without any problems, you can close the message box in Excel Online.

b) Activate the Microsoft Edge window and close the **Excel Online** tab.

Files - OneDrive	Develetech Holiday Sch ✕

This is the equivalent of selecting **File→Close** in Excel 2016.

c) Close the Microsoft Edge browser window. If prompted, close all open tabs.

d) In the Excel 2016 window, if a message about a newer version appears, select the **Reopen Document** button.

✕ SERVER...	A newer version is available.	Reopen Document

e) Observe the updated workbook.

◢	A	B	C	D
1	Day	Date	Holiday	Days
2	Wed	1-Jan	New Year's Day	1
3	Mon	19-Jan	Martin Luther King, Jr. Day	1
4	Mon	16-Feb	Presidents Day	1
5	Mon	25-May	Memorial Day	1
6	Fri	3-Jul	Independence Day Observed	1
7	Mon	7-Sep	Labor Day	1
8	Thu	27-Nov	Thanksgiving	1
9	Thu	24-Dec	Christmas Eve	1
10	Fri	25-Dec	Christmas	1
11			**Total Days**	

You should see the Days data in column D and the Total Days text in C11, along with any other edits that were made to the file in Excel Online.

6. Select **File→Close** to close the file without saving it.

TOPIC D

Enter Cell Data

Excel has an incredible array of information types that you can work with in your workbooks. You'll need to be familiar with what these data types are and how Excel deals with them. Having a working knowledge of how Excel "sees" data is an important first step to developing the skills you'll need to crunch your numbers and keep track of your important information. In this topic, you'll use fundamental Excel features to help you enter data.

Data Types

One of the most fundamentally important things to understand about Excel is that it is not a "what you see is what you get" type of environment. Often, the value or text that appears within a cell is not what is actually stored in the cell. A simple example of this is the result of a calculation. If you have a formula entered in a cell, by default, the cell will display the result of the formula. For example, if the cell contains a formula that is the equivalent of "1 + 1," the cell will display the result of that formula: 2. But 2 is not the actual cell data; the formula is. Although this may, at first, not seem highly important, as you begin to work with the more complex functionality in Excel, it will become a critical concept to understand.

 Note: When you're in **Edit** mode, the cell displays its actual content, similar to the way the **Formula Bar** displays cell content. So if a cell contains a formula, while you edit the content, the cell displays the formula. When you're in **Enter** mode, Excel displays the formula result in the cell.

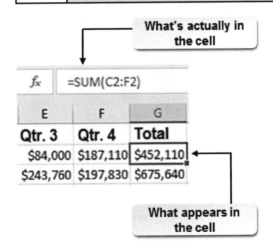

Figure 1-23: The difference between what you see in a cell and what's actually in the cell.

Although Excel cells can contain an incredible array of content, there are really only a few general categories of data that you'll work with on a regular basis.

Data Category	Description
Values	Numeric constants that do not change unless you edit the cell contents. Examples include 1, 345, 11.6, and .002.
Labels/text	Alphanumeric text not used to perform calculations or store numeric values. These can largely be viewed as labels for related sets of data on a worksheet. Examples include "Sales," "Q1," and "Total."

Data Category	Description
Formulas	Mathematical equations used to perform calculations or data analysis. Formulas are dynamic, so the displayed value can change if you change the cell data "feeding" the formula.
Dates and times	Date and time values. These can be used both as simple labels or as part of certain mathematical or logical operations.

The Cut, Copy, and Paste Commands

Although Excel is different from other Office applications such as Word and PowerPoint®, you'll find some of the functionality is quite similar. The **Cut**, **Copy**, and **Paste** commands are a good example of this. You will use the **Cut**, **Copy**, and **Paste** commands either to make a copy of cell data and place it in another cell, or to remove data from one cell and put it in another. Copied data is temporarily stored on a Microsoft Office tool known as the clipboard. Data on the clipboard can be reused in other locations on the same worksheet, within the same workbook, and in other workbooks and applications. The **Cut**, **Copy**, and **Paste** commands are displayed in the **Clipboard** group on the **Home** tab.

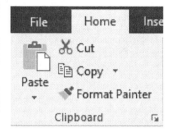

Figure 1-24: The Clipboard group displays the Cut, Copy, and Paste commands.

To refresh your memory, or in case you are not familiar with the **Cut**, **Copy**, and **Paste** commands, the following table offers a description of each.

Command	Performs This Action
Cut	Removes data from the selected cell or removes the selected data, and places a copy of it on the clipboard.
Copy	Makes a copy of the data in the selected cell or a copy of the selected data, and places the copy on the clipboard.
Paste	Places the data that was most recently added to the clipboard in the destination cell or location.

One important distinction to make in Excel regarding the use of these commands is the difference between using **Cut**, **Copy**, and **Paste** on entire cells versus using them on selected data. If you select a cell, using the **Cut** or the **Copy** command will affect all of the data within the cell; remember that what you see isn't necessarily the data in the cell. You can also select a portion of the cell data to cut or copy. You can do this within the cell if it's in **Edit** mode, or in the **Formula Bar** with the desired cell selected. The same is true of the **Paste** command. You can either paste the clipboard content into an entire cell or you can place it alongside other cell content in a cell in either **Edit** mode or in the **Formula Bar**.

When you use the **Cut** or the **Copy** command to copy content to the clipboard, Excel displays an animated, dashed-line box, often referred to as "marching ants" or a marquee selection, around your selection to help you verify that you have copied the correct content. After you paste the content and begin to perform another task, Excel stops displaying the marquee selection.

E	F	G
Qtr. 3	Qtr. 4	Total
$84,000	$187,110	$452,110
$243,760	$197,830	$675,640
$100,700	$110,925	$429,125
$88,000	$61,670	$342,670
$105,000	$192,215	$592,215

The Undo and Redo Commands

Inevitably, as you work with Excel, you will make a mistake. Fortunately, Excel, like many other Office applications, provides you with the **Undo** and **Redo** commands to help you correct errors as you work. The **Undo** command will cancel out the last action you performed, or the last several actions you performed, so you can correct any mistakes you've made while working with your workbooks. The **Undo** command works on a wide variety of actions, including entering data/typing text, performing calculations, adding objects to your worksheets, and formatting worksheets and worksheet objects. Once you've used the **Undo** command, Excel activates the **Redo** command, which will cancel out the last undo action or a series of undo actions.

By default, the **Undo** and **Redo** commands are available on the **Quick Access Toolbar**.

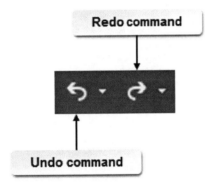

Figure 1-25: The Undo and Redo commands on the Quick Access Toolbar.

 Note: Excel Online App
The **Undo** and **Redo** buttons are located on the **Home** tab in Excel Online.

The AutoFill Feature

Excel 2016 includes a number of features meant to make your life a bit easier. One of these is the *AutoFill* feature. The AutoFill feature attempts to recognize an existing pattern in the data you have already entered, and then apply that pattern to filling in additional cells. Let's look at an example.

Say you enter the following values into the following cells in column **A: A1**: 1, **A2**: 2, **A3**: 3, and **A4**: 4. Clearly, you are attempting to create a sequential numbered list in the first column, or at least that's what Excel will assume. If you use the AutoFill feature to fill in the remaining cells in column **A**, Excel will follow the pattern and fill in the remaining cells with 5, 6, 7, 8, 9, 10, and so on. If you would like AutoFill to recognize a repeating pattern, say 1, 2, 3, 1, 2, 3, you would need to enter at least two cycles of the pattern to be sure Excel recognizes it as a pattern and not a sequence of numbers. If you start with only a single value, Excel will simply repeat it. AutoFill works for text as well as numeric values, so Excel would, for example, recognize a pattern such as lettering the first column instead of numbering, entering the days of the week, or entering the months of the year.

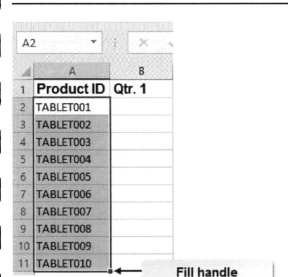

Figure 1-26: A column of cells populated by the AutoFill feature.

To use the AutoFill feature, you must first select the sequence of cells you want the pattern to be based on. When you select a cell or a range, Excel displays the cell or range within a solid green border. At the bottom-right corner of the border, Excel displays a **fill handle**. To use the AutoFill feature, you simply drag the **fill handle** until the border surrounds the desired range of cells, and then release it. When the mouse pointer is directly over the **fill handle**, it is displayed as a thin black

plus symbol. **+**

The AutoFill feature can also assist you with entering duplicate text entries in the same column. If you begin to type something into a cell that matches the beginning of another cell's content, Excel will attempt to automatically complete the entry for you to match the existing content. If you intended to enter a duplicate entry, you can simply press the **Enter** key, and Excel will automatically complete the entry. However, as you type, if the sequence of characters deviates from the other cell's content, Excel will stop displaying the entry and will simply let you continue to type the desired cell content. This works only with entries that consist of just text or a combination of text and numbers. Excel will not automatically complete duplicate entries of numeric values.

AutoFill Options

Excel 2016 also provides you with several options for deciding how to apply AutoFill when you use the feature. After you release the **fill handle**, Excel displays a small icon on the lower-right side of the range. Selecting that icon opens a menu, providing you with access to a series of options for choosing how to apply the AutoFill. These options can change depending on the type of data you have entered into the range.

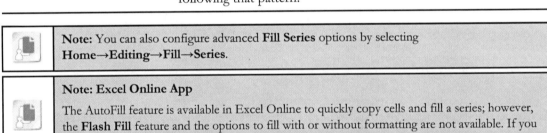

Figure 1-27: The AutoFill options in Excel 2016.

The following table describes the most commonly used AutoFill options.

AutoFill Option	Description
Copy Cells	Ignores any recognizable pattern and fills the remaining cells with the same data the originally selected cells contain.
Fill Series	The default AutoFill option. Excel applies the pattern it recognizes in filling the remaining cells.
Fill Formatting Only	Applies any formatting in the originally selected cells to the remaining cells without populating the cells with content.
Fill Without Formatting	Fills the remaining cells with data based on the recognized pattern while ignoring any formatting applied to the originally selected cells.
Flash Fill	If Excel recognizes a pattern in cell entries in one column based on the cells in other columns, it can fill in the remaining cell entries following that pattern.

> **Note:** You can also configure advanced **Fill Series** options by selecting **Home→Editing→Fill→Series**.

> **Note: Excel Online App**
>
> The AutoFill feature is available in Excel Online to quickly copy cells and fill a series; however, the **Flash Fill** feature and the options to fill with or without formatting are not available. If you want to use these AutoFill options, you must open the workbook in Excel 2016.

Flash Fill

In addition to being an AutoFill option, the *Flash Fill* feature can automatically recognize patterns across rows as you enter data, and then copy those patterns down a column of entries. The key difference between this and the AutoFill feature is that it depends on a recognizable pattern based on the entries in cells in other columns. Essentially, you can use this feature to combine entries, or parts of entries, from cells in the same row to another cell in that row, and then copy that combined data down a column. Let's look at a simple example to illustrate the point.

Suppose you have a worksheet that lists employee names. The last names are in column **A** and the first names are in column **B**. But you also need a column for each employee's email address. These email addresses always follow the same pattern: *firstname.lastname@develetech.com*. So, in the first row in column **C**, you manually type the first employee's first name followed by a period, then the employee's last name, then *@develetech.com*. Excel can recognize that this data is based on the entries in the first two columns, and then it can copy all of the names down column **C**, following the pattern, for each of the employees. You have to begin entering subsequent entries by following the same pattern before it can do so. Flash Fill can end up saving you an incredible amount of time.

 Note: The Flash Fill feature cannot recognize patterns in a column and then copy the pattern across a row. It works only down columns.

 Note: The Flash Fill feature will work only if there are no empty columns between the original data and the column you're trying to fill following a pattern. There can, however, be columns of data that don't relate to the pattern in between the cells containing the original data and the cells you are trying to fill.

	A	B	C
1	**Last Name**	**First Name**	**Email Address**
2	Silva	John	john.silva@develetech.com
3	Maddox	Sandy	sandy.maddox@develetech.com
4	Koval	Aaron	aaron.koval@develetech.com
5	Lindgren	Michael	michael.lindgren@develetech.com
6	Sykes	Emilia	emilia.sykes@develetech.com
7	Lee	Albert	albert.lee@develetech.com
8	Gilgamos	Francisco	francisco.gilgamos@develetech.com
9	Matthews	Trent	trent.matthews@develetech.com
10	Anderson	Linda	linda.anderson@develetech.com
11	Smith	Caroline	caroline.smith@develetech.com
12	Wagner	Leonard	leonard.wagner@develetech.com
13	Roberts	Thomas	thomas.roberts@develetech.com
14	Avellone	Xavier	xavier.avellone@develetech.com
15	Clarke	Janine	janine.clarke@develetech.com
16	Chen	Erica	erica.chen@develetech.com

Figure 1-28: The Flash Fill feature recognizes that cell C3 is following the pattern of C2 using data from its adjacent cells. It can then fill in the pattern for the rest of the cells in column C.

The Clear Command

Because you need to enter data into worksheet cells, it stands to reason that you will also need to delete cell data from time to time. The most basic method of doing this is to select the cell that contains the data you wish to remove and then press the **Delete** key. Excel also provides an alternative with the **Clear** command, which gives you access to a number of options for removing cell content that don't always include removing everything from the cell. The **Clear** command is available in the **Editing** group on the **Home** tab.

The following table describes each of the **Clear** command options.

Clear Command Option	Clears
Clear All	Everything from the selected cell(s).
Clear Formats	Only formatting applied to the selected cell(s). The content is left in place, including any existing comments.
Clear Contents	Only the contents of the selected cell(s), but not the formatting.
Clear Comments	Only comments from the selected cell(s).
Clear Hyperlinks	Hyperlinks from cell contents. The formatting is left in place, including formatting applied to the text when the hyperlink was created.
Remove Hyperlinks	Hyperlinks and all formatting.

Note: Excel Online App

To clear comments or hyperlinks, you must right-click the cell containing the content to be removed and then select **Remove Comment** or **Remove Hyperlink** from the context menu.

Access the Checklist tile on your CHOICE Course screen for reference information and job aids on How to Enter Data in Worksheet Cells.

ACTIVITY 1-6
Entering Cell Data

Data Files

C:\091055Data\Getting Started with Microsoft Office Excel 2016\My New Products.xlsx

C:\091055Data\Getting Started with Microsoft Office Excel 2016\Future Products.txt

Before You Begin

Excel 2016 is open.

Scenario

Your colleague has emailed you a text file with some additional new products that Develetech will be adding to its catalog. In order to keep track of the new product lines all in one place, you decide to add the new items to the **My New Products.xlsx** workbook file. In addition to tracking the cost and quantity of your new products, you also want to list each product's unique number and product code as identifiers. These will be used both internally and on the public-facing online store to assist with inventory. These identifiers follow certain patterns, so rather than wasting time entering them manually for each product, you'll let Excel do the work for you.

---

1. Open the **My New Products.xlsx** file.

   a) Select **File→Open**.

   b) From the **Open** screen, ensure that **Recent** is selected and, in the **Today** list, select **My New Products.xlsx**.

2. Open the **Future Products.txt** file.

   a) On the Windows 10 taskbar, select the **File Explorer** icon.

   b) In File Explorer, navigate to the **C:\091055Data\Getting Started with Microsoft Office Excel 2016** folder.

   c) Double-click the **Future Products.txt** file.

3. Copy and paste the new product names into the **My New Products.xlsx** workbook.

   a) Select all of the text in the **Future Products.txt** file.

   b) Press **Ctrl+C** to copy the text to the clipboard.

   c) On the taskbar, select the **Excel** icon to switch back to the **My New Products.xlsx** workbook.

   d) Select cell **A4**, and then select **Home→Clipboard→Paste**.

e) Ensure that the new product names appear in the worksheet.

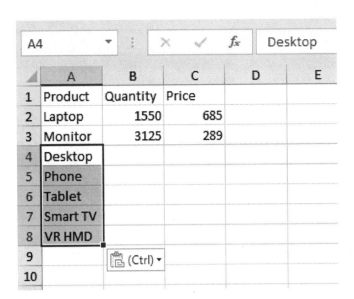

f) Select your text editor's icon on the taskbar to switch back to the **Future Products.txt** file, and then close the file.

4. **Use the AutoFill feature to add unique product numbers for each new product entry.**

   a) Select cell **D1**, type *Prod. #* and then press **Enter**.
   b) In cell **D2**, type *101* and then press **Enter**.
   c) In cell **D3**, type *102* and then press **Enter**.
   d) Select the range **D2:D3**, then place the mouse pointer over the **fill handle** until it appears as a thin, black plus symbol.

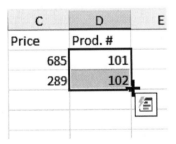

   e) Double-click the **fill handle**.

    Note: You can also drag the **fill handle** manually, but double-clicking is a faster way of populating every cell down a column that has adjacent row data.

   f) Verify that Excel filled in the remaining cells through 107 as expected.

5. **Use Flash Fill to quickly generate a product code based on the product name and number.**

   a) Select cell **E1**, type *Prod. Code* and then press **Enter**.
   b) In cell **E2**, type *Lap-101* and press **Enter**.

c) In cell **E3**, type *M* and then verify that Excel has predicted the product codes for the rest of the products.

D	E
Prod. #	Prod. Code
101	Lap-101
102	Mon-102
103	Des-103
104	Pho-104
105	Tab-105
106	Sma-106
107	VR -107

d) Press **Enter** to complete the Flash Fill.

6. Save and close the **My New Products.xlsx** file, but leave the Excel application open.

TOPIC E

Use Excel Help

As you become more familiar with some of Excel's more advanced functionality, you are likely to encounter commands you are unfamiliar with or have questions about how to perform certain tasks. Excel 2016 comes packaged with its own Help system that can assist you in finding answers to your questions. Taking the time to learn how to use Excel Help now could save you countless hours of research down the road.

Microsoft Excel Help

Microsoft Excel Help provides you with access to articles that can answer your Excel questions and show you how to perform various tasks within the application. Excel Help checks Microsoft Office's support website for these articles, which can include text, screenshots, and video. In order to access Help articles, you must have an active Internet connection. To access the Excel Help system, press the **F1** key. You can also reach Help on specific topics by searching for the topic in

Tell Me, or you can select the **Microsoft Excel Help** button in the top-right corner of the Excel UI while in the **Backstage** view. This opens your web browser to a Help article on that particular **Backstage** command.

> **Note: Excel Online App**
>
> You can access the Excel Online Help window by selecting **File→Help→Help**. Another option is to enter a keyword in the **Tell Me** search box and then select the **Get Help on** item in search results pane. Once open, the Excel Online Help window works the same as the Excel 2016 Help window.

The Help Task Pane

When you open the Excel Help system, Excel displays the **Help** task pane. You can use the **Help** task pane to search for, browse through, and review the various web articles available to you.

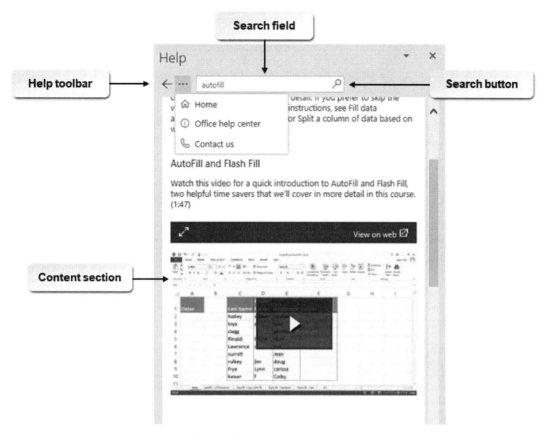

Figure 1-29: The Excel 2016 Help window.

The **Help** task pane is divided into a number of sections and displays a variety of commands to help you locate the desired Help resources. The following table describes each of these in some detail.

Help Task Pane Element	Is Used To
Help toolbar	Navigate back through Help search results, go to the Help home page, open the Microsoft Office help center website in your browser, and contact Microsoft about an issue with Excel.
Search field	Enter search terms for locating Help resources.
Search button	Execute Help searches.
Content section	Display the results of a search or the contents of an online Help article.

 Access the Checklist tile on your CHOICE Course screen for reference information and job aids on How to Use Excel Help.

ACTIVITY 1–7
Using Excel Help

Before You Begin
Excel 2016 is open.

Scenario
As you've been working with Excel more and more, you have come across some features that you have some questions about. You have heard there is a particular command that you might have use for, but you want to learn more about what it does first. You decide to use the Excel Help system to find out more about the application.

---

1. Open Excel Help.
   a) Press **F1**.
   b) Verify that the **Help** task pane opened.

2. Search for Excel Help resources online.
   a) In the **Search** field, type *freeze panes* and select the magnifying glass button.
   b) In the search results, select the **Freeze panes to lock rows and columns** link.
   c) Review the content.
   d) On the **Help** toolbar, select the ellipsis button ⋯ and then select **Home**.

3. Close the **Help** task pane.

Summary

In this lesson, you used some of the most basic Excel 2016 functionality, which laid the foundation you will need to begin developing your Excel knowledge and skills. You navigated the Excel user interface, used Excel commands, created and saved a basic workbook, entered cell data, and used the Excel Help system. As you build upon these foundational skills, you will begin to unlock Excel's robust functionality and discover the power that lies within your organizational data.

Do you think you'll prefer to use the mouse or the keyboard navigation options as you develop your workbooks?

Compared to other desktop apps you've worked with, what is your impression of Excel 2016's UI?

Note: Check your CHOICE Course screen for opportunities to interact with your classmates, peers, and the larger CHOICE online community about the topics covered in this course or other topics you are interested in. From the Course screen you can also access available resources for a more continuous learning experience.

2 | Performing Calculations

Lesson Time: 1 hour, 30 minutes

Lesson Introduction

The true power of Microsoft® Office Excel® 2016 lies in its ability to help you analyze your organizational data. Excel contains an incredible array of functionality to help you do this, particularly when it comes to working with numerical data. In order to take full advantage of Excel's abilities to quickly, efficiently, and accurately calculate data, you must first understand how Excel thinks, and how to tell it what to do. In this lesson, you'll do just that.

Lesson Objectives

In this lesson, you will:

- Create worksheet formulas.

- Insert functions.

- Reuse formulas and functions.

TOPIC A

Create Worksheet Formulas

Imagine trying to maintain a spreadsheet that contains important financial figures that constantly change. Every time a single value changes, you might have to change entire rows or columns of data. Keeping up with such calculations manually is not only impractical and tedious, but it is also unnecessary and, in some cases, nearly impossible. Why not have Excel do it for you? Performing calculations is one of the most critical, foundational tasks in Excel, forming the basis for nearly all of the data analysis you'll need to perform. By gaining a solid, clear understanding of how Excel performs such calculations, you'll save yourself valuable time, avoid a ton of headaches, and ensure a level of accuracy not possible when performing the same calculations on your own.

Excel Formulas

Excel *formulas* perform simple or complex mathematical computations in worksheets. You can use formulas to perform tasks such as adding up a row or a column of numbers, multiplying sales figures by commission rates, and applying tax to sales. One of the key benefits of using formulas in Excel is that you can change some of the values used in the formulas and, by default, Excel will automatically adjust the calculations accordingly.

It is important to remember that, in Excel, what you see isn't necessarily what you get. When you enter a formula into a worksheet cell, by default, Excel will display the result of calculating the formula in the cell, and not the formula itself.

Excel can perform calculations by using fixed numbers, or by referring to values in other cells. This is one of the truly powerful features of using Excel to perform calculations. Excel 2016 provides you with an incredible array of options for performing calculations in your workbooks and worksheets.

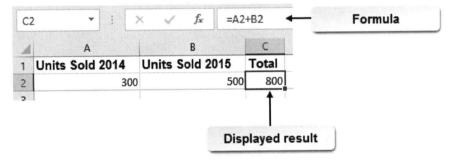

Figure 2–1: A formula in a worksheet cell.

The Formula Bar

You can enter Excel formulas directly into worksheet cells or you can use the *Formula Bar*. As you've seen, the **Formula Bar** allows you to edit cell contents and select, navigate to, and view the contents of selected cells. It's also useful for quickly inserting pre-existing formulas. Additionally, to the left of the **Formula Bar** text box are buttons that provide supplementary options.

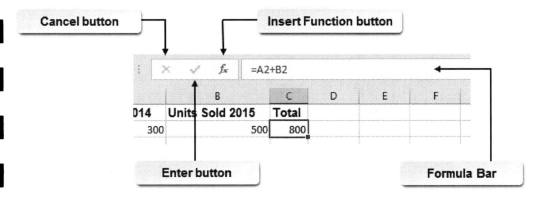

Figure 2-2: Elements of the Formula Bar.

The following table describes the **Formula Bar** options in greater detail.

Formula Bar Option	Description
Cancel button	The **Cancel** button is displayed only when a cell is in **Edit** mode or **Enter** mode. Selecting the **Cancel** button will undo any changes you have made to a cell since selecting it and will keep that cell active. Basically, it reverts the cell back to its state before you began editing it.
Enter button	The **Enter** button is essentially the same as pressing **Ctrl+Enter**. When you select the **Enter** button, Excel enters whatever content is in the active cell and keeps the cell active.
Insert Function button	The **Insert Function** button opens the **Insert Function** dialog box, providing you with access to a wide variety of pre-existing Excel formulas.

Note: Excel Online App

The elements and process used to create Excel formulas are exactly the same in Excel Online. The only minor difference is the absence of the **Cancel** and **Enter** buttons on the **Formula Bar**.

Elements of Excel Formulas

The first rule of using formulas in Excel is that all formulas begin with an equal sign. This may seem a bit counter-intuitive at first, as you are used to seeing figures on both sides of a formula when it's written out. But Excel displays formula results in cells, which takes care of the result side of the equal sign. You enter the expression side of a formula *after* the equal sign.

To understand this better, let's first look at a simple mathematical formula. Formulas basically consist of an expression on one side of the equal sign and a result on the other. Expressions consist of a series of constants, variables, and mathematical operators. Operators indicate where to perform such basic computations as adding, subtracting, multiplying, dividing, calculating exponents, and so on. Here are the basic elements of a mathematical formula as written on paper.

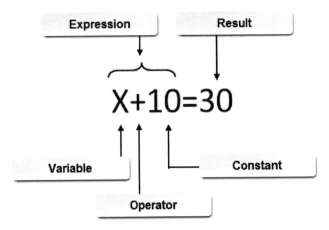

Figure 2-3: A basic mathematical formula.

Excel formulas work pretty much the same way. When you enter a formula in a worksheet cell, the cell displays the result. The equal sign and the mathematical expression make up the content that's actually entered in the cell. In Excel formulas, you can think of constants as numbers you manually enter into formulas, and variables as references to other cells. When you manually type a number into an Excel formula, that number remains the same unless you manually edit it; this is referred to as "hard coding" the value in the formula. When you enter a cell reference in an Excel formula, the result of the calculation will change if you change the value in the referenced cell.

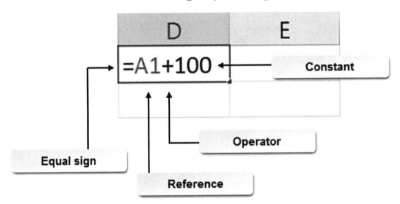

Figure 2-4: An Excel formula.

Basic Excel formulas consist of the following elements: the equal sign, constants, references, and mathematical operators.

Excel Formula Element	Description
Equal sign	The equal sign defines cell content as a formula. The equal sign tells Excel to perform a calculation based on the formula components and then to display the result of the calculation in the cell. All formulas in Excel must start with an equal sign.
Constants	Numbers and text that do not change unless manually altered.
References	Essentially, the variables in Excel formulas. When you include a reference to a cell or a range, Excel uses the value(s) from that cell or range to perform the calculation.
Mathematical operators	Symbols that specify the kind of calculation that Excel should perform on the elements of a formula.

Common Mathematical Operators

Excel uses a set of the most commonly used mathematical operators to perform a wide variety of calculations. These are simply symbols Excel uses to identify the calculations it should perform.

Mathematical Operator	Symbol	Function/Operation
Parentheses	( )	Groups a set of constants, references, and operators into a single value within a formula.
Caret	^	Exponentiation
Asterisk	*	Multiplication
Forward slash	/	Division
Plus sign	+	Addition
Minus sign	-	Subtraction

The Order of Operations

Excel gives precedence to certain mathematical operators over others. This is how Excel determines which operation to perform first, second, third, and so on in a complex formula. It is important that you understand how Excel will compute a formula before you create one to ensure that Excel will perform the calculation exactly as you want it to. The following is the order of operations, from first to last:

- Parentheses
- Exponents
- Multiplication and division
- Addition and subtraction

It's important to understand that, in some cases, Excel also reads formulas from left to right. So if two or more operators fall in the same order of precedence, such as in a formula with both the addition and the subtraction operators, Excel will perform the leftmost calculation first.

 Note: While often used for subtraction, the minus sign (−) can also be used to denote a negative value. In these cases, the minus sign takes greater precedence than exponents, allowing you to calculate the exponential value of a negative number. Percentage signs (%) also take higher precedence than exponents.

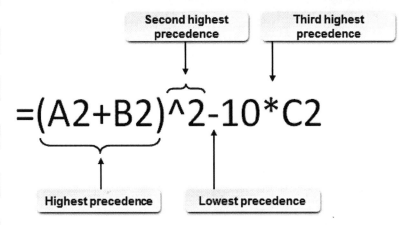

Figure 2–5: Excel performs mathematical computations in a specific order.

Reference Operators

Mathematical operators aren't the only type of operator you will use to work with the data in your workbooks. In fact, there are four different kinds of operators you can use to perform calculations. *Reference operators* are one of the most important. Reference operators tell Excel which cell or range values to use as variables in your formulas. There are three reference operators: the comma, the colon, and the space.

Reference Operator	Symbol	Function
Comma	,	The comma is used as a union operator, which tells Excel to include each reference in a series of references. This is similar to how you would use a comma when writing a serial list; you are telling Excel to include each of the references. So, A1,B3,C5 tells Excel to include the values in each of these three cells.
Colon	:	The colon is used as a range operator, which you've already seen when selecting a range of cells. The colon tells Excel to include all cells in a range between the cell references on either side of the colon. For example, A1:A10 tells Excel to include the values in every cell from A1 to cell A10.
Space	N/A	A blank space is an intersection operator. This tells Excel to look for a value in the cell where two ranges intersect. For example, A9:J9 E2:E22 tells Excel to look for the value in the cell where these two ranges intersect, which in this case would be the value in cell E9. If you have a spreadsheet of salespeople as the rows and their quarterly sales as the columns, you can use an intersection to find how well Salesperson X did in Q3. While you might be able to find this information by simply looking at the spreadsheet, this can become a hassle in larger spreadsheets that require scrolling through multiple pages.

Note: Excel reads a blank space only as an intersection operator if no other operator is present between cell or range references. If you enter another reference operator between the cell or range references, Excel will read the operator and ignore the spaces. So, A1:A3, A5, A6 is the same, to Excel, as A1:A3,A5,A6. Here, the spaces don't matter because of the commas. Excel will not look for the intersection, which in this case makes sense as the cells don't actually intersect.

	A	B	C	D	E	F	G	H	I	J	K	L
1	Employee Name	Region	Qtr. 1	Qtr. 2	Qtr. 3	Qtr. 4	Total	Average	Highest	Lowest		Matthews' Q3
2	Silva	Northeast	$115,500	$65,500	$84,000	$187,110	$452,110	$113,027.50	$187,110	$65,500		=A9:J9 E2:E22
3	Maddox	Northeast	$113,500	$120,550	$243,760	$197,830	$675,640	$168,910.00	$243,760	$113,500		
4	Koval	West	$104,500	$113,000	$100,700	$110,925	$429,125	$107,281.25	$113,000	$100,700		
5	Lindgren	South	$79,500	$113,500	$88,000	$61,670	$342,670	$85,667.50	$113,500	$61,670		
6	Sykes	North	$125,000	$170,000	$105,000	$192,215	$592,215	$148,053.75	$192,215	$105,000		
7	Lee	West	$120,550	$274,060	$76,000	$142,320	$612,930	$153,232.50	$274,060	$76,000		Intersection operation
8	Gilgamos	West	$128,000	$243,760	$151,500	$92,215	$615,475	$153,868.75	$243,760	$92,215		
9	Matthews	South	$113,000	$292,225	$84,000	$102,270	$591,495	$147,873.75	$292,225	$84,000		
10	Anderson	North	$113,500	$243,240	$184,275	$147,150	$688,165	$172,041.25	$243,240	$113,500		
11	Smith	Southwest	$116,500	$123,000	$106,900	$211,020	$557,420	$139,355.00	$211,020	$106,900		
12	Wagner	Northeast	$119,000	$138,500	$63,000	$88,950	$409,450	$102,362.50	$138,500	$63,000		
13	Roberts	South	$274,130	$296,120	$120,500	$118,335	$809,085	$202,271.25	$296,120	$118,335		
14	Avellone	Southweest	$156,000	$115,500	$88,500	$171,050	$531,050	$132,762.50	$171,050	$88,500		
15	Clarke	West	$251,120	$86,500	$76,000	$136,650	$550,270	$137,567.50	$251,120	$76,000		

Figure 2-6: This intersection will return the value $84,000.

Access the Checklist tile on your **CHOICE** Course screen for reference information and job aids on **How to Create Formulas.**

ACTIVITY 2–1
Creating Worksheet Formulas

Data File

C:\091055Data\Performing Calculations\New Product Income.xlsx

Before You Begin

Excel 2016 is open.

Scenario

Develetech plans to introduce five new products. Company management wants you to analyze the projected sales figures to determine how much the company can plan to profit from the new items. You have entered the sales estimates into an Excel worksheet. Now, you must use Excel formulas to get Excel to perform the calculations for you.

1. Open the **New Product Income.xlsx** file.

   a) If necessary, select **File→Open**.
   b) From the **Open** screen, select **Browse**.
   c) In the **Open** dialog box, navigate to the **C:\091055Data\Performing Calculations** folder.
   d) Select the **New Product Income.xlsx** file and then select **Open**.

2. Calculate the sales before tax based on the sales estimates for each product.

   a) Select cell **B8**.

b) Type *=b2+b3+b4+b5+b6* and press **Enter**.

	A	B
1	New Product	Est. Sales
2	Desktop	55350
3	Phone	109600
4	Tablet	78900
5	Smart TV	89488
6	VR HMD	59400
7		
8	Sales Before Tax	392738
9	Tax Rate	8%
10	Sales With Tax	
11	Expenses	81980
12	Profit	

Note: Although Excel displays cell and range references, and many other elements of formulas and functions, in all capital letters, it is not necessary to type them in all capital letters. Excel's functionality enables it to determine what is a formula or function and what is standard text based on the context of your cell data. Excel will automatically display formulas and functions in all capital letters, even if you type them as lowercase letters.

c) Verify that the sum of the values in the range **B2:B6** is displayed in cell **B8**.

3. Calculate sales with tax.
   a) Select cell **B10**.
   b) Type *=b8+(b8*b9)* and press **Enter**.
   c) Verify that Excel performed the calculation as expected.

	A	B
1	New Product	Est. Sales
2	Desktop	55350
3	Phone	109600
4	Tablet	78900
5	Smart TV	89488
6	VR HMD	59400
7		
8	Sales Before Tax	392738
9	Tax Rate	8%
10	Sales With Tax	424157.04
11	Expenses	81980
12	Profit	

4. Subtract expenses from sales before tax to calculate the estimated profit on the new product sales.

a) Select cell **B12**.

b) Type *=b8-b11* and press **Enter**.

c) Verify that Excel performed the calculation as expected.

	A	B
1	New Product	Est. Sales
2	Desktop	55350
3	Phone	109600
4	Tablet	78900
5	Smart TV	89488
6	VR HMD	59400
7		
8	Sales Before Tax	392738
9	Tax Rate	8%
10	Sales With Tax	424157.04
11	Expenses	81980
12	Profit	310758
13		

5. Save the file as *My New Product Income.xlsx* and close the workbook.

a) Select **File→Save As**.

b) From the **Save As** screen, if necessary, select **This PC**, and then, in the **Current Folder** section, select the **Performing Calculations** folder.

c) In the **Save As** dialog box, in the **File name** field, type *My New Product Income* and select **Save**.

d) Close the workbook.

TOPIC B

Insert Functions

You've learned the usefulness of basic formulas, but at some point, you will likely need to use more complex formulas that involve numerous cell and range references. Excel 2016 provides you with the ability to do this quickly and easily through a massive set of built-in formulas. Excel includes functionality to help you fill in and interpret these formulas, enabling you to focus more on the information you need to extract from your data and less on the mathematical operations themselves. Taking the time to learn how to use this functionality now will save you time, effort, and possibly a few headaches down the road.

Functions

In Excel, *functions* are simply built-in, predefined formulas that you can quickly and easily insert into worksheet cells. Like formulas, all functions begin with an equal sign. Unlike formulas, in functions the equal sign is followed by the function name and then a set of *arguments* in parentheses, which are separated by commas. Arguments can be cell references, constants, formulas, or even other functions or logical values. Functions use their arguments in specific ways to calculate a result. The function name is typically the name, or an abbreviated version, of the actual mathematical function. For example, you would use the SUM function to find the sum of a group of numbers and you would use the EXP function to calculate an exponential expression. Each function has its own specific structure and order of arguments. You can manually type functions into worksheet cells or you can enter them by using various commands and dialog boxes.

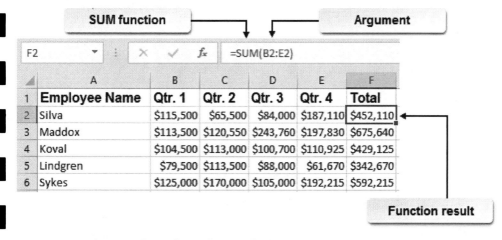

Figure 2-7: The SUM function with a single argument.

The Function Library Group

Excel 2016 provides you with a central location for accessing all of its available functions: the **Function Library** group. The **Function Library** group contains a set of menus that organize Excel functions according to specific categories for ease of reference. The **Function Library** group also provides you with access to the **Insert Function** button, which is the same as the **Insert Function** button on the **Formula Bar**, and the AutoSum feature. You can access the **Function Library** group on the **Formulas** tab.

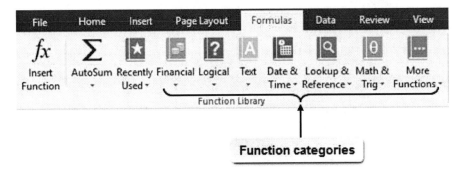

Figure 2-8: The Function Library group.

The following table provides a brief description of the function categories in the **Function Library** group.

Category	Provides You with Access To
Recently Used	The functions you have most recently used. When you first install Excel, you can access a set of commonly used functions from this menu.
Financial	Functions used to perform business calculations, such as determining loan repayment figures, determining the future value or net present value of an investment, and calculating asset depreciation.
Logical	Functions that determine if an argument is true or false, or if it meets other logical conditions.
Text	Functions that change text values, such as making text all capital letters or converting numbers into dollar amounts.
Date & Time	Functions that allow you to incorporate dates and times into calculations. You might use these, for example, to determine how many work days occur between two specific dates.
Lookup & Reference	Functions that allow you to look up a particular cell value or reference from a range or table given specific criteria.
Math & Trig	Formulas that perform a number of different mathematical or trigonometric calculations.
More Functions	A set of menus that contain some higher-level and less commonly used functions, such as engineering and statistical functions.

Note: Excel Online App

The basics of function syntax and how to insert functions is the same regardless of the Excel version you are using. However, in Excel Online, you do not have the same ability to step through building a function one argument at a time. According to Microsoft, some workbook functions behave differently in the browser window. For detailed information on workbook function differences, go to **https://support.office.com**.

The Insert Function Dialog Box

The **Insert Function** dialog box enables you to search for and insert into cells any of the available functions in Excel 2016. The **Insert Function** dialog box also displays a brief description of whatever function you have selected and provides a link to open the **Excel 2016 Help** window, which automatically displays help content on the currently selected function. You can access the

Insert Function dialog box by selecting the **Insert Function** button either on the **Formula Bar** or in the **Function Library** group.

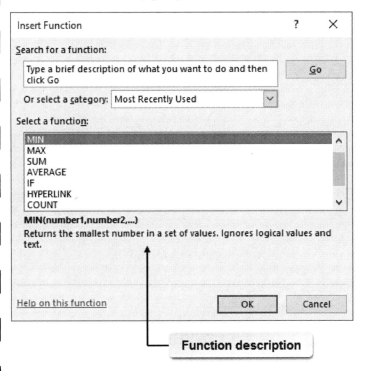

Function description

Figure 2-9: The Insert Function dialog box.

The following table describes the various elements of the **Insert Function** dialog box.

Insert Function Dialog Box Element	Use This To
Search for a function field	Enter a description of what you would like a function to do. For example, you could type "add numbers together" or "find the average of a set of numbers." The **Insert Function** dialog box will use this as a search query to find the appropriate function.
Go button	Execute a function search.
Or select a category drop-down menu	Filter the available functions by category. If you perform a search, this menu defaults to the **Recommended** setting and the search results will appear in the **Select a function** menu. Even if you've entered a search query, if you change the setting here to any category other than **Recommended**, the **Select a function** menu displays all functions in the selected category, effectively ignoring the search query.
Select a function menu	View a list of available functions depending on your search query or your selection in the **Or select a category** drop-down menu.
Function description	View a brief description of the currently selected function.
Help on this function link	Open the **Excel 2016 Help** window to display an article about the currently selected function.

 Note: Excel Online App

The **Insert Function** button is available on the **HOME** and **INSERT** tabs but it opens a simplified version of the **Insert Function** dialog box that you see in Excel 2016.

The Function Arguments Dialog Box

When you insert a function using the categorized menus in the **Function Library** group or the **Insert Function** dialog box, Excel displays the **Function Arguments** dialog box. You can use this dialog box to enter the required and optional arguments for the function, view descriptions of the function and its arguments, and view a preview of the function results given the currently entered arguments. The **Help on this function** link performs the same task here as it does in the **Insert Function** dialog box.

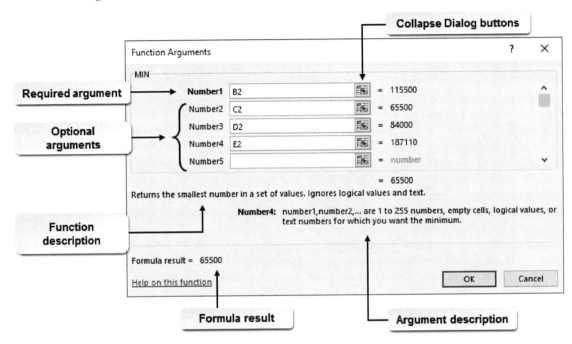

Figure 2-10: The Function Arguments dialog box assists you with the process of entering function arguments.

The following table describes the various elements of the **Function Arguments** dialog box.

Function Arguments Dialog Box Element	Use This To
Required argument fields	Enter the required arguments for the function. The required argument names appear in bold text.
Optional argument fields	Enter the desired optional arguments for the function. The optional argument names appear in non-bold text.
Collapse Dialog button	Minimize the **Function Arguments** dialog box to graphically select cell and range references directly on your worksheets. This command appears in numerous dialog boxes, wherever you have the option of manually selecting a cell or range. Once you collapse a dialog box, this becomes the **Expand Dialog** button, which you can use to restore the dialog box to its full size.
Function description	View a brief description of the function.
Argument description	View a brief description of the currently selected argument.
Formula result	Preview the function result given the currently entered arguments.

 Note: Excel Online App
This feature and function-building guidance is not available in Excel Online.

Graphical Cell and Range Reference Entry

Excel 2016 provides you with a useful graphical method for entering cell and range references for a number of purposes, including for use in formulas and functions. Whenever you need to enter a cell or range reference, you have the option of typing the reference manually or selecting the reference graphically right from the worksheet. This is why the **Function Arguments** dialog box provides the **Collapse Dialog** buttons. These minimize the dialog box, providing you with easier access to your worksheets for the purpose of graphically selecting references. To graphically select a reference, you can simply select the cell or the range with mouse clicks or by dragging the mouse (or by using the appropriate equivalent action on a touchscreen device), and then either press the **Enter** key or select the **Expand Dialog** button in the minimized dialog box.

> **Note:** If you are manually typing a formula or function, once you've graphically selected a range, you can simply enter the next formula element or type a comma and then enter the next function argument.

After you graphically select a cell or range reference, Excel displays the marquee selection to help you verify that you have selected the correct cell or range. When you have finished entering the reference, the marquee selection goes away.

B2			×	✓	*fx*	=AVERAGE(B2:E6)	

	A	B	C	D	E	F
1	**Employee Name**	**Qtr. 1**	**Qtr. 2**	**Qtr. 3**	**Qtr. 4**	**Total**
2	Silva	$115,500	$65,500	$84,000	$187,110	$452,110
3	Maddox	$113,500	$120,550	$243,760	$197,830	$675,640
4	Koval	$104,500	$113,000	$100,700	$110,925	$429,125
5	Lindgren	$79,500	$113,500	$88,000	$61,670	$342,670
6	Sykes	$125,000	$170,000	$105,000	$192,215	$592,215

Figure 2-11: Graphically selecting cell and range references is a quick and easy alternative to typing them.

The AutoSum Feature

Adding up the values in a row or a column is the single most common mathematical calculation most people perform in Excel. As such, Excel provides you with a fast and easy way to do this: the AutoSum feature. The AutoSum feature enables you to calculate the total of the values in a row or a column simply by selecting a single button and then pressing **Enter** or **Tab**. Using the AutoSum feature inserts a SUM function in the active cell.

The AutoSum feature will automatically try to guess which cells you would like to add together if you use it on a cell in a row or a column that contains values. AutoSum first looks for cells above, then looks for cells to the left of the active cell. You can also manually edit the group of cells or the range that the AutoSum feature should include as arguments in the SUM function. If there are no values in the row and the column associated with a cell and you insert the SUM function, you must manually enter the arguments in the SUM function.

You can access the AutoSum feature by selecting **Formulas→Function Library→AutoSum** or by using the **Alt+=** keyboard shortcut. For ease of access purposes, Excel also displays the **AutoSum** button in the **Editing** group on the **Home** tab.

> **Note:** You do not have to use the AutoSum feature to insert a SUM function. You can also simply type the SUM function into a cell or access the SUM function from the **Math & Trig** menu in the **Function Library** group.

◢	A	B	C	D	E	F	G	H
1	**Employee Name**	**Qtr. 1**	**Qtr. 2**	**Qtr. 3**	**Qtr. 4**	**Total**		
2	Silva	$115,500	$65,500	$84,000	$187,110	=SUM(B2:E2)		
3	Maddox	$113,500	$120,550	$243,760	$197,830	SUM(**number1**, [number2], ...)		
4	Koval	$104,500	$113,000	$100,700	$110,925			
5	Lindgren	$79,500	$113,500	$88,000	$61,670			
6	Sykes	$125,000	$170,000	$105,000	$192,215			

Figure 2-12: The AutoSum feature correctly guesses that the sum in F2 should use B2:E2 as its argument.

Note: Excel Online App

The **AutoSum** button and commonly used functions list are the same in appearance and function in Excel Online.

Other Commonly Used Functions

The **AutoSum** button in the **Function Library** group also provides you with quick access to some other commonly used Excel functions. When you select the **AutoSum** drop-down arrow, Excel displays a menu that allows you to insert one of these other common functions into the active cell.

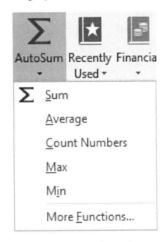

Figure 2-13: The other commonly used functions available from the AutoSum button.

You can use the functions available from the **AutoSum** drop-down arrow to perform the following tasks.

Function	Use To
SUM	Add the values entered in the cells that are specified in the arguments.
AVERAGE	Calculate the average of the values entered in the cells specified in the arguments.
COUNT	Find the number of cells, out of those that have been specified in the arguments, that contain numeric entries.
MAX	Find the largest single numeric value out of all of the values entered in the cells specified in the arguments.
MIN	Find the smallest single numeric value out of all of the values entered in the cells specified in the arguments.

> **Note:** Similar functions to COUNT include COUNTA, which finds the number of cells that contain any type of value, and COUNTBLANK, which finds the number of cells that contain no value at all.

Basic Function Syntax

In order to understand exactly how an Excel function works, you must understand its *syntax*. A function's syntax is simply the structure necessary to properly express the function and to define its arguments. As stated earlier, all Excel functions begin with an equal sign followed by the function name. The function name is followed by a set of parentheses that contains the function's arguments; the arguments are separated by commas. Remember that depending on the particular function you are using, arguments can include constants, cell or range references, logical values such as TRUE or FALSE, formulas, and even other functions.

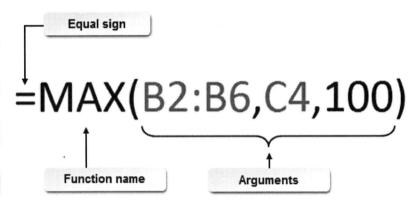

Figure 2-14: The basic elements of an Excel function.

Functions can contain both required and optional arguments. In function syntax, optional arguments are notated by using square brackets [ ]. The SUM function, as an example, contains one required argument and up to 254 optional arguments. Excel must have at least one number to return a result. Excel can sum up to 255 values with a single SUM function. So the first argument (value) is required, and the rest are optional.

Each function has a unique syntax and requires different specific arguments. If all of the arguments for a function are valid, the function will return a result in a cell. If one or more of the arguments in a function are invalid, Excel will return an error, which you will have to correct. Let's take a look at the syntax for each of the commonly used functions mentioned so far.

The SUM Function

Syntax: =SUM(number 1, [number 2], ...)

> **Note:** The ellipsis (...) in function syntax indicates that the same type of argument can carry out up to the maximum number of arguments for the function. In this case, it's up to 255 arguments, which is the maximum number of supported arguments in an Excel 2016 function.

Description: Adds the values specified by the arguments. For this function, the arguments can be constants, cell or range references, or both.

The following table includes examples of the SUM function in action.

To Add These Numbers	Enter This Function
The values in cells A1 through A10	=SUM(A1:A10)
The values in cells A1 through A10, in cell B3, and in cell D17	=SUM(A1:A10, B3, D17)

To Add These Numbers	Enter This Function
The values in cells A1 through A10, in cell B3, in cell D17, and the numbers 14 and 7	=SUM(A1:A10, B3, D17, 14, 7)

The AVERAGE Function

Syntax: =AVERAGE(number 1, [number 2], ...)

Description: Adds the values specified by the arguments and then divides the total by the number of individual values. In other words, the AVERAGE function calculates the average (arithmetic mean) of the specified values. For this function, the arguments can be constants, cell or range references, or both.

The following table includes examples of the AVERAGE function in action.

To Find the Average of These Numbers	Enter This Function
The values in cells A1 through A10	=AVERAGE(A1:A10)
The values in cells A1 through A10, in cell B3, and in cell D17	=AVERAGE(A1:A10, B3, D17)
The values in cells A1 through A10, in cell B3, in cell D17, and the numbers 14 and 7	=AVERAGE(A1:A10, B3, D17, 14, 7)

The COUNT Function

Syntax: =COUNT(value 1, [value 2], ...)

Description: Counts the number of cells specified in the arguments that contain a numeric entry. For this function, the arguments can be cell or range references, or both.

The following table includes examples of the COUNT function in action.

To Count the Number of Numeric Entries in These Cells	Enter This Function
A1 through A10	=COUNT(A1:A10)
A1 through A10, B7, and F11	=COUNT(A1:A10, B7, F11)
All cells from A1 through D10	=COUNT(A1:D10)

 Note: The COUNT function will also count constants if you include them as arguments. However, it is more intended to count numeric cell entries.

The MAX Function

Syntax: =MAX(number 1, [number 2], ...)

Description: Returns the largest numeric value out of all numeric values in the arguments. For this function, the arguments can be constants, cell or range references, or both.

The following table includes examples of the MAX function in action.

To Return the Largest Numeric Value from These Sources	Enter This Function
The values in cells A1 through A10	=MAX(A1:A10)
The values in cells A1 through A10, B13, and C22	=MAX(A1:A10, B13, C22)
The values in cells A1 through A10, and the number 78	=MAX(A1:A10, 78)

The MIN Function

Syntax: =MIN(number 1, [number 2], ...)

Description: Returns the smallest numeric value out of all numeric values in the arguments. For this function, the arguments can be constants, cell or range references, or both.

The following table includes examples of the MIN function in action.

To Return the Smallest Numeric Value from These Sources	Enter This Function
The values in cells A1 through A10	=MIN(A1:A10)
The values in cells A1 through A10, B13, and C22	=MIN(A1:A10, B13, C22)
The values in cells A1 through A10, and the number 78	=MIN(A1:A10, 78)

 Note: To explore how Excel handles dates in calculations, view the LearnTO **Calculate Dates in Excel** presentation from the **LearnTO** tile on the CHOICE Course screen.

The Formula AutoComplete Feature

The Formula AutoComplete feature is a dynamic feature that anticipates the function you want to use in a cell. When you type an equal sign into a cell, and then begin typing the name of a function, Excel displays a pop-up menu with all of the available functions that begin with the characters you have already typed. This allows you to select the desired function, and then simply enter the required arguments to complete it. The Formula AutoComplete feature also displays a tooltip that describes whatever function you select from the pop-up menu. The Formula AutoComplete feature can save you time otherwise spent navigating the extensive **Function Library** group for the function you're looking for. It can also help you quickly select a function when you can't remember its exact name.

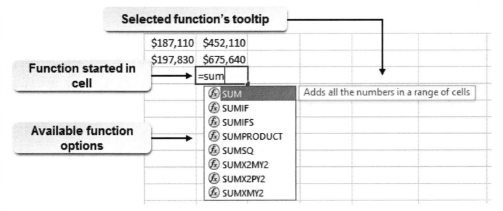

Figure 2-15: Excel displays the available function options and their descriptions as you type the function name.

The Formula AutoComplete feature also provides you with assistance when entering function arguments. As you enter the arguments for the selected formula, Excel displays a different tooltip that highlights the specific argument you're currently entering. This helps you keep track of which arguments you've entered and which ones you still need to enter. When you're done entering all necessary arguments, simply press **Enter** or **Tab**, and Excel will automatically add the closing parenthesis and enter the function.

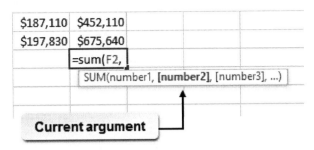

Figure 2–16: This tooltip highlights where you are within the function syntax.

 Access the Checklist tile on your **CHOICE** Course screen for reference information and job aids on How to Insert Functions.

ACTIVITY 2-2
Inserting Functions

Data File

C:\091055Data\Performing Calculations\Sales Contest.xlsx

Before You Begin

Excel 2016 is open.

Scenario

You've launched a sales contest to reward Develetech's best performing sales reps. To track their progress, you created a worksheet to store and perform calculations on the sales figures for each of the reps. You're trying to analyze the numbers to determine which sales reps will win prizes. You want to start by calculating each rep's total sales, average quarterly sales, and highest and lowest quarterly sales.

1. Open the **Sales Contest.xlsx** workbook file.

2. Calculate the total sales for the first two sales reps: Silva and Maddox.
   a) Select cell **F4**.
   b) Select **Formulas→Function Library→AutoSum**.
   c) Verify that the cell range **B4:E4** is selected on the worksheet and that it appears in the active cell and in the **Formula Bar**.
   d) Press **Enter**.
   e) Perform the same calculation for Maddox.

3. Calculate the average quarterly sales for the same two sales reps.
   a) Select cell **G4** and type *=av*
   b) From the **Formula AutoComplete** pop-up menu, double-click **AVERAGE**.
   c) On the worksheet, select the range **B4:E4**.
   d) Add a closing parenthesis and press **Enter**.
   e) Perform the same calculation for Maddox.

Total	Average	Highest
452110	113027.5	
675640	168910	

4. Determine the highest quarterly sales total for the same two sales reps.
   a) Select cell **H4**.
   b) Select **Formulas→Function Library→Insert Function**.
   c) In the **Insert Function** dialog box, in the **Search for a function** field, type *max* and select **Go**.
   d) In the **Select a function** menu, ensure that **MAX** is selected, and then select **OK**.

e) In the **Function Arguments** dialog box, to the right of the **Number1** field, select the **Collapse Dialog** button.

f) On the worksheet, select the range **B4:E4** and then select the **Expand Dialog** button.

> **Note:** You may need to move the **Insert Function** dialog box to select the range.

g) In the **Function Arguments** dialog box, select **OK**.

h) Repeat the process for Maddox.

Total	Average	Highest	Lowest
452110	113027.5	187110	
675640	168910	243760	

5. Determine the lowest quarterly sales for the same two sales reps.

a) Select cell I4.

b) Select **Formulas→Function Library→AutoSum drop-down arrow→Min**.

c) On the worksheet, select the range **B4:E4** and press **Enter**.

d) Ensure that cell I5 is selected and then select **Formulas→Function Library→More Functions→Statistical→MIN**.

e) In the **Function Arguments** dialog box, to the right of the **Number1** field, select the **Collapse Dialog** button.

f) Select the range **B5:E5** and press **Enter**.

g) In the **Function Arguments** dialog box, select **OK**.

Total	Average	Highest	Lowest	Commission
452110	113027.5	187110	65500	
675640	168910	243760	113500	

6. Save the workbook to the **C:\091055Data\Performing Calculations** folder as *My Sales Contest.xlsx* and leave the workbook open.

TOPIC C

Reuse Formulas and Functions

Imagine that you're totaling the sales figures for individual associates to calculate their commissions. You'll likely need to apply the same formula or function to each row. If your organization employs hundreds, or even thousands, of sales associates, this could be an incredibly lengthy, tedious process. Being able to create one set of formulas or functions and then apply it to every row would be far easier. Excel, much like a word-processing application, provides you with a number of methods to reuse nearly any of your content, including formulas and functions, basically by using a variety of copy and paste techniques. This functionality represents one of the most useful time-saving features of Excel. By reusing your content, you can eliminate the hassle and reduce the likelihood of entering numerous errors in your workbooks. All of this will allow you to avoid repetitive tasks and hours of troubleshooting so you can focus on more important tasks.

Formulas and the Cut, Copy, and Paste Commands

As with other worksheet content, if you want to reuse your Excel formulas and functions, you can do so by using the **Cut**, **Copy**, and **Paste** commands. By default, if a cell contains a formula or a function and you cut or copy its content to the clipboard, when you paste the content to another cell, Excel pastes the formula in the destination cell. Although the destination cell will display the result of the formula or function, as it did in the source cell, the content is still the formula. This functionality forms the basis of how you can reuse formulas and functions throughout your worksheets and workbooks.

Drag-and-Drop Editing

In addition to using the **Cut**, **Copy**, and **Paste** commands to move content, you can use Excel's drag-and-drop editing functionality. When you select a cell or a range, the cell or range is displayed with a solid green border around it. If you place the mouse pointer over the green border anywhere other than above the **fill handle**, Excel displays the mouse pointer as a move icon. When the move pointer appears, you can click and drag the selected cell or range and drop it in place anywhere else on the worksheet. This effectively cuts and pastes all content within the selection to the new location.

If you press and hold down the **Ctrl** key while performing this procedure, the mouse pointer changes into the copy pointer. By using the copy pointer, you can drag a copy of the content in the selected cell(s) to a new location. This is the same as copying and pasting the content.

The Paste Options

Excel 2016 provides you with a number of different options for pasting copied content into other cells. This is because there will be occasions where you want to paste certain elements of a cell's content into another cell, but not the exact contents. Let's look at an example to clarify this. What if you want to paste a formula's numerical result in another cell, without bringing the actual formula along with it? Situations like this are where Excel's paste options come in handy.

When you copy a cell's contents to the clipboard, a number of paste options become available from the **Paste** drop-down menu, which you can access from the **Paste** drop-down arrow in the **Clipboard** group. These options are also available from the **Paste Options** button if you paste the content by using the **Paste** button or the **Ctrl+V** keyboard shortcut. If you access the paste options from the ribbon, placing the mouse pointer over the various option icons will display a temporary preview of what the content will look like if you select that option.

Note: The paste options are not available if you cut a cell's content. They are available only when you copy and paste.

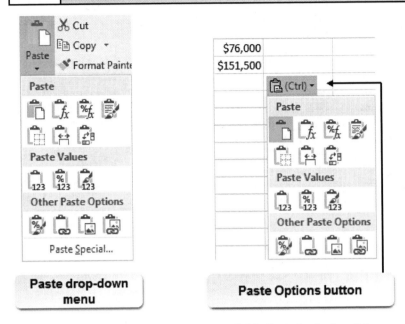

Paste drop-down menu

Paste Options button

Figure 2-17: The paste options are available from both the ribbon and the Paste Options button.

The following table describes the various paste options.

Paste Option	Will Paste
Paste	All of the copied cells' contents.
Formulas	Just the formulas from the copied cells.
Formulas & Number Formatting	The formulas and any applied number formatting from the copied cells.
Keep Source Formatting	All of the copied cells' content along with all applied formatting.
No Borders	All of the copied cells' content and formatting except for the border formatting.
Keep Source Column Widths	All of the copied cells' content and formatting. This option will also adjust the column width for the column the destination cells are in to match the column width of the copied cell.
Transpose	All of the contents and formatting from a group of copied cells. This option will also switch rows to columns and vice versa.
Values	Just the values from the copied cells without formulas or formatting.
Values & Number Formatting	Just the values and any number formatting from the copied cells without formulas or other types of applied formatting.
Values & Source Formatting	Just the values and any applied formatting from the source cells without the formulas.
Formatting	Just the formatting from the copied cells without any cell content.

Paste Option	Will Paste
Paste Link	The content from the selected cells into the new cells and will create a link between the cells. If you make any changes to the copied cells, those changes will be reflected in the new cells. This option works only for certain types of content, such as formulas that contain absolute references.
Picture	The displayed content from the copied cells as a picture. The pasted content will no longer behave like values, formulas, functions, text, and so on.
Linked Picture	The displayed content from the copied cells as a picture and create a link between the picture and the copied cells. The pasted content will no longer behave like values, formulas, functions, text, and so on, but changes made in the copied cells will be reflected in the pasted picture.

 Note: Some of the paste options described in this table cover features or options that have not yet been discussed. Most of these will be covered either later in this course or in other courses in the Excel 2016 series.

The Paste Special Options

Excel 2016 provides you with several other paste options that you can access by using the **Paste Special** dialog box. Here you will find many of the same paste options you've already seen, but you will also find a few more. These include the ability to paste review markup such as comments and validation formatting (which restricts the type of data that a user can enter into cells) along with several options for performing basic mathematical operations. You can access the **Paste Special** dialog box by selecting **Home→Clipboard→Paste drop-down arrow→Paste Special**.

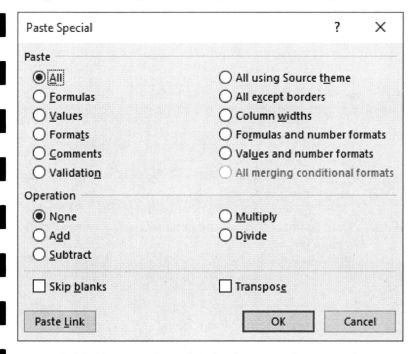

Figure 2-18: The Paste Special dialog box provides you with access to additional paste options.

The following table describes some of the **Paste Special** options that are not available with the other paste options.

Paste Special Option	Description
Add	Adds the value in the copied cell to the value entered in the destination cell.
Subtract	Subtracts the value in the copied cell from the value entered in the destination cell.
Multiply	Multiplies the value in the destination cell by the value in the copied cell.
Divide	Divides the value in the destination cell by the value in the copied cell.
Skip blanks	If the range you copy includes blank cells, these will be omitted when you paste the content to the destination range of cells.

Note: Excel Online App

There is no **Paste Special** dialog box in Excel Online, and you are limited to the following **Paste Special** options: **Formulas**, **Values**, and **Formatting**.

Relative References

Before you explore how cutting, copying, and pasting relate to reusing formulas, you will first need to understand how cell and range references work. In Excel, there are three types of references: relative, absolute, and mixed. *Relative references* are the default in Excel. A relative reference is a cell or a range reference that will change when you move or copy a formula from one cell to another. In other words, the reference is relative to the location of the cell. To see how this works, take a look at this simple example.

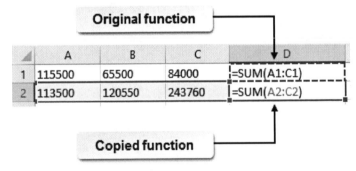

Figure 2-19: With relative references, when you move a formula or function, the cell references change.

In this example, the formula from cell **D1** has been copied and pasted into cell **D2**. The formula in cell **D1** adds the values in cells **A1**, **B1**, and **C1**. But because the range reference in the formula is a relative reference, what it's telling Excel is to look at the cell three spaces to the left of the formula, the cell two spaces to the left of the formula, and the cell one space to the left of the formula to find the values to add. So when you copy and paste the formula into cell **D2**, it still looks for the values in the cells three spaces to the left, two spaces to the left, and one space to the left. This is why the reference has changed from **A1:C1** to **A2:C2**, as those are now the cells the correct number of spaces away from the formula. If you were to paste the same formula into cell **D3**, the range reference would change to **A3:C3**, and so on.

Relative references are one of the keys to understanding just how powerful and useful Excel can be. This forms the basis for how Excel can apply the same calculation to thousands of rows and columns of data.

Absolute References

On the other hand, *absolute references* refer to particular cells and do not change when you move or copy formulas to other cells. In Excel, absolute references are indicated by using the dollar sign ($) before the row and column header. So, if **A1** is a relative reference, then **A1** is an absolute reference. You use absolute references whenever you want to apply a formula to multiple cells but still want part of the calculation to include a value entered into a specific cell. Common examples of this include multiplying a sales figure by the sales tax rate or a sales rep's total sales by the commission rate. Rather than having to enter the same multiplier in every row or column of data, you can simply place that value in a single cell on your worksheet, and then include an absolute reference to that cell in the formula. When you move or copy that formula to the other sales figures, each is now multiplied by the same value.

In the following example, the cells in column **D** contain formulas with relative references. These were copied from cell **D2** to the other cells in the column. By default, the cells in column **D** would display the sales totals for each sales rep for the first two quarters. The formulas in column **E** are multiplying the sales totals from column **D** by a fixed rate. In this case, it's the sales commission rate in cell **G4**. Because the formula in cell **E2** contains an absolute reference to cell **G4**, when copied to cell **E3**, the formula still references the same cell. Notice, however, that the formula is referencing the sales total in cell **D3**, not **D2**, because that is a relative reference in the formula.

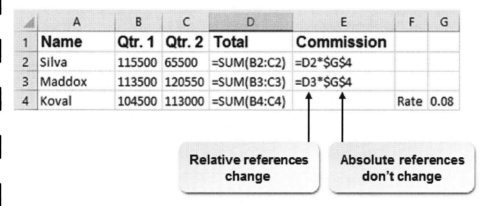

Figure 2-20: Absolute references do not change when copying or moving formulas.

Note: Excel Online App

To apply absolute references, you must type the dollar sign as you enter the cell reference. The **F4** key activates the web browser address bar and does not toggle between absolute, relative, and mixed references.

Mixed References

Mixed references are cell or range references in which either the column or the row header is absolute, but the other reference is relative. The cell reference **A$1** would be a mixed reference. In this example, the column header, **A**, is relative and will change if used in a formula that is copied or moved to another cell. But the row header, **$1**, is absolute, so if you move the formula, it will reference different columns, but in the same row. Mixed references are typically used less than relative and absolute references, but they can be quite handy. You would use a mixed reference when you need to copy a formula across multiple rows and columns and you need the formula to look, for example, for values in the same column but in different rows. Let's take a look at a simple example to see how this works.

In the following example, the worksheet contains a list of three products, each with their base price. Rows 6 and 7 show the percentages that the prices have been marked down for the last three years. Columns E through H will calculate the price for each product, for each year, after the markdown is applied. The basic formula that would go in cell **F2** would be: **=B2*(1-B7)**. This multiplies the desktop's base price by its remaining percentage after the markdown is applied for the year 2013.

	A	B	C	D	E	F	G	H
1	**Product**	**Base Price**			**Price Per Year**	2013	2014	2015
2	Desktop	685			Desktop			
3	Smartphone	249			Smartphone			
4	Tablet	375			Tablet			
5								
6	**Year**	2013	2014	2015				
7	**Decrease**	0.1	0.15	0.18				

However, when you use AutoFill to apply this formula to the other products, you would need the formula to keep looking in row 7, as this is where the markdown percentages are. Otherwise, Excel will assume you want to move down a row for each new product. Likewise, when you AutoFill this formula horizontally, across the different years, you'll need Excel to keep looking in column B where the base prices are. So, you'll need to adjust the aforementioned formula in cell **F2** to the following: **=$B2*(1-B$7)**. Notice the two mixed references—Excel will always look in column B for the base prices, while still moving down the column for each product; and it will always look in row 7 for the markdown percentages, while still moving across the row for each year.

	A	B	C	D	E	F	G	H
1	**Product**	**Base Price**			**Price Per Year**	2013	2014	2015
2	Desktop	685			Desktop	=$B2*(1-B$7)	=$B2*(1-C$7)	=$B2*(1-D$7)
3	Smartphone	249			Smartphone	=$B3*(1-B$7)	=$B3*(1-C$7)	=$B3*(1-D$7)
4	Tablet	375			Tablet	=$B4*(1-B$7)	=$B4*(1-C$7)	=$B4*(1-D$7)
5								
6	**Year**	2013	2014	2015				
7	**Decrease**	0.1	0.15	0.18				

Mixed references

Figure 2-21: Mixed references applied to the example.

 Note: To quickly cycle through relative, absolute, and mixed references in Excel formulas, select the cell with the formula, place the insertion point next to or within the reference in the formula in the **Formula Bar**, and press the **F4** key. If you press the key multiple times, the reference will cycle through all possible combinations.

AutoFill and Formulas

As mentioned with mixed references, you can use the AutoFill feature to quickly and easily copy and paste a formula across columns and rows. This is one of the most useful features Excel has to offer.

Let's say you have a worksheet that lists quarterly sales for your sales team. You want the final column to display the total sales for each sales rep for the entire year. So you enter a SUM function for the first sales rep in the **Total** column. Now you want to copy and paste that formula, using relative references, all the way down the **Total** column. If your company has only 5 or 10 sales reps, copying and pasting would likely be just fine. But what if your organization has thousands of sales reps? Copying and pasting the formula could take hours. However, you can also simply select the cell containing the formula and, by using the **fill handle**, drag the formula down the entire column all at once. If there is one trick you remember about Excel, this should be it.

You can also double-click the **fill handle** to automatically fill all cells in a column with a formula or function. This feature does not work to fill across a row. Also, if there are any gaps in your data, the formula or function will not copy all the way down the column. If you have any empty rows in your data, Excel will fill in the column's cells only up to the first empty row.

	A	B	C	D	E	F	G
1	Name	Qtr. 1	Qtr. 2	Qtr. 3	Qtr. 4	Total	
2	Silva	$115,500	$65,500	$84,000	$187,110	$452,110	
3	Maddox	$113,500	$120,550	$243,760	$197,830	$675,640	
4	Koval	$104,500	$113,000	$100,700	$110,925	$429,125	
5	Lindgren	$79,500	$113,500	$88,000	$61,670	$342,670	
6	Sykes	$125,000	$170,000	$105,000	$192,215	$592,215	
7							
8							

Figure 2-22: The AutoFill feature enables you to copy and paste multiple instances of a formula in one easy step.

Worksheet References

You've seen how Excel formulas can reference cells in various ways on a worksheet. But what if you want to include values from cells on another worksheet in one of your formulas? Excel workbooks often contain multiple worksheets. It would be a waste of time and effort to have to copy and paste data from one worksheet just to be able to use that data in calculations on another. Fortunately, you don't have to. Excel 2016 allows you to create references to cells on other worksheets for use in a number of different ways, including as references in functions and formulas.

Creating a reference to cells on another worksheet is as simple as adding the worksheet name and an exclamation point directly before the cell or range reference. Let's look at a simple example using the default worksheet names you would find in a new blank workbook. If you have a formula on **Sheet1** and you would like that formula to reference cell **D3** from the worksheet **Sheet2**, you would include the following reference in the formula: **Sheet2!D3**. Excel allows you to rename your worksheets, so be sure to include the correct worksheet name when creating references to cells on other worksheets.

Note: You can also graphically select cells and ranges on other worksheets for use as references in formulas. You do the same as you would for references on the same worksheet, except you switch to the correct worksheet to select the cell or range.

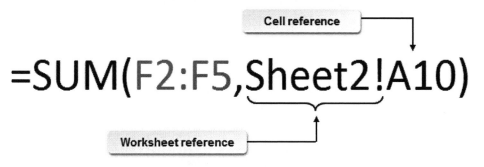

Figure 2-23: A reference to a cell on another worksheet.

Excel Errors

As you begin to enter and reuse more and more data in your Excel worksheets, you'll be more likely to occasionally encounter an error. This is especially true as you work with complex formulas and functions. There are a number of common issues that can cause errors in Excel, each returning a unique error message. It is important to understand what causes these errors and how to resolve them.

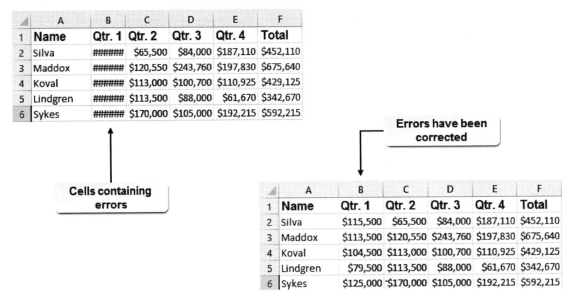

Figure 2-24: A series of number signs indicates that a column is too narrow to display all cell content.

The following table lists some of the common Excel error messages, what they mean, and possible solutions.

Error Message	What It Means	What to Do
#####	The most common cause of this error, which is sometimes referred to as "railroad tracks," is that a column is too narrow to display all cell content. You may also see this error if dates or times in your worksheets contain negative values.	Either adjust the column width to accommodate cell content or correct your date or time entries.
#VALUE!	An Excel formula has encountered an unexpected value (for example, text where it thinks numeric values should be).	Correct the data entry or the cell reference in the formula, or enter a different formula.
#DIV/0!	A formula you have entered is forcing Excel to divide a value by zero. This can happen either when zero is the value in the cell or a cell contains no value at all.	Correct the data entry or the cell reference in the formula, or enter a different formula.
#REF!	This error indicates an invalid reference. One common cause is deleting a cell that a formula references.	Update the formula or restore the deleted cell.
#NULL!	You have tried to reference the intersection of two ranges that do not actually intersect.	Correct the intersection reference.

One other common error indicator you'll encounter occasionally is a green triangle icon in the top-left corner of a cell. This indicates some other type of error involving formulas that still returns a valid value. Most commonly, users encounter this error indicator when they enter a formula in a cell that doesn't match other formulas entered into adjacent cells. So, while the formula itself is valid and returns a valid value, Excel recognizes that it doesn't seem to match surrounding formulas and flags it as a possible mistake.

When you select a cell containing an error indicator, Excel displays a drop-down menu. This menu indicates the type of error Excel flagged, provides you with access to options for correcting or ignoring the error, and provides access to Help resources about the particular error.

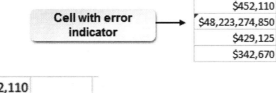

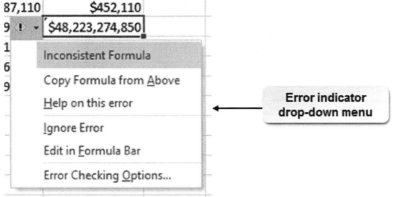

Figure 2–25: Here, the user mistakenly multiplied a set of values instead of adding them, which doesn't match the surrounding data.

 Note: Excel Online App

The ##### error message appears when the column is too narrow to display all cell content. However, when an error in the formula occurs, the cell just displays 0.

 Access the Checklist tile on your CHOICE Course screen for reference information and job aids on How to Reuse Formulas and Functions.

ACTIVITY 2-3
Reusing Formulas and Functions

Before You Begin
The **My Sales Contest.xlsx** file is open.

Scenario
You need to complete your analysis of the sales figures for all sales reps so you can announce the contest winners at an upcoming meeting. You decide to reuse the functions you have already created for Silva and Maddox for the remaining sales reps rather than create new functions for each one. Because you also need to provide commission payment figures to the payroll department before the meeting, you decide to use the same worksheet to perform the commission calculations.

1. Use the existing functions to calculate the total and average quarterly sales for the remaining sales reps.
   a) Select cell **F5**.
   b) Press **Ctrl+C** to copy the cell's contents to the clipboard.
   c) Select the range **F6:F27** and then press **Ctrl+V** to paste the function to the selected range of cells.
   d) Verify that the function has been copied into the remaining cells in the column.
   e) Select cell **G5**.
   f) Place the mouse pointer over the **fill handle** until it is displayed as a thin black plus symbol.

Average	Highest	Lowest
113027.5	187110	65500
168910	243760	113500

   g) Double-click the **fill handle**.
   h) Verify that the function has been copied into the remaining cells in the column.

2. Use the AutoFill feature to fill in the highest and lowest quarterly sales figures down the remaining cells in columns H and I.

3. Calculate the annual sales commission figure for Silva by using the commission rate in cell **M3**.
   a) Select cell **J4**.
   b) Type *=f4*m3* and press **Ctrl+Enter**.

4. Reuse the formula to calculate the commission for Maddox.
   a) Double-click the **fill handle** in cell **J4**.
   b) Verify that the figure that appears in cells **J5:J27** is **0**.

5. Modify the commission formula to include an absolute reference to the commission rate in cell **M6**.

a) Select cell **J4**.

b) In the **Formula Bar**, place the insertion point immediately before or after **M3** in the formula.

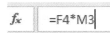

c) Press the **F4** key to switch the relative reference to an absolute reference.

d) Ensure that **M3** is now displayed as **M3** in the **Formula Bar** and press **Enter**.

6. AutoFill the modified formula in **J4** to the rest of the cells in column **J**.

7. Ensure that the formula now returns the appropriate values.

Lowest	Commission
65500	18084.4
113500	27025.6
100700	17165
61670	13706.8
105000	23688.6
76000	24517.2
92215	24619

8. Save and close the workbook file.

Summary

In this lesson, you created Excel formulas, inserted functions into cells, and reused formulas and functions in other cells. These basic tasks will form the foundation of your ability to work with and analyze your organizational data. This will enable you to extract actionable organizational intelligence from your data so that you can make sound business decisions.

Which formulas and functions do you see yourself using most in your daily life? How does that relate to your current role?

How do you see the AutoFill feature saving you time and effort? Can you think of uses for it not covered so far?

 Note: Check your CHOICE Course screen for opportunities to interact with your classmates, peers, and the larger CHOICE online community about the topics covered in this course or other topics you are interested in. From the Course screen you can also access available resources for a more continuous learning experience.

3 | Modifying a Worksheet

Lesson Time: 45 minutes

Lesson Introduction

From time to time, you'll need to make changes to your worksheets and workbooks. What if the changes you need to make go beyond simply re-entering a formula or updating a value? What if you need to add a whole new column or row to your worksheet? What if that column or row is in the middle of existing data? Also, what if you discover you've made the same mistake over and over? Or, what if you need to check your spelling throughout all worksheets in a workbook? Microsoft® Office Excel® 2016 provides you with a wide variety of options for making significant changes like these to your worksheets. Understanding how this functionality works will help you keep your documents updated without throwing away all of the valuable work you've already done.

Lesson Objectives

In this lesson, you will:

- Insert, delete, and adjust cells, columns, and rows.

- Search for and replace data.

- Check the spelling in a worksheet.

TOPIC A

Insert, Delete, and Adjust Cells, Columns, and Rows

At some point in your data entry process, the amount of text you need to display in a cell may be more than the cell can hold. Or, perhaps, your organization will create a new metric by which certain figures are tracked. To include information on the new metric, you may have to add a row or a column right in the middle of existing data. Or maybe you want to view your data in a different way to focus more on one element of a system than another. When situations like these arise, you'll need to be able to modify the cells, columns, and rows in your worksheets to suit your needs. Excel 2016 provides you with a number of commands and features that allow you to make these kinds of changes.

The Insert and Delete Options

Adding new information at the end of a column or row is easy. But what if you need to add a cell, a row, or a column in the middle of existing data? For this, the **Cells** group on the **Home** tab provides you with access to the **Insert** and **Delete** commands. These commands enable you to add a single cell, a group of cells, or even entire rows or columns anywhere you need them.

If you select either the **Insert** or the **Delete** button, Excel will insert or delete whatever you currently have selected. If you select a cell or a group of cells and then select **Insert**, Excel will insert a cell or a group of cells. If you select an entire row and then select **Delete**, Excel will delete the entire row. Excel defaults to pushing cells or rows down to make room for new ones when adding cells or rows. It defaults to pushing them up to "fill in the space" when you delete them. Excel also defaults to pushing columns to the right to make room for new columns, and pushing them to the left to "fill in the space" when you delete columns.

The **Insert** and **Delete** options provide you with additional functionality for inserting and deleting cells. If you insert or delete a cell or a group of cells by using either the **Insert Cells** or the **Delete Cells** command from the drop-down menus, Excel displays either the **Insert** dialog box or the **Delete** dialog box. These provide you with options for shifting cells in a particular direction or inserting or deleting an entire row or column even if you've selected only a cell or group of cells.

 Note: You can also access the **Insert** and **Delete** dialog boxes by right-clicking a selected cell or range, and then selecting either **Insert** or **Delete**.

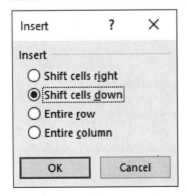 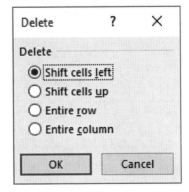

Figure 3-1: The Insert and Delete dialog boxes.

> **Note: Excel Online App**
>
> When inserting and deleting rows, columns, or selected ranges, you must select the exact row, column, or range to be affected before you select the **HOME→Cells→Insert** and **HOME→Cells→Delete** commands. In Excel Online, the command is immediately executed without displaying a dialog box containing additional options.

Width and Height Adjustments

There will, undoubtedly, be instances in which you need to enter data or formulas in worksheet cells that spill over beyond cell borders. When this happens, you'll need to adjust the size of the cells in your worksheets. To adjust cell sizes, you must either adjust row heights, column widths, or both. Excel 2016 provides you with several options for adjusting cell sizes in your worksheets.

The first method is to simply click and drag row or column borders to adjust them manually. To do this, place the mouse pointer directly over the desired border in either the row or column header until it appears as a dark line with a double arrow. 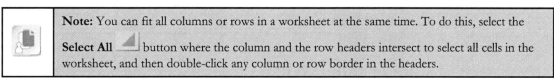 Then click and drag the border until the row or the column is the desired height or width. When you adjust row and column heights manually, drag either the bottom border of the desired row or the right-hand border of the desired column.

Figure 3-2: Click and drag column or row borders to manually adjust cell size.

You can also manually fit row heights or column widths to match cell content. To do this, double-click the appropriate row or column border in the row and column headers. When you use this method, Excel will fit the row or the column to accommodate the greatest amount of cell content in the row or column. As with manually dragging rows or columns to the desired size, when you double-click to fit them, you double-click the lower border for a row and the right-hand border for a cell.

> **Note:** You can fit all columns or rows in a worksheet at the same time. To do this, select the **Select All** ◢ button where the column and the row headers intersect to select all cells in the worksheet, and then double-click any column or row border in the headers.

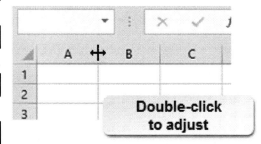

Figure 3-3: When the mouse pointer is displayed as a line with a double arrow, you can double-click row or column borders to fit them to cell content.

You can also use the AutoFit feature in Excel to automatically adjust row height or column width to match cell content. You can access the AutoFit commands by selecting **Home→Cells→Format**. To use the AutoFit feature, select any cell or range within the row(s) or the column(s) that you would like to adjust and then select either the **AutoFit Row Height** or the **AutoFit Column Width** command from the **Format** drop-down menu.

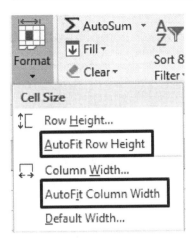

Figure 3–4: The AutoFit feature adjusts row height or column width to match cell content.

Finally, you can use the **Row Height** and **Column Width** dialog boxes to adjust cell size. To adjust cell size by using this method, simply select a cell in the desired row, open the appropriate dialog box, enter the desired height or width value, and then select **OK**. You can access the **Row Height** and the **Column Width** dialog boxes by selecting either **Home→Cells→Format→Row Height** or **Home→Cells→Format→Column Width**.

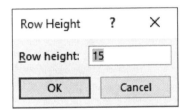 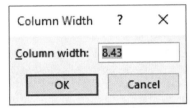

Figure 3–5: The Row Height and the Column Width dialog boxes.

Note: Excel Online App

You must use the mouse techniques (drag borders, double-click, and right-click) to adjust the width and height and hide and unhide rows and columns. In Excel Online, the commands are not available on the **HOME** tab.

The Hide and Unhide Commands

The **Hide** and **Unhide** commands enable you to suppress the visibility of particular rows or columns in your worksheets. These commands can come in handy in large worksheets that have more rows or columns than can fit on the screen at once, or if your worksheets contain extraneous information or calculation data that doesn't need to be displayed. When you hide rows or columns, they remain in the worksheet and all references to cells in the hidden rows or columns remain intact. You can access the **Hide** and **Unhide** commands by selecting **Home→Cells→Format→Hide & Unhide**.

Note: You can also access the **Hide** and **Unhide** commands by selecting a row, a column, or multiple rows or columns, right-clicking anywhere within the selection, and then selecting either **Hide** or **Unhide**.

◢	A	G	H
1	**Employee Name**	**Total**	**Average**
2	Silva	$452,110	$113,027.50
3	Maddox	$675,640	$168,910.00
4	Koval	$429,125	$107,281.25
5	Lindgren	$342,670	$85,667.50
6	Sykes	$592,215	$148,053.75

Figure 3-6: Columns B through F are hidden.

 Access the **Checklist** tile on your **CHOICE** Course screen for reference information and job aids on **How to Insert, Delete, and Adjust Cells, Columns, and Rows.**

ACTIVITY 3-1
Adjusting Cells, Columns, and Rows

Data File

C:\091055Data\Modifying a Worksheet\Sales Data.xlsx

Before You Begin

Excel 2016 is open.

Scenario

You have been asked to present data about your sales team to company leadership at an important, upcoming meeting. They would like to gauge the performance of individual members of your sales team. You have prepared an Excel worksheet that you will use to present the information to attendees. But, as you're reviewing the worksheet, you feel some of the information isn't necessary to present, so you decide to hide some of the columns. You also feel some of the columns take up too much space for the data in them, so you want to adjust their widths. In addition, one of your sales reps recently left the company, so you'll need to delete her information.

1. Open the **Sales Data.xlsx** workbook.

2. Adjust the column widths for columns **A** and **B**.
   a) Select the column header for column **A** to select the entire column.
   b) Select **Home→Cells→Format→AutoFit Column Width**.
   c) In the column headers, place the mouse pointer over the border between columns **B** and **C** until it is displayed as a vertical line with two arrows.
   d) Double-click the border between columns **B** and **C** to AutoFit the column width to the cell contents.

3. Hide the columns containing the quarterly sales data.
   a) Select the column header for column **C**, press and hold down **Shift**, and then select the column header for column **F**.

   > **Note:** Alternatively, you can drag to select the range.

   b) Release **Shift**.
   c) Ensure that the range **C:F** is selected.
   d) Select **Home→Cells→Format→Hide & Unhide→Hide Columns**.

   > **Note:** Alternatively, you can right-click the column headers and select **Hide**.

e) Verify that column headers **B** and **G** now appear beside each other with nothing in between.

B	G
Region	Total
Northeast	452110
Northeast	675640

4. Delete the row containing information for the former employee, Smith.

   a) Select any cell within row **14**.

   b) Select **Home→Cells→Delete drop-down arrow→Delete Sheet Rows**.

   c) Verify that Smith's data is gone, and that Wagner is now in row **14**.

5. Save the workbook to the **C:\091055Data\Modifying a Worksheet** folder as *My Sales Data.xlsx*

TOPIC B

Search for and Replace Data

Consider that you mistakenly entered the wrong data in your worksheets—and not only that, but you made the same mistake over and over again throughout the workbook. If your worksheets contain thousands of rows' and columns' worth of data, having to find and correct multiple errors would be a painstaking, time-consuming process. But you're in luck; Excel 2016 includes a number of options to help you find and correct mistakes throughout your workbooks quickly and easily.

The Find Command

You can use the **Find** command to locate specific content within your worksheets and workbooks. When you select the **Find** command, Excel opens the **Find and Replace** dialog box with the **Find** tab automatically selected. From the **Find** tab, you can search your workbooks and worksheets for a number of different types of content, including values, formulas, formatting, and review markup. You can search for individual instances of the content you're searching for or view a list of all instances of content matching your search query at once. Excel provides you with a number of options for configuring your search queries to find the precise information you're looking for. To access the **Find** command, select **Home→Editing→Find & Select→Find** or press **Ctrl+F**.

 Note: You can direct Excel to search only within a particular range by selecting that range before selecting the **Find** command.

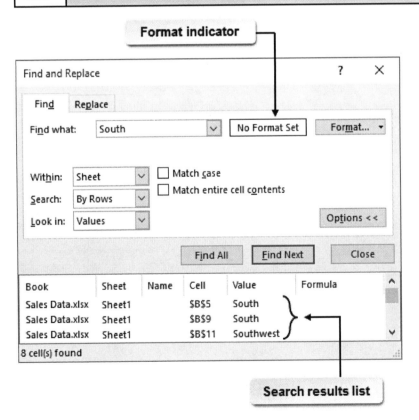

Figure 3-7: The Find and Replace dialog box with the options expanded.

The following table describes the various elements of the **Find** tab in the **Find and Replace** dialog box.

Find Tab Element	Use This To
Find what field	Enter your search query. This is the content Excel will search for in the workbook or worksheet.
Options button	Expand or collapse additional options in the **Find and Replace** dialog box.
Format indicator	Determine whether or not you have selected a particular format to search for. If you have not selected a format, the indicator displays the text *No Format Set*. If you have selected a format, the indicator displays the text *Preview**.
Format button	Select the type of formatting you wish to search for. Selecting the **Format** button opens the **Find Format** dialog box, which allows you to select the type of formatting you wish to search for. Selecting the **Format** drop-down arrow also gives you the option to manually select a worksheet cell to set the desired formatting to search for or to clear formatting from the search query.
Within drop-down menu	Decide between searching the current worksheet or the entire workbook.
Search drop-down menu	Choose whether to search by row or by column.
Look in drop-down menu	Tell Excel to search within cells containing values, formulas, or comments.
Match case check box	Require an exact casing match in order for Excel to return search results.
Match entire cell contents check box	Require an exact content match within a cell in order for Excel to return a search result.
Find All button	Display a list of all instances of content matching your search query at the bottom of the **Find and Replace** dialog box. When you select a search result from the list, Excel automatically navigates to and selects the matching cell.
Find Next button	Cycle among all cells with content matching the search query. Excel automatically navigates to and selects each cell containing matching content in the order it finds them.
Search results list	Review search results when you use the **Find All** command and to select cells containing content that matches the search query.

Note: Excel Online App

The Find command is scaled down to only search for specific cell content in your worksheet. You can either press **Ctrl+F**, **Shift+F3**, or select **HOME→Editing→Find** on the ribbon to open the **Find** dialog box. You can repeat the **Find** command down throughout the worksheet by pressing **Shift+F4**.

The Replace Command

Like the **Find** command, the **Replace** command will also search for specific content within your workbooks and worksheets. But you can use the **Replace** command to switch out the old, incorrect data with the updated or correct data. Excel provides you with the same options for configuring your searches when using the **Replace** command, with the additional option of entering the content you would like to replace the incorrect content with. As with the **Find** command, you can apply the

Replace command for one instance of your search query at a time or for all matching instances at once. The keyboard shortcut for the **Replace** command is **Ctrl+H**.

 Note: As with the **Find** command, you can direct the **Replace** command to search for and replace only content within a particular range by first selecting the range and then selecting the **Replace** command. Also, the **Look in** options are restricted to only **Formulas** on the **Replace** tab.

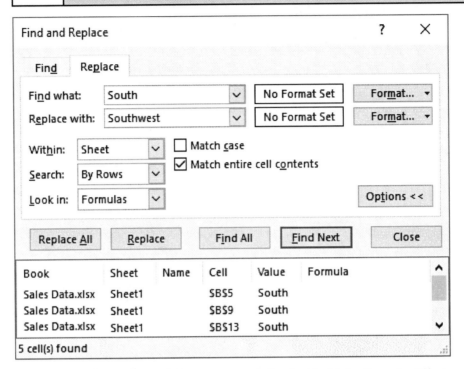

Figure 3-8: The Replace tab is a near match for the Find tab; the only difference is the ability to specify the content you want to replace the old content with.

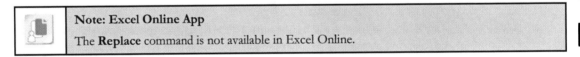 **Note: Excel Online App**

The **Replace** command is not available in Excel Online.

The Go To Dialog Box

You can use the **Go To** dialog box to quickly navigate to and select any cell within a workbook or worksheet. This works in much the same way as using the **Name Box** to navigate. You simply enter the desired cell reference and then select **OK** to navigate to a cell. If you would like to navigate to a cell on a different worksheet within the same workbook, include the name of the desired worksheet followed by an exclamation point (!) before the cell reference. Although this isn't really necessary in smaller worksheets, if you have thousands of rows and columns in a large worksheet, this can make navigation far easier.

The main advantage of using the **Go To** dialog box over the **Name Box** is that the **Go To** dialog box saves a list of the cells to which you have previously navigated. This way, if you use particular cells often in a worksheet, you can quickly jump back to them when you need to edit data. You can access the **Go To** dialog box by selecting **Home→Editing→Find & Select→Go To** or by pressing the **F5** key.

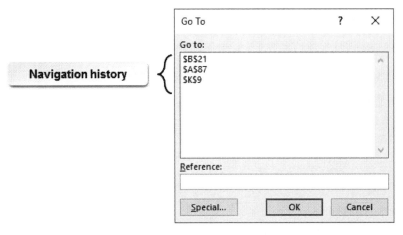

Figure 3-9: The Go To dialog box remembers your navigation history.

Note: Excel Online App

Using the **Go To** command, you are limited to simply navigating to a cell reference. To open the **Go To** dialog box, you must press **Ctrl+G**.

The Go To Special Dialog Box

The Go To Special feature is far more powerful than the Go To feature. Whereas the **Go To** dialog box allows you to navigate directly to a particular cell, the **Go To Special** dialog box allows you to select multiple cells that all meet particular criteria. This feature is handy when you want to avoid manually navigating through a large worksheet to select multiple cells by pressing and holding down the **Ctrl** key. But the feature also works well for finding a single cell in a worksheet that meets the desired search criteria or for selecting a contiguous range of cells that all meet the criteria. The **Go To Special** feature works only on the currently selected worksheet.

When you use this feature, selected cells behave as they normally do when you select a range. So you can add formatting to all of the cells at once, delete the content of all of the cells, or use the **Tab** and **Enter** keys to navigate among the selected range to enter data one cell at a time. You can access the **Go To Special** dialog box by selecting **Home→Editing→Find & Select→Go To Special** or by accessing the **Go To** dialog box and selecting the **Special** button.

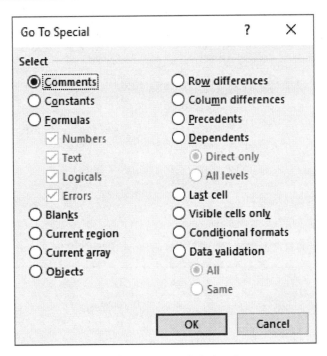

Figure 3-10: The Go To Special dialog box.

The **Go To Special** dialog box provides you with a wide array of criteria for selecting cells and ranges.

Option	Select This To
Comments radio button	Select all cells containing comments.
Constants radio button	Select all cells containing constants. Using the check boxes below, you can restrict the search to select only cells containing: • **Numbers** • **Text** • **Logicals**—this option will not select instances of TRUE or FALSE that are the result of a logical function, only cases in which you've typed TRUE or FALSE as text. Also, Excel differentiates TRUE and FALSE from all other text when using this option.
Formulas radio button	Select cells containing formulas. Using the check boxes below, you can restrict the search to select only cells containing formulas that return: • **Numbers** • **Text** • **Logicals**—this option *will* select instances of TRUE or FALSE that are the result of a logical function. • **Errors**
Blanks radio button	Select all blank cells within a dataset or a selected range.
Current region radio button	Select all cells in the same region as the currently selected cell or range.
Current array radio button	Select all cells in the same array as the currently selected cell or range, if the selected cell is part of an array.

Option	Select This To
Objects radio button	Select all objects on the worksheet. This option does not select worksheet cells, only objects on the worksheet.
Row differences radio button	Select all cells in the same row as the selected cell that do not contain the same content as the selected cell.
Column differences radio button	Select all cells in the same column as the selected cell that do not contain the same content as the selected cell.
Precedents radio button	Select all cells that contain data feeding the formula in the selected cell.
Dependents radio button	Select all cells that contain formulas that the currently selected cell is feeding.
Direct only radio button	Restrict the **Precedents** option or the **Dependents** option to select only those cells directly feeding or fed by the currently selected cell.
All levels radio button	Set the **Precedents** option or the **Dependents** option to select all cells feeding or fed by the currently selected cell.
Last cell radio button	Select the last cell containing data or formatting in a worksheet.
Visible cells only radio button	Select all non-hidden cells.
Conditional formats radio button	Select all cells containing conditional formatting or all cells containing the same conditional formatting as the currently selected cell.
Data validation radio button	Select all cells containing data validation or all cells containing the same data validation as the currently selected cell.
All radio button	Set the **Conditional formats** option to select all cells containing conditional formatting or to set the **Data validation** option to select all cells containing data validation.
Same radio button	Restrict the **Conditional formats** option to select only cells containing the same conditional formatting as the currently selected cell, or to restrict the **Data validation** option to select only cells containing the same data validation criteria as the currently selected cell.

Note: Excel Online App

The **Go To Special** is not available in Excel Online.

Access the Checklist tile on your CHOICE Course screen for reference information and job aids on How to Search for and Replace Data.

ACTIVITY 3-2
Searching for and Replacing Data

Before You Begin
The **My Sales Data.xlsx** file is open.

Scenario
You have received notification from the human resources department that one of your sales reps has been transferred to a different region, and another was recently married and has changed her name. You decide to use the **Find** command to locate the employee information without having to manually search the worksheet so you can update the records. Additionally, Develetech has recently consolidated the sales teams from two regions into one. You realize it would be easier to use the **Replace** command to update all of the records at once rather than to do so one at a time.

---

1. Change the regional information for the transferred employee.
   a) Select **Home→Editing→Find & Select→Find**.
   b) In the **Find and Replace** dialog box, ensure that the **Find** tab is selected.
   c) In the **Find what** field, type *clarke* and select **Find Next**.
   d) Ensure that Excel navigated to cell A17.
   e) Select cell **B17**, type *Southwest* and press **Enter**.

    Note: You can leave the **Find and Replace** dialog box open when you edit cell B17. If the dialog box is obstructing your view, you can drag it elsewhere.

2. Update the married sales rep's last name.
   a) If you previously closed the **Find and Replace** dialog box, select **Home→Editing→Find & Select→Find**, and then ensure that the **Find** tab is selected.
   b) In the **Find what** field, double-click **clarke** and type *king*, then press **Enter**.
   c) Ensure that Excel navigated to cell A23.
   d) Close the **Find and Replace** dialog box, type *Connor* in cell A23, and then press **Enter**.

3. Change all instances of **West** region entries to **Southwest**.
   a) Select cell **A1**.
   b) Select **Home→Editing→Find & Select→Replace**.
   c) In the **Find and Replace** dialog box, ensure that the **Replace** tab is selected.
   d) In the **Find what** field, double-click **king** and type *West*
   e) In the **Replace with** field, type *Southwest*
   f) Select the **Options** button.
   g) Check the **Match entire cell contents** check box and select the **Find Next** button.
   h) Ensure that Excel selected an instance of **West** in the **Region** column and select the **Replace** button.
   i) Verify that Excel changed the previous instance of **West** to **Southwest**, and then selected another instance of **West** in the **Region** column.
   j) To change all other instances of **West** to **Southwest**, select the **Replace All** button.

---

k) In the **Microsoft Excel** message box, select **OK**.

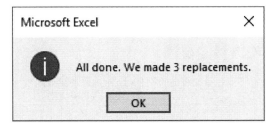

l) Close the **Find and Replace** dialog box.

4. Save the workbook.

TOPIC C

Use Proofing and Research Tools

Although you may not always be asked to do so, it's likely that at some point you will have to share your workbooks with your colleagues. Whether you're presenting your workbooks in front of a live audience, sharing some data with colleagues in a meeting, or emailing your workbook files to other people, you'll want to make sure all of your content is correct before doing so. In addition to ensuring that you have the correct data and formulas in your worksheets, you'll want to make sure everything is spelled correctly and that you're using all terminology correctly. This is why Excel 2016 includes spelling check and other functionality you can use to ensure your content is ready to present to others. Understanding how to use this functionality can help you make sure your worksheets are accurate and look professional.

The Spelling Dialog Box

You can use the **Spelling** dialog box to inspect your worksheets for spelling errors. Excel 2016's spelling check feature flags any text that Excel doesn't recognize as spelling errors and then lets you decide how to resolve the errors. Excel uses a set of built-in dictionaries to compare the text in your worksheets to. If a word is not in the currently selected dictionary, Excel will flag it as an error. Keep in mind, however, not all words that aren't in the dictionary are actual spelling errors, such as proper nouns. If a word that Excel believes is an error is similar to other words in the dictionary, the **Spelling** dialog box displays a list of suggested corrections that you can choose from to replace the misspelling.

 Note: Unlike some other applications, such as Microsoft Office Word, Excel does not mark spelling errors with red underlines. Don't rely on on-screen markup to flag spelling errors in your worksheets. You must run spelling check manually.

You can also add words to the dictionary so that Excel no longer flags them as spelling errors. This can be useful if you include a lot of names in your worksheets, which may be the case for people who manage sales or HR, or if you use a lot of job-related jargon or terminology in your worksheets. You can inspect only one worksheet at a time using the **Spelling** dialog box.

You can access the **Spelling** dialog box by selecting **Review→Proofing→Spelling** or by pressing the **F7** key. You can direct Excel to check the spelling in only a particular range by first selecting it and then opening the **Spelling** dialog box.

 Note: Excel Online App

The spell check feature and other proofing tools are not available in Excel Online. You must open the worksheet in Excel 2016 in order to use the tools described in this topic.

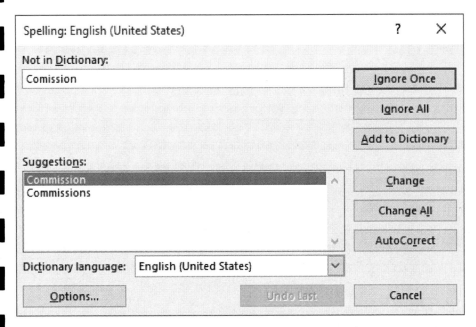

Figure 3-11: The Spelling dialog box detecting an error and suggesting corrections.

The **Spelling** dialog box contains a number of commands and options you can use to configure exactly how you search for and resolve spelling errors.

Spelling Dialog Box Option	Description
Not in Dictionary field	Displays the word that the spelling checker does not recognize and has flagged as a possible error.
Suggestions list	Displays a list of suggested alternatives for the flagged word from the currently selected dictionary.
Dictionary language drop-down menu	Allows you to select the desired dictionary against which Excel checks for spelling errors.
Ignore Once button	Ignores the currently selected instance of a misspelled word.
Ignore All button	Ignores all instances of the currently selected misspelled word throughout a worksheet.
Add to Dictionary button	Adds the term in the **Not in Dictionary** field to the currently selected dictionary so Excel no longer flags it as a misspelling. The dictionary is shared by other Microsoft Office apps, so any terms you add will also be active in those apps.
Change button	Replaces the currently selected instance of the word in the **Not in Dictionary** field with the word selected in the **Suggestions** list.
Change All button	Replaces all instances of the word in the **Not in Dictionary** field throughout a worksheet with the word selected in the **Suggestions** list.
AutoCorrect button	Adds the word in the **Not in Dictionary** field to the AutoCorrect feature so that, whenever you type the flagged word, Excel automatically replaces it with the word selected in the **Suggestions** list.
Options button	Opens the **Excel Options** dialog box with the **Proofing** tab selected.

Spelling Dialog Box Option	Description
Undo Last button	Reverts the last corrected instance of a word back to its original spelling.
Cancel button	Cancels the current spelling check and closes the **Spelling** dialog box.

The AutoCorrect Feature

Excel 2016 also includes a feature that can help you avoid spelling errors as you type them—*AutoCorrect*. The AutoCorrect feature automatically changes common misspellings to the correct spelling as you type. For example, if you type *teh* in a cell, Excel will automatically change it to *the*. AutoCorrect can also automatically format text as you type it, such as creating a hyperlink when you type a web address or an email address, and insert certain mathematical symbols when you type particular keystrokes. When you install Excel 2016, AutoCorrect is preconfigured with a set of terms it will automatically correct, but you can customize this to suit your needs.

The Thesaurus Task Pane

Excel 2016 also includes a handy feature you can use if you simply want to search for synonyms, antonyms, or related terms for a particular word or phrase: the **Thesaurus** task pane. In the **Thesaurus** task pane, you have the option of selecting from a handful of default dictionaries Excel can search to return results.

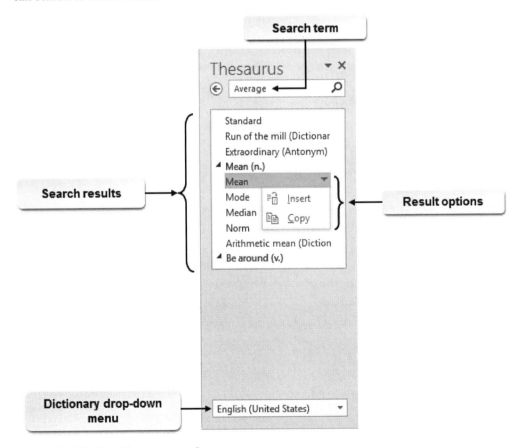

Figure 3-12: The Thesaurus task pane.

The following table describes the various elements of the **Thesaurus** task pane.

Thesaurus Task Pane Element	Is Used To
Back button	Navigate back to the previous term.
Synonyms await field	Enter a word or a phrase you want to find synonyms, antonyms, or related terms for.
Search button	Execute a search query.
Search results	Review search results, or select a particular term from the search results to perform a search on that term. You can also select the drop-down arrow next to a result to copy the term to the clipboard or insert the term into the active cell on your worksheet.
Dictionary drop-down menu	Select the dictionary you want the **Thesaurus** task pane to search.

The Insights Task Pane

Excel 2016 can also help you perform research on your data from a number of online resources. The **Insights** task pane uses the active cell's contents as a search query to run in Microsoft's Bing® search engine. It can also automatically incorporate the content of surrounding cells to refine the search. The results of the search are displayed as text and images on the **Explore** tab of the **Insights** task pane, and can come from a variety of different web-based resources, including:

- The introductory paragraph and image from the relevant article on Wikipedia, a free encyclopedia.
- The definition of a term from the *Oxford English Dictionary*.
- Additional relevant Wikipedia articles in the **Explore with Wikipedia** section.
- Relevant images in the **Bing image search** section.
- Additional relevant web pages in the **Web search** section.

For most results, you can either select the **More** link to expand the content of the result, or you can select the result itself to navigate to that web page in your browser. The **Define** tab of the task pane may also display a term's definition, if applicable.

With a cell selected, you can access the **Insights** task pane by selecting **Review→Insights→Smart Lookup** or by right-clicking the cell and selecting **Smart Lookup** from the contextual menu. You can also select **Smart Lookup** on any **Tell Me** search. You cannot conduct a search from within the **Insights** task pane itself, however.

> **Note:** Like the Excel Help system, you must be connected to the Internet in order to use the **Insights** task pane.

> **Note:** Before you can use the **Insights** task pane, you must agree to the privacy policy.

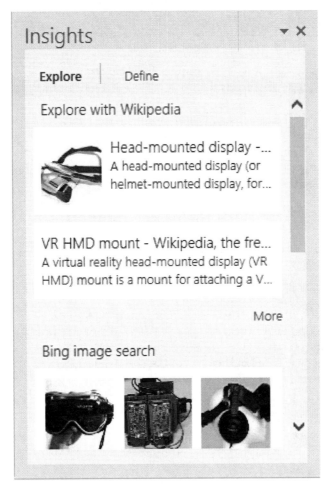

Figure 3-13: The Insights task pane displaying results for a cell whose contents are "VR HMD".

 Access the Checklist tile on your **CHOICE** Course screen for reference information and job aids on **How to Check a Worksheet's Spelling and Perform Research.**

ACTIVITY 3-3
Checking the Spelling in a Worksheet

Before You Begin
The **My Sales Data.xlsx** workbook file is open.

Scenario
You would like to both project your worksheet to attendees at the upcoming meeting and create printed handouts. Before you do, you want to make sure there are no spelling errors in the file. You decide to use the spelling check feature to check the worksheet for you.

1. Prepare to check the spelling in the worksheet.

   a) Select cell **A1** so Excel begins to check the spelling from the beginning of the sheet.

    Note: You can also press **Ctrl+Home** to return to cell **A1**.

   b) Select **Review→Proofing→Spelling** to open the **Spelling** dialog box.

2. Check the worksheet's spelling.

   a) In the **Spelling** dialog box, in the **Not in Dictionary** field, verify that Excel has identified **Comission** as a misspelled word.

   b) In the **Suggestions** list, ensure that **Commission** is selected, and then select the **Change** button.

    Note: You may need to relocate the **Spelling** dialog box on screen to view which cells Excel identifies as having misspelled words.

   c) Verify that Excel has flagged another instance of the misspelling **Comission**.

   d) To correct all instances of **Comission**, select **Change All**.

   e) Verify that Excel has flagged **Koval** as a misspelled word.

   f) As this is a proper noun and you do not wish to correct it, select **Ignore All**.

   g) Select **Ignore All** for **Gilgamos** and **Avellone**, as these are also proper nouns.

   h) Verify that Excel flags **Southweest** as a misspelled word.

   i) In the **Suggestions** list, ensure that **Southwest** is selected, and then select **Change**.

   j) Select **Ignore All** for the remaining flagged terms.

   k) In the **Microsoft Excel** message box, select **OK** to confirm that the spelling check completed.

3. Save and close the workbook.

Summary

In this lesson, you modified worksheets by inserting, deleting, and adjusting cells, columns, and rows; searching for and replacing cell data; and performing a spelling check. Understanding how to modify your worksheets will give you the flexibility you'll need to build upon existing workbooks without having to start from scratch whenever significant changes are needed. This means you'll always be able to produce and develop functional, professional-looking workbooks without wasting your valuable time.

In your own worksheets, when would adjusting or hiding columns come in handy?

How will Excel's search-and-replace functionality make previous tasks you've performed easier?

Note: Check your CHOICE Course screen for opportunities to interact with your classmates, peers, and the larger CHOICE online community about the topics covered in this course or other topics you are interested in. From the Course screen you can also access available resources for a more continuous learning experience.

4 Formatting a Worksheet

Lesson Time: 1 hour, 30 minutes

Lesson Introduction

Large worksheets with thousands, or perhaps millions, of data entries can be difficult to read. This can be especially true if you're working with a variety of data types, such as text, dollar amounts, percentages, and more. You may need to organize your data according to department, region, job role, or other important distinctions. And some data is simply more important than other data, and should stand out even at first glance. Fortunately, Microsoft® Office Excel® 2016 allows you to present data in a wide variety of formats that can suit your specific needs. Understanding how to use and, perhaps more importantly, when and why to use these formatting options, will help you make your worksheets easy to read, professional in their appearance, and more useful.

Lesson Objectives

In this lesson, you will:

- Apply text formats.

- Apply number formats.

- Align cell contents.

- Apply styles and themes.

- Apply basic conditional formatting.

- Create and use templates.

TOPIC A

Apply Text Formats

Differences in letter size, color, and style make it easy for the eye to pick out particular information in what is often a sea of clutter—think of how a news article's headline is typically larger than the article's contents. This is meant to draw your eye to the most important information first, and also allows you to easily skim pages to locate the exact information you're looking for with ease. This is really no different with spreadsheets. Excel 2016 provides you with a number of options to help you create spreadsheets that are easy to read and interpret, and that allow the important information to stand out. This will also help you add a level of visual appeal, which can facilitate a greater level of engagement when you present your data to others, that would simply not be possible by using a single, monotonous type of font.

 Note: For tips on how to effectively organize and apply formatting to your worksheets, access the LearnTO **Design Effective Workbooks** presentation from the **LearnTO** tile on the CHOICE Course screen.

Fonts

When people talk about *fonts* and typefaces, there is often a lot of confusion surrounding the topic. Essentially, a font is a physical collection of characters, whether it is part of a computer file or a collection of metal pieces to be used in a printing press, and the typeface is the overall design and appearance of the characters in a font. In this course, the word font may be used interchangeably to refer to both a physical font and the typeface design. What's really important to remember is that when you change the font in your worksheets, letters, numbers, punctuation, and other characters will look different.

You can use different fonts and different font sizes to change the appearance of the text and data in your worksheets for a number of reasons. Differing fonts and font sizes can help distinguish certain content from other content, give certain data prominence over other data, or simply make your worksheets more visually pleasing. In addition to changing the design of the text in your worksheets, changing fonts can also affect the spacing between characters.

Font	FONT	font	Font	Font
Font	FONT	font	Font	Font
Font	FONT	font	Font	Font
Font	FONT	font	Font	Font
Font	FONT	font	Font	Font

Figure 4–1: The same text repeated in different fonts and sizes.

The Font Group

The **Font** group on the **Home** tab provides you with access to the most commonly used commands for adjusting the fonts in your worksheets. From here you can change the font type, size, and color in your worksheets. You will also find commands in the **Font** group for applying particular formatting to your fonts, such as bolding, italics, and underlining.

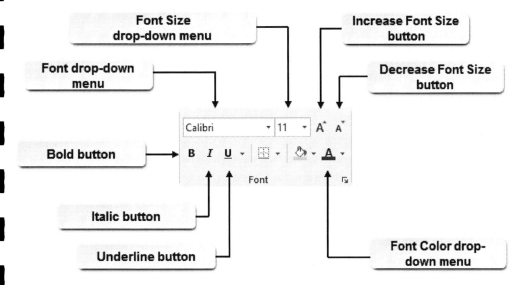

Figure 4-2: The Font group on the Home tab.

Use the commands in the **Font** group to configure the text in your worksheets.

Font Group Command	Use This To
Font drop-down menu	Change the font type.
Font Size drop-down menu	Change the font size. You can either select one of the predefined font sizes from the drop-down menu or manually type the desired font size.
Increase Font Size button	Cycle up through the predefined font sizes to make your worksheet font bigger.
Decrease Font Size button	Cycle down through the predefined font sizes to make your worksheet font smaller.
Bold button	Bold the currently selected text.
Italic button	Italicize the currently selected text.
Underline button	Underline the currently selected text.
Font Color drop-down menu	Change the color of the currently selected text.

Note: Excel Online App

On the **HOME** tab, the **Font** group also contains a **Double Underline** button; however, it does not contain the buttons used to increase and decrease the font size. Additionally, there is no dialog box launcher to open the **Format Cells** dialog box. You must open the workbook in Excel 2016 to access these additional settings.

Live Preview

Live Preview is a dynamic feature of Excel 2016 that allows you to see what a particular formatting change will look like before you actually apply it. This feature can help you quickly assess which particular formatting you would like to apply to the content and objects in your worksheets. The Live Preview feature works with a number of different formatting options, including font formatting, cell styles, and **Paste** command options.

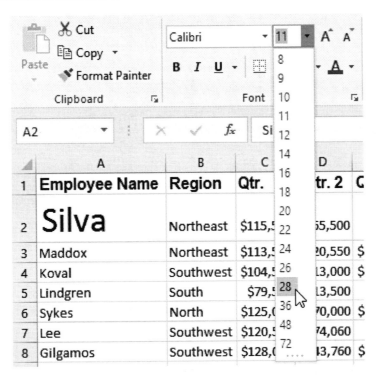

Figure 4–3: Live Preview displays a formatting change to cell A2 before the change is applied.

 Note: Excel Online App

Live Preview is available when changing the **Fill Color** or the **Font Color**, but it's not available to preview **Font** and **Font Size** changes.

The Format Cells Dialog Box

You can access all of the commands and options for formatting your worksheet fonts, along with a wide variety of other formatting options, in the **Format Cells** dialog box. Think of the **Format Cells** dialog box as an extension of the common formatting commands you will find in the various ribbon groups. It is divided into six tabs that are grouped by specific categories of cell content formatting. You can access the **Format Cells** dialog box by selecting the dialog box launcher in either the **Font**, **Alignment**, or **Number** group on the **Home** tab.

 Note: Alternatively, you can open the **Format Cells** dialog box by right-clicking a selected cell and then selecting **Format Cells** or by selecting **Home→Cells→Format→Format Cells**.

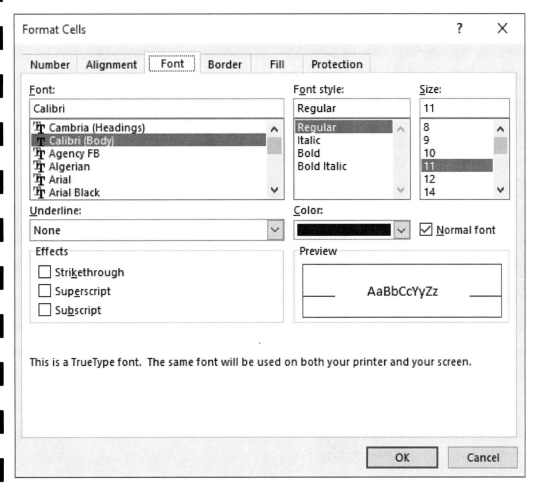

Figure 4-4: The Format Cells dialog box.

The following table identifies the types of formatting commands and options you will find on the **Format Cells** dialog box tabs.

Format Cells Dialog Box Tab	Contains Commands For
Number	Formatting numeric data for a wide variety of purposes. Number formatting configures the display and behavior of numbers for figures such as monetary amounts, dates, times, percentages, and fractions.
Alignment	Controlling the placement of data within cells. You can use these commands to align data with a particular cell border, to center content within a cell, to display text at different angles, and to control the relationship between the content and the cell borders.
Font	Applying a variety of formatting to your worksheet fonts. You can use these commands to change the type, size, and color of your fonts, and to add effects such as bolding, underlining, and italics.
Border	Applying a variety of formatting to your cell borders. You can use these commands to configure the width, color, and style of your cell borders.
Fill	Adding color, gradient shading, or patterns as cell backgrounds.
Protection	Protecting your cell content.

The Colors Dialog Box

In addition to the common font colors available from the **Font Color** drop-down menu, a wider range of color options and the ability to customize your font color are available in the **Colors** dialog box. The **Colors** dialog box is divided into two tabs: the **Standard** tab and the **Custom** tab. The **Standard** tab provides you with access to a wide range of preconfigured color and grayscale options, while the **Custom** tab lets you customize color options by using two different color models. In addition to using the **Colors** dialog box to customize your font color, you can use it to apply color formatting to a number of other items, such as cell backgrounds and borders. You can access the **Colors** dialog box by selecting **More Colors** from any of the color drop-down menus.

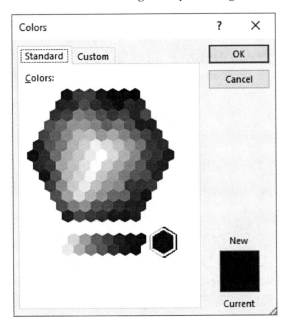 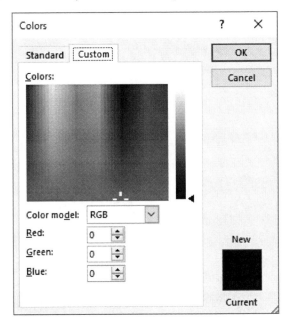

Figure 4-5: The Standard and Custom tabs in the Colors dialog box.

 Note: Excel Online App
You are limited to using the colors that are available from the **Font Color** drop-down menu.

 Access the Checklist tile on your CHOICE Course screen for reference information and job aids on How to Modify Fonts.

Hyperlinks

A *hyperlink* is simply a link within a document that, when selected, performs a particular action, such as navigating to a different location within the document, opening another document, creating a new document, navigating to a web page, or starting an email. In Excel 2016, you can create a hyperlink within a worksheet cell or out of an object. When you select the text in the cell or the object, Excel performs the designated action. The default text formatting for hyperlinks in Excel 2016 is blue, underlined text. You can modify the formatting, however, to suit your needs.

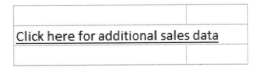

Figure 4-6: Worksheet text formatted as a hyperlink.

> **Note:** When you wish to select a cell containing a hyperlink, it's sometimes a best practice to select a nearby cell, and then use keyboard navigation to select it, especially if the text spills over into other cells. This is because it's sometimes difficult to select the cell instead of the text. When you place the mouse pointer over a cell containing a hyperlink, pay attention to the shape of the mouse pointer. If it looks like the standard thick white cross, you can select the cell; if it looks like a finger pointing, you can select the hyperlink text.

The Insert/Edit Hyperlink Dialog Box

You will use the **Insert Hyperlink** dialog box and the **Edit Hyperlink** dialog box to create and modify hyperlinks in your worksheets. These are, essentially, the same dialog box; the only differences are that the **Insert Hyperlink** dialog box opens when the active cell does not already contain a hyperlink, and the **Edit Hyperlink** dialog box opens when the active cell contains a hyperlink. The **Edit Hyperlink** dialog box also displays the **Remove Link** button.

The buttons in the **Link to** section of the **Insert Hyperlink** and **Edit Hyperlink** dialog boxes provide access to the various commands and options needed to create, configure, and modify worksheet hyperlinks. You can access the **Insert Hyperlink** and **Edit Hyperlink** dialog boxes by selecting **Insert→Links→Hyperlink**.

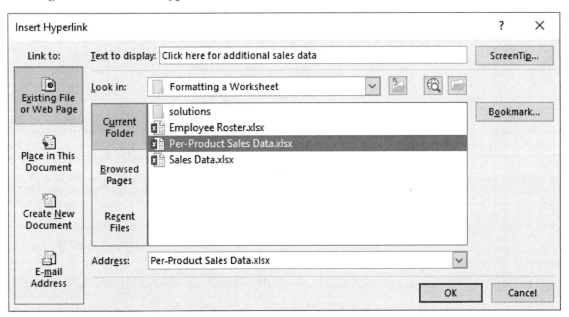

Figure 4–7: The Insert/Edit Hyperlink dialog box.

Although most of the commands available in the **Insert Hyperlink** and the **Edit Hyperlink** dialog boxes change depending on the type of hyperlink you're creating, there are a few elements that are always displayed.

Dialog Box Element	Use This To
Link to section buttons	Select the type of hyperlink you wish to create or edit. Selecting each of these will display a different set of commands for configuring the hyperlink.
Text to display field	Enter the text you want to display in the cell once you create or edit the hyperlink. If there is already text in the cell, Excel automatically displays it here. Any changes you make here will overwrite the existing cell text.

Dialog Box Element	Use This To
ScreenTip button	Open the **Set Hyperlink ScreenTip** dialog box, which allows you to enter text that will appear in a small pop-up box when a user points the mouse pointer at the text or object containing the hyperlink.

Note: Excel Online App

The scaled-down version of the **Insert Hyperlink** dialog box enables you to insert links to URLs, places in the current workbook, and email addresses.

Access the Checklist tile on your CHOICE Course screen for reference information and job aids on How to Insert and Edit Hyperlinks.

The Format Painter

You can probably already tell that applying a variety of different formatting to a large number of cells throughout a worksheet can quickly become a tedious, painstaking task. Excel 2016 includes a tool that can help make this process easier: the **Format Painter**. You can think of the **Format Painter** much as you would a standard paint brush. Whatever color you dip a paintbrush into is the color you can paint on a canvas. When you use the **Format Painter**, you are "dipping" the brush into the formatting of whatever cell you select and then "painting" that formatting onto another cell or range.

The **Format Painter** essentially copies and pastes just the formatting from one cell or range to another cell or range. The content of the affected cells remains intact. You cannot select which type of formatting you wish to transfer to the new cell or cells; whatever formatting is applied to the source cell is fully applied to the destination cells. If you double-click the **Format Painter** command, the **Format Painter** enters sticky mode. When in sticky mode, you can apply the copied formatting to any number of other cells. You must exit sticky mode to be able to select another cell or range without applying the copied formatting.

By using the **Format Painter**, you can reapply existing formatting to other cells on the same worksheet, to other worksheets in the same workbook, and in other open workbook files. You can access the **Format Painter** from the **Clipboard** group on the **Home** tab.

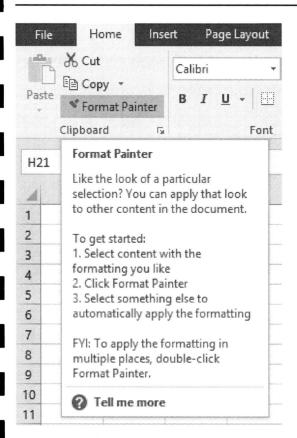

Figure 4-8: The Format Painter enables you to quickly and easily apply formatting to any number of cells in your workbooks.

Note: Excel Online App

The **Format Painter** button is not available in Excel Online; however, you can copy only cell formatting by using the two-step procedure. First, select the cell containing the desired formatting and select **HOME→Clipboard→Copy**. Then, select the destination cell or range and select **HOME→Clipboard→Paste→Paste Formatting**.

Access the Checklist tile on your **CHOICE Course** screen for reference information and job aids on **How to Use the Format Painter**.

ACTIVITY 4-1
Formatting Text in a Worksheet

Data Files

C:\091055Data\Formatting a Worksheet\Sales Data.xlsx

C:\091055Data\Formatting a Worksheet\Per-Product Sales Data.xlsx

Before You Begin

Excel 2016 is open.

Scenario

You have updated and checked the spelling of the worksheet you plan to present at the upcoming meeting. Your supervisor requested that you include all sales data in your presentation, so you have already unhidden the hidden sales data columns. Now you would like to make the worksheet more visually appealing and easier to read for the meeting attendees. You decide to start by making some text formatting changes to the worksheet text. Also, you want to include a link to a document containing supplemental sales data. You plan on emailing a copy of the workbook file to everyone attending the meeting, and you feel the additional information may be helpful.

---

1. Open the **Sales Data.xlsx** workbook file.

2. Change the worksheet font.
   a) At the intersection of the row and column headers, in the top-left corner of the worksheet, select the
      Select All button ◢ to select the entire worksheet.
   b) Select **Home→Font→Font drop-down arrow** and then, from the **Font** drop-down list, select **Arial**.

3. Format the worksheet title so it stands out from the rest of the text.
   a) Select cell **A1**.
   b) Select **Home→Font→Font Color drop-down arrow** and then, in the **Standard Colors** section, select **Blue**.

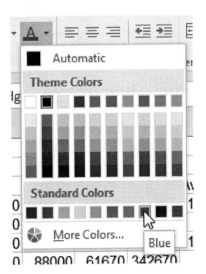

   c) Select **Home→Font→Bold**.

   d) Select **Home→Font→Font Size drop-down arrow**, and then select **16**.

4. Format the column labels to distinguish them from the cells containing data and increase the font size for the sales rep names.

   a) Select the range **A4:L4**.

   b) Change the font size to **12** and make the text bold.

   c) Select the range **A5:A27** and change the font size to **12**.

   d) Adjust the column widths as necessary to accommodate the column labels.

5. Apply the column label formatting to the commission rate, number of employees, and resigned employees cells.

   a) Select cell **A4**.

   b) Select **Home→Clipboard→Format Painter**.

   c) Select the range **N1:N3** and release the mouse button.

   d) Verify that Excel pasted the formatting as expected.

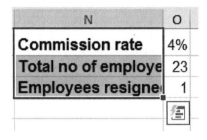

   e) Adjust the column width as necessary to accommodate the new formatting.

6. Add a hyperlink that links to the **Per-Product Sales Data.xlsx** workbook.

   a) In the **Sales Data.xlsx** workbook, select cell **Q3**.

   b) Select **Insert→Links→Hyperlink**.

   c) In the **Insert Hyperlink** dialog box, in the **Link to** section, ensure that **Existing File or Web Page** is selected.

   d) In the **Text to display** field, type *Click here for additional sales data*

   e) Select the **ScreenTip** button.

   f) In the **Set Hyperlink ScreenTip** dialog box, in the **ScreenTip text** field, type *Per-Product Sales Data* and select **OK**.

g) In the **Current Folder** list, select the **Per-Product Sales Data.xlsx** file and select **OK**.

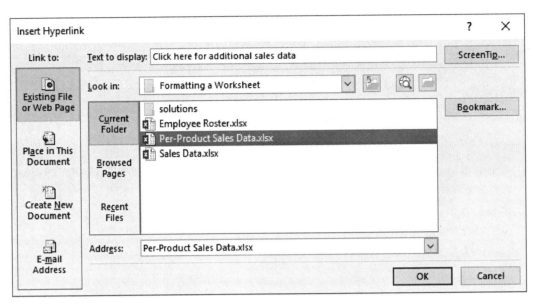

7. Verify that the newly added hyperlink works as expected.
    a) Select cell **Q3**.
    b) Verify that the **Per-Product Sales Data.xlsx** workbook file opens.
    c) Hover your cursor over the **Excel** icon on the taskbar and verify that you can select either workbook to switch between them.
    d) Close the **Per-Product Sales Data.xlsx** workbook.

8. Save the **Sales Data.xlsx** file to the **C:\091055Data\Formatting a Worksheet** folder as *My Sales Data.xlsx*

TOPIC B

Apply Number Formats

People who work with data in Excel worksheets will need to express and work with that numeric data in a variety of ways. For example, an accountant may want all numbers to appear with a dollar sign, or other currency symbol, and show only two decimal places. An engineer may need to work with far more decimal places to achieve a higher level of accuracy for sensitive calculations. Someone who manages a team of people and is in charge of work schedules and coordinating paid leave will need to be able to work with dates and times. Excel 2016 provides these options and much more when it comes to expressing numeric values. By understanding how these different number formats work, and by knowing how and when to apply them, you'll have the flexibility needed to work with and analyze all of your numeric data.

Number Formats

Number formats change the display of numeric data in Excel worksheets. By applying number formatting to your worksheet cells, you can control the display of such items as currency figures, dates and times, fractions, decimal places, and negative numbers. It's important to remember that, as with much of what is displayed in worksheet cells, number formatting affects only how data is displayed, not what data is actually stored in the cells. Excel 2016 includes a variety of preset number formatting options and provides you with the ability to create custom number formats. You can access all of the number formatting options on the **Number** tab of the **Format Cells** dialog box. Additionally, you can format cells by using the default settings for any of the number format categories. You can select these defaults from the **Number Format** drop-down menu, located in the **Number** group on the **Home** tab.

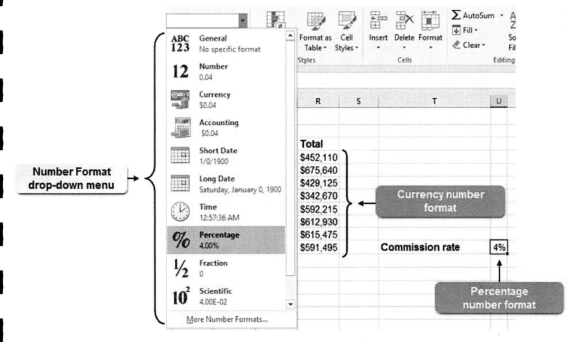

Figure 4–9: Various number formats applied to worksheet cells.

Number Format Categories

Excel 2016's number formatting options are arranged by categories, which are grouped according to function, for ease of use. The following table describes the various number formatting categories as displayed on the **Number** tab in the **Format Cells** dialog box.

 Note: The quick-access number formats that are available from the **Number Format** drop-down menu are arranged in a slightly different configuration of categories.

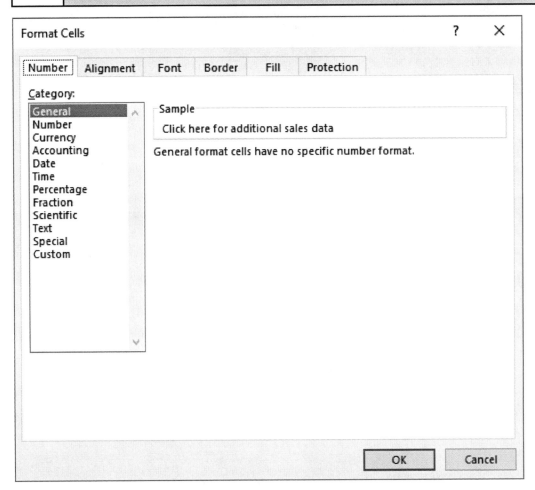

Figure 4-10: The Number tab in the Format Cells dialog box.

Number Format Category	Enables You To
General	Display numeric data in cells exactly as you enter it. This is the default number formatting in Excel worksheets and, essentially, applies no specific number formatting to your data.
Number	Control how many decimal places are displayed, how negative numbers are displayed, and whether or not Excel uses commas to separate degrees of 1,000.
Currency	Control how many decimal places are displayed, whether or not to display currency symbols, and how Excel displays negative numbers.
Accounting	Control how many decimal places are displayed and whether or not to display currency symbols.

Number Format Category	Enables You To
Date	Display dates by using a variety of long and short date formats. Excel uses serial numbers to represent specific dates (0 represents Dec. 31, 1899; every subsequent number represents the number of days that have passed since then.) This is how Excel is able to apply a variety of date formats in your worksheets.
Time	Display times by using a variety of time formats. This can include military time and whether or not to display AM and PM to distinguish morning and night time values from each other. Excel uses serial numbers to represent times, much as it does with dates. These numbers represent the percentage of the day that has passed since midnight.
Percentage	Automatically display numeric values as a percentage and control the number of decimal places that are displayed. Basically, this format multiplies the cell value by 100 and adds the percent sign.
Fraction	Display decimal values as fractions, control how many digits are displayed in the numerator and the denominator, and round non-whole number values to the nearest fraction value.
Scientific	Display large numeric values in scientific notation and control the number of decimal places that are displayed.
Text	Treat numeric data as textual data. Numbers will be displayed exactly as you enter them but cannot be used in calculations.
Special	Display specific numeric data types, such as phone numbers, Social Security numbers, and ZIP codes, in the correct format. Special formatting is also useful for working with lists and database tables.
Custom	Specify the exact number formatting you require.

Note: Excel Online App

The **Number Format** dialog box contains the same number format categories that can be applied to your workbook cells. However, you cannot create new custom number formats, but the existing custom formats are available to use.

Custom Number Formats

If none of the existing number formatting options fit your particular needs, you can create and apply custom number formatting. Excel uses strings of code to create number formats. By selecting the **Custom** category on the **Number** tab in the **Format Cells** dialog box, you can view the code strings for the predetermined number formats. To create your own custom format, you can start with one of the existing code strings and modify it to suit your needs. Custom formats are saved along with the workbook file and will not be available in other workbooks. You cannot delete or alter the existing, predefined formats; when you create a custom format, you are working with a copy of the original code.

In the code strings, there is a significant difference between a number sign (#) and a zero (0). Zeros represent digits that will always appear in cells, even when the value is zero. Number signs represent numbers that can, but don't have to, appear. For example, consider entering the value 3.1000 in a cell. If the number format applied to the cell has the code string #.####, it will appear as 3.1. If the code string is #.0000, it will appear as 3.1000. Many other symbols appear in code strings—dollar signs to show monetary formats, for example, or commas to separate factors of one thousand.

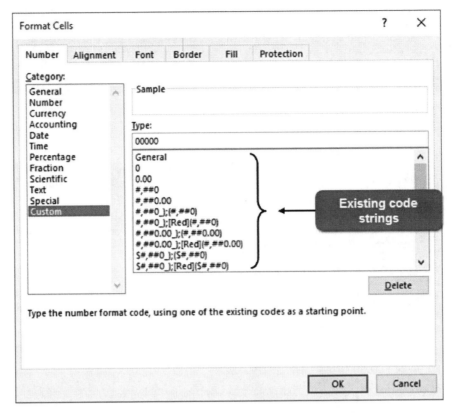

Figure 4-11: The existing code strings for custom number formats.

Note: The full range of options for customizing number formats and in-depth coverage of the formatting code are beyond the scope of this course. For more information on customizing number formats, visit **office.microsoft.com**.

Access the Checklist tile on your **CHOICE Course** screen for reference information and job aids on **How to Apply Number Formats**.

ACTIVITY 4-2
Applying Number Formats

Before You Begin
The **My Sales Data.xlsx** workbook file is open.

Scenario
Your sales data worksheet is looking better and better. But you still see opportunities to make it easier to read. You decide that the worksheet would be easier to interpret if you applied the currency format to the dollar amounts. Also, you feel that adding the date to the worksheet will help give meeting attendees a better idea of how current the information is.

1. Format the quarterly and total sales data as currency with no decimal places displayed.
   a) Select the range **C5:G27**.
   b) Select **Home→Number→dialog box launcher**.
   c) In the **Format Cells** dialog box, ensure that the **Number** tab is selected.
   d) In the **Category** section, select **Currency**.
   e) Set the **Decimal places** spin box to **0** and then select **OK**.

2. Format the remaining sales data as currency with two decimal places displayed.
   a) Select the range **H5:K27**.
   b) Select **Home→Number→dialog box launcher**.
   c) In the **Format Cells** dialog box, on the **Number** tab, in the **Category** section, select **Currency**.
   d) Ensure that the **Decimal places** spin box is set to **2** and then select **OK**.

3. Add the date to the worksheet and apply date formatting to suit your needs.
   a) Select cell **Q1**.
   b) Enter the current date in the mm/dd/yyyy format, and then press **Ctrl+Enter**.
   c) Select **Home→Number→dialog box launcher**.
   d) In the **Format Cells** dialog box, on the **Number** tab, in the **Category** section, ensure that **Date** is selected.
   e) In the **Type** list, scroll to the bottom, select **14-Mar-2012**, and then select **OK**.
   f) Ensure that Excel applied the date formatting to cell **Q1**.

4. Save the workbook.

TOPIC C

Align Cell Contents

So far, you have formatted worksheets by applying formatting to text and numbers. You may also want to consider making your worksheets easier to read and interpret by controlling where data is displayed within cells. Would it be easier to view row totals if the numbers were displayed to the left or the right of the final cell? Should a worksheet title be displayed centered along the top of the worksheet or all the way to the left? The answers to these questions and more will largely depend on your particular needs. Familiarizing yourself with the text alignment options available in Excel 2016 will prove to be yet another asset in keeping your organizational data orderly, readable, and functional.

Alignment Options

Excel 2016 provides you with the ability to control where your content appears horizontally and vertically within your worksheet cells. By default, Excel aligns numeric data to the right side and along the bottom of worksheet cells, and textual data to the left side and along the bottom of worksheet cells.

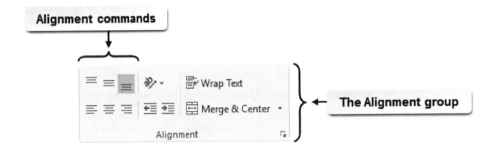

Figure 4-12: A worksheet with data aligned in various ways.

There are six basic alignment options in Excel, which appear in the **Alignment** group on the **Home** tab.

Alignment Option	Command Button	Aligns Text
Top Align		Vertically along the top of the cell.
Middle Align		Centered vertically in the cell.
Bottom Align		Vertically along the bottom of the cell.
Align Left		Horizontally to the left side of the cell.
Center		Centered horizontally in the cell.
Align Right		Horizontally to the right side of the cell.

The Indent Commands

You can use the indent commands to increase or decrease the amount of space between cell data and cell borders. If your cell content is aligned to the left side of cells, selecting the **Increase Indent** command will move the content to the right, increasing the amount of space between the left cell border and the content. Selecting the **Decrease Indent** command will move the content to the left. The opposite is true of content aligned to the right side of cells. If your content is centered within the cell, selecting the **Decrease Indent** command has no effect, while selecting the **Increase Indent** command will automatically change the alignment to left aligned and then increase the amount of space between the left border and the content.

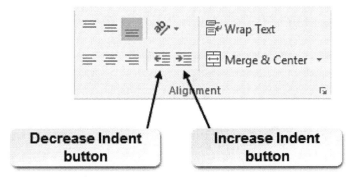

Figure 4-13: The indent commands on the ribbon.

 Note: Excel Online App

While the six alignment options are available, the **Indent** commands are not available in Excel Online.

The Wrap Text Command

By default, when a cell contains a large amount of text, the text spills over into the next column if the adjacent cells are empty. Excel truncates the display of the text if the adjacent cells are populated. Often, neither of these options is what worksheet users are looking for. But you can use the **Wrap Text** command to automatically adjust row height to accommodate large amounts of text while preserving column width. When the **Wrap Text** command is enabled on a cell, and the textual content in that cell exceeds the column width, Excel automatically drops the text down to the next line by increasing the row height of the row containing the cell. This feature enables you to preserve your worksheet layout while still allowing worksheet users to view all of the content in cells.

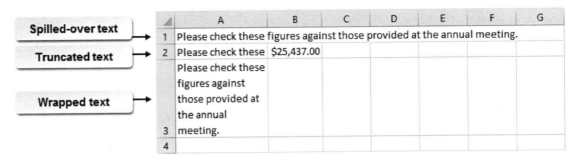

Figure 4-14: The ways in which text appears when its contents exceed normal cell boundaries.

Note: Excel Online App

The **Wrap Text** command is available in Excel Online, but the text orientation options are not.

Orientation Options

In order to display data in a worksheet legibly, you may need to change the orientation of some of your text. For example, if a column's header text takes up more horizontal space than the data in the column's cells, you might want to change the display angle to avoid having to make the column too wide. Not only does this make your worksheet layout more visually appealing, but it can also help you fit more columns on the same screen or printed page. Excel 2016 provides you with a number of preset orientation options. You can also specify an exact orientation angle in the **Format Cells** dialog box from the **Orientation** section on the **Alignment** tab. Changing cell orientation can affect row height and column width.

	A	B	C	D	E	F	G
1	Employee Name	Region	Qtr. 1	Qtr. 2	Qtr. 3	Qtr. 4	Total
2	Silva	Northeast	$115,500	$65,500	$84,000	$187,110	$452,110
3	Maddox	Northeast	$113,500	$120,550	$243,760	$197,830	$675,640
4	Koval	Southwest	$104,500	$113,000	$100,700	$110,925	$429,125
5	Lindgren	South	$79,500	$113,500	$88,000	$61,670	$342,670
6	Sykes	North	$125,000	$170,000	$105,000	$192,215	$592,215
7	Lee	Southwest	$120,550	$274,060	$76,000	$142,320	$612,930

Figure 4-15: Column header cells angled counterclockwise.

You can access the preset orientation options from the **Orientation** button in the **Alignment** group on the **Home** tab. These options cannot be used in conjunction with one another, and are not configurable. Essentially, you can only toggle these on or off, or switch from one orientation preset to another. You can, however, use orientation and alignment options in conjunction with one another to achieve the desired text placement.

Orientation Preset Option	Description
Angle Counterclockwise	Rotates the text in the selected cell or range 45 degrees counterclockwise.
Angle Clockwise	Rotates the text in the selected cell or range 45 degrees clockwise.

Orientation Preset Option	Description
Vertical Text	Orients the text in the selected cell or range vertically from top to bottom, but keeps the letters, numbers, and symbols upright.
Rotate Text Up	Rotates the text in the selected cell or range 90 degrees counterclockwise.
Rotate Text Down	Rotates the text in the selected cell or range 90 degrees clockwise.
Format Cell Alignment	Opens the **Format Cells** dialog box with the **Alignment** tab automatically selected. From here, you can set more precise orientation configurations.

The Merge & Center Options

In Excel 2016, you can merge multiple, contiguous cells across either rows or columns into a single cell, and revert merged cells back to individual cells. It is important to note, however, that this can have a significant effect on the data in those cells. Excel will display a warning message if you attempt to merge cells in such cases. If you revert a merged cell back to individual cells, lost data will not be recovered. You can, however, use the **Undo** command to restore the data if you mistakenly merge cells.

	A	B	C	D	E	F	G	H	I	J	K	L
1												
2						Sales Ledger						
3												
4	Employee Name	Region	Qtr. 1	Qtr. 2	Qtr. 3	Qtr. 4	Total	Average	Highest	Lowest	Commission	Employee ID

Figure 4-16: The worksheet's title is merged and centered across cell range A1:L3.

You can access the **Merge & Center** options from the **Merge & Center** drop-down arrow in the **Alignment** group on the **Home** tab.

Merge & Center Option	Description
Merge & Center	Merges all selected cells across rows and columns into a single cell and centers the text horizontally in the new, larger cell. Only the data in the top-leftmost cell is retained.
Merge Across	Merges selected cells together one row at a time. Only the data from the leftmost cell in each row is retained and the data is not centered.
Merge Cells	Merges all selected cells across rows and columns into a single cell. Only the data in the top-leftmost cell is retained and it is not centered.
Unmerge Cells	Reverts a merged cell back into the original, individual cells. Data that was lost in the merge process is not restored.

Note: Excel Online App

The **Merge & Center** command is simplified to only the standard command. The other options are not available in Excel Online.

Access the Checklist tile on your CHOICE Course screen for reference information and job aids on How to Align Cell Contents.

ACTIVITY 4–3
Aligning Cell Contents

Before You Begin

The **My Sales Data.xlsx** workbook file is open.

Scenario

Your worksheet is coming along nicely. You have formatted the text and applied number and date formatting to make it easier to read and interpret. But you still feel some of the text doesn't line up quite right, and you would like to make adjustments. Specifically, you want to align some of the column labels with the cell content for their respective columns, ensure the title formatting applies to all of the title text, center the worksheet title above the worksheet data, and use the **Wrap Text** command to make one of the cells seem less crowded.

1. Right-align some of the column labels.

   a) Select the range **C4:L4**.

   b) Select **Home→Alignment→Align Right**.

   c) Align the cells in range **L5:L27** to the right.

2. Merge and center the title text over the sales data.

   a) Select the range **A1:L3**.

   b) Select **Home→Alignment→Merge & Center**.

   c) Select **Home→Alignment→Middle Align**.

3. Revise the text in cell **N2** and then wrap the text to better fit the column width.

   a) Select cell **N2**, type *Total number of employees* and press **Enter**.

   b) Verify that Excel truncates the display of the text in cell **N2**.

N	O
Commission rate	4%
Total number of employ	23
Employees resigned	1

   c) Select cell **N2** and then select **Home→Alignment→Wrap Text**.

4. Save the workbook.

TOPIC D

Apply Styles and Themes

If you create and analyze data in a number of large worksheets on a regular basis, you'll quickly find that individually applying formatting to the various sections, data types, and worksheet elements can be a massive, tedious chore. This sense of monotony and wasted effort will only grow as you create multiple worksheets with the same type of formatting requirements over and over. The good news is that Excel provides you with a number of options for quickly applying a variety of formatting options to your worksheet cells. This will not only save you time and effort, but can also help you consistently present data to your audiences in ways that are clear and instantly recognizable.

Cell Styles

If you looked at a large number of Excel worksheets from a number of different organizations in a variety of fields, you would probably quickly notice that a lot of them contain very similar data types. Sales figures, column and row totals, calculations, and column and row labels are just a few of these. Because a fairly small variety of data types appear over and over in many, if not most, worksheets, it would make sense to have a way to distinguish these data types from other types of data quickly and easily. Fortunately, there is a way—by using *cell styles*.

A cell style is a unique set of formatting options that you can apply to a cell or a range on a worksheet. Styles can include any type of formatting options, and you can select from a wide variety of predefined cell styles or create custom styles. In addition to visual formatting options, styles can include cell protection options to prevent people from altering your important organizational data. You can access the commands you will use to apply cell styles to your worksheets and create new styles from the **Cell Styles** command in the **Styles** group on the **Home** tab.

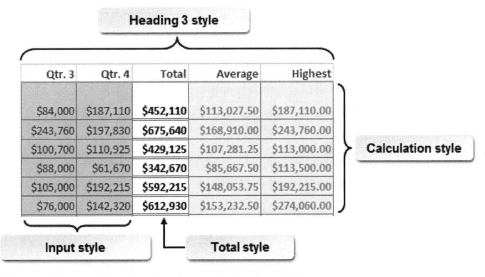

Figure 4-17: Predefined cell styles applied to a worksheet.

> **Note: Excel Online App**
>
> The **Cell Styles** command is not available in Excel Online. You must open the workbook in Excel 2016 if you want to apply, create, or merge cell styles. Everything in this topic applies to Excel 2016 only.

Galleries

For many types of formatting options, Excel 2016 and other Office 2016 applications present you with a visually oriented type of menu for making selections: *galleries*. Galleries behave very much like standard drop-down or pop-up menus but, instead of simply listing your options in the form of text, galleries present your options in the form of thumbnail images or icons that give you an indication of what the formatting options will look like once applied. Most galleries also use the Live Preview feature, so when you place the mouse pointer over an option in a gallery, Excel displays a temporary preview of what the formatting will look like on the selected cells.

When you select the **Cell Styles** command on the ribbon, Excel displays the **Cell Styles** gallery. This particular gallery presents you with several predefined styles divided into various functional sections. For example, if you wanted to highlight where sales performance is strongest or weakest in your worksheet, you might apply any of the styles from the **Good, Bad and Neutral** section. Remember that you are not confined to using just the predefined styles in this gallery—you may also define your own custom styles that will appear in a **Custom** section of the **Cell Styles** gallery.

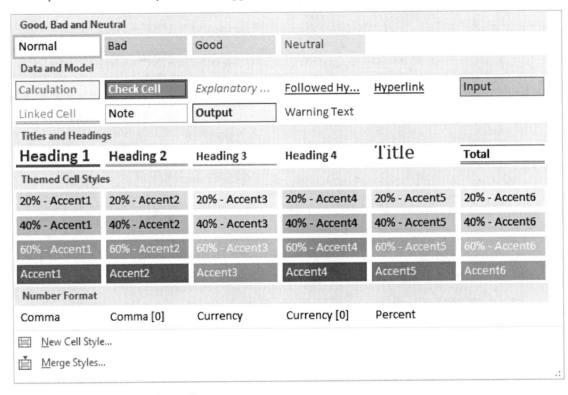

Figure 4–18: The Cell Styles gallery.

The Style Dialog Box

You will use the **Style** dialog box to modify existing cell styles and create custom cell styles. The **Style** dialog box contains a set of formatting option check boxes that you can use to quickly toggle particular formatting options on and off. From the **Style** dialog box, you can also access the **Format Cells** dialog box, where you can make more detailed changes to your cell styles. You can access the **Style** dialog box by selecting **Home→Styles→Cell Styles→New Cell Style** or by selecting **Home→Styles→Cell Styles**, right-clicking an existing cell style, and then selecting **Modify**.

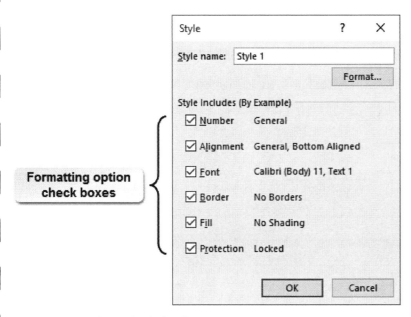

Formatting option check boxes

Figure 4-19: The Style dialog box.

The Merge Styles Dialog Box

By default, Excel saves custom cell styles with the associated workbook file and they are not available in other workbooks. However, Excel 2016 provides you with a tool you can use to import custom styles from existing workbooks into other workbooks: the **Merge Styles** dialog box. The **Merge Styles** dialog box searches all open workbook files for custom styles that you can merge into the active workbook file. You can access the **Merge Styles** dialog box by selecting **Home→Styles→Cell Styles→Merge Styles**.

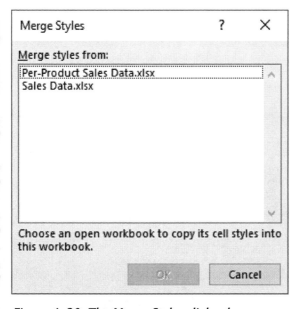

Figure 4-20: The Merge Styles dialog box.

Access the Checklist tile on your CHOICE Course screen for reference information and job aids on How to Work with Cell Styles.

Themes

Themes are collections of formatting options that you can apply to an entire workbook, as opposed to a particular cell or range. Theme formatting includes colors, fonts, and effects but, unlike cell styles, does not include number formatting, cell protection, alignment, or fill formatting. Several predefined themes are included with Excel 2016, and you can manually set the formatting of a workbook and then save it as a new custom theme.

You can use Excel themes to create numerous workbooks that all have a consistent, professional look. Customizing themes enables you to apply organizational branding across all of your spreadsheet documents. You can access the **Themes** gallery by selecting **Page Layout→Themes→Themes**. By default, all new, blank workbooks have the Office theme applied to them.

 Note: Changing theme formatting does not affect the default text in cells without cell styles applied to them.

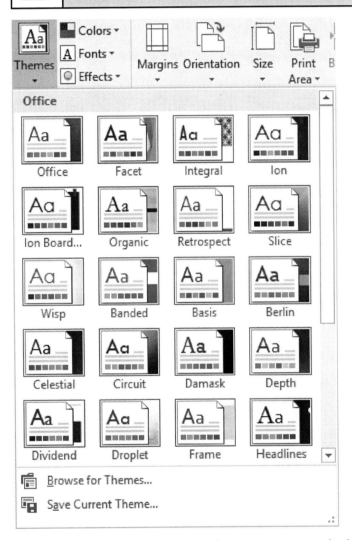

Figure 4–21: Themes make it easy for you to create multiple workbooks that all have a consistent look and feel.

 Note: Excel Online App

The **Themes** command is not available in Excel Online. You must open the workbook in Excel 2016 if you want to apply or modify themes.

Theme Components

As previously mentioned, Excel themes consist of colors, fonts, and effects. More specifically, and more accurately, Excel themes contain combinations of multiple fonts and colors and a predefined set of theme effects. In order to fully understand how changing theme formatting will affect your worksheets, let's take a closer look at what each of the formatting components does.

Theme Colors

All Excel themes, both pre-existing and custom, contain a set of 12 colors: 4 text and background colors, 6 accent colors, and 2 hyperlink colors. The colors that appear on the **Colors** button in the **Themes** group on the **Page Layout** tab represent the text and background colors for the currently applied theme. When you select the **Colors** button, the gallery that appears enables you to view the accent and the hyperlink colors for all of the included themes and your custom themes. If you select **Page Layout→Themes→Colors→Customize Colors**, Excel displays the **Create New Theme Colors** dialog box, which enables you to customize the theme colors and lets you view what, exactly, is affected by each color selection.

 Note: Applying various themes to your workbooks will also change the available colors in the **Theme** section of both the **Fill Color** and the **Font Color** drop-down menus.

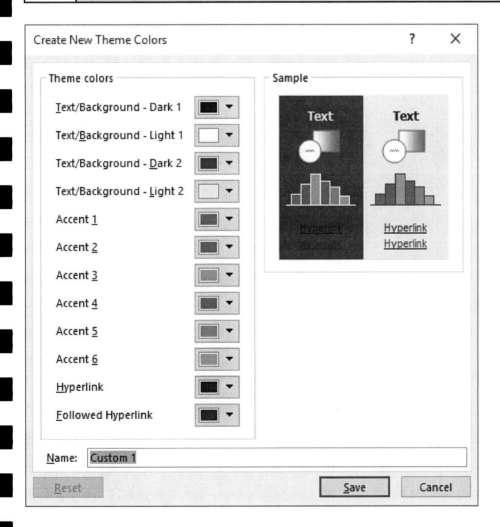

The following table describes in detail what each of the theme colors affects.

Theme Color Element	Description
Text/Background - Dark 1	Defines the default text color for the workbook. This will be the text color for all data displayed in cells unless otherwise formatted, along with the color of text displayed on light-colored backgrounds in graphical objects such as charts and in cells with light-colored fills.
Text/Background - Light 1	Defines the default color of text displayed on dark backgrounds in graphical objects and in cells with dark-colored fills.
Text/Background - Dark 2	Defines the default dark background color for graphical objects.
Text/Background - Light 2	Defines the default light background color for graphical objects.
Accent 1-6	Defines the color of graphical objects such as the individual bars or lines on a graph that represent different sets of data.
Hyperlink	Defines the default color of hyperlink text for the theme.
Followed Hyperlink	Defines the color of hyperlink text once it's been selected.

Theme Fonts

All Excel themes, both pre-existing and custom, contain two fonts: a heading font and a body font. The heading font defines the default font type for the **Title** cell style, and the body font defines the font type for labels, titles, and other text on some graphical objects, such as charts. You can access the theme fonts by selecting **Page Layout→Themes→Fonts**. You can also define a set of custom theme fonts by using the **Create New Theme Fonts** dialog box, which you can access by selecting **Page Layout→Themes→Fonts→Customize Fonts**.

 Note: The theme fonts do not affect the default font type for cell data. That is an application-wide setting, which is also customizable. The default font type for cell data is Calibri.

Theme Effects

All Excel themes contain a set of effects that define how graphical elements, such as line styles, line weights, object shading, and drop shadows, appear on worksheets. You cannot customize theme effects in Excel, but Excel 2016 includes a gallery of 15 predefined theme effect configurations. You can access the theme effects by selecting **Page Layout→Themes→Effects**.

Custom Themes Considerations

You have already seen that Excel themes can be customized. But there are a few important points to keep in mind when it comes to creating custom themes. The first is that you may want to find an existing theme that contains some of the formatting options you desire and then make the necessary changes to tweak the theme to suit your needs. This is far easier than trying to build one from scratch. Also, Excel saves all themes to a default folder that is installed along with Excel. Do not save your custom themes in any other folders. Excel will look for custom themes only in the default directory.

Excel enables you to create custom sets of theme colors and custom theme fonts, as well as entire custom themes. Each will be displayed at the top of their respective galleries in a section called **Custom** once saved.

 Access the Checklist tile on your CHOICE Course screen for reference information and job aids on How to Apply and Manage Themes.

Guidelines for Using Themes

 Note: All of the Guidelines for this lesson are available as checklists from the **Checklist** tile on the CHOICE Course screen.

Applying themes is an important step in enhancing the visual appeal of your workbooks, and keeping that visual appeal consistent across multiple documents. Take the following guidelines into account when using themes.

Use Themes

When using themes:

- Apply themes to worksheets whenever possible. It will be more difficult to format a worksheet's data without a theme applied.
- If you don't like any of the default themes, create a custom theme and set each individual element (fonts, colors, effects) to your liking.
- Keep in mind that themes are meant to facilitate reuse—think of how your themes could enhance future workbooks.
- Be consistent with themes across worksheets or related workbooks.
- Keep in mind that manually changing the format of data outside of themes will override that theme format. For example, if you change the text color in one cell to red, it will stay red even if you change the theme of the worksheet.
- Make sure that your cell styles work with your themes—if you change a worksheet's theme, it may also alter the formatting of any cell styles you have applied.
- When creating custom themes, choose colors that blend well together. Having an excessive amount of disparate colors that clash with one another can be eye-straining to your readers.
- Choose disparate colors primarily to highlight specific parts of your data, but keep this to a minimum. Consider the saying, "When everything is bold, nothing is."
- Likewise, choose an easily readable font at an appropriate size. Large, ornate fonts may be acceptable in worksheet titles, but the raw data itself needs to be visually efficient.

ACTIVITY 4-4
Applying Cell Styles and Themes

Before You Begin
The **My Sales Data.xlsx** workbook file is open.

Scenario
You like the progress you have made formatting the sales data worksheet, but you think it's important for the people who will be viewing the worksheet at the sales meeting to be able to distinguish between raw data and data that has been calculated using formulas and functions. You'd also like to set off the sales reps' names a bit more from the rest of the worksheet data. So, you decide to apply cell styles to differentiate among the various data types. You also feel it would be a good idea to modify the default **Title** cell style to align more with your current formatting. You want to use the modified cell style in other sales-related workbooks to ensure consistency. After reviewing your worksheet cell styles, you decide to go with a slightly more subtle color palette for the worksheet. By applying a different theme to the workbook, you'll be able to consistently change the color palette throughout.

1. Apply the **Title** cell style to the worksheet title.
   a) Select cell **A1**.
   b) Select **Home→Styles→Cell Styles**.
   c) In the **Cell Styles** gallery, in the **Titles and Headings** section, select **Title**.

2. Modify the **Title** cell style to use the text formatting you applied earlier.
   a) Select **Home→Styles→Cell Styles**, and then right-click the **Title** cell style and select **Duplicate**.
   b) In the **Style** dialog box, in the **Style name** field, type *Sales Department Title*
   c) Select **Format**.
   d) In the **Format Cells** dialog box, select the **Font** tab.
   e) In the **Font style** section, select **Bold**.
   f) In the **Size** section, select **16**.
   g) Select the **Color** drop-down menu, then, in the **Standard Colors** section, select **Blue**.
   h) Select **OK**.
   i) In the **Style** dialog box, ensure that the **Font** check box is checked, uncheck the **Number** check box, and then select **OK**.

3. Verify that Excel saved the modified cell style.
   a) Select **Home→Styles→Cell Styles**.
   b) In the **Cell Styles** gallery, in the **Custom** section, place the mouse pointer over the modified cell style to view its ScreenTip.
   c) Verify that the ScreenTip appears as **Sales Department Title**.
   d) Select the custom style to apply it.

4. Apply a cell style to the items in the **Employee Name** column and the quarterly sales columns.
   a) Select the range **A5:A27**.
   b) Select **Home→Styles→Cell Styles**, and then, in the **Themed Cell Styles** section, select **20% - Accent6**.
   c) Apply the same cell style to the raw sales data in **C5:F27**.

5. Apply a cell style to cells containing formulas or functions.
   a) Select the range **G5:K27**.
   b) From the **Cell Styles** gallery, in the **Data and Model** section, select the **Output** cell style.
   c) Deselect the range to view the newly applied cell style.

Employee Name	Region	Qtr. 1	Qtr. 2	Qtr. 3	Qtr. 4	Total	Average	Highest	Lowest	Commission
Silva	Northeast	$115,500	$65,500	$84,000	$187,110	$452,110	$113,027.50	$187,110.00	$65,500.00	$18,084.40
Maddox	Northeast	$113,500	$120,550	$243,760	$197,830	$675,640	$168,910.00	$243,760.00	$113,500.00	$27,025.60
Koval	Southwest	$104,500	$113,000	$100,700	$110,925	$429,125	$107,281.25	$113,000.00	$100,700.00	$17,165.00
Lindgren	South	$79,500	$113,500	$88,000	$61,670	$342,670	$85,667.50	$113,500.00	$61,670.00	$13,706.80
Sykes	North	$125,000	$170,000	$105,000	$192,215	$592,215	$148,053.75	$192,215.00	$105,000.00	$23,688.60
Lee	Southwest	$120,550	$274,060	$76,000	$142,320	$612,930	$153,232.50	$274,060.00	$76,000.00	$24,517.20

6. Preview several themes to determine how they will affect the overall look of your workbook.
   a) Select **Page Layout→Themes→Themes**.
   b) In the **Themes** gallery, point the mouse pointer at various themes to preview them.

 Note: Remember, the text in cells without cell styles applied to them will not be affected by changing the theme.

7. Select the **Savon** theme to apply it to the workbook.

8. Save the workbook.

TOPIC E

Apply Basic Conditional Formatting

As your Excel skill level increases and you begin to perform more and more data analysis with the information in your workbooks, you may find yourself looking for a way to make certain bits of information stand out based on particular conditions. For example, if you're analyzing the budgets for various departments, you may want to highlight in red any departments that have exceeded their budgets. Rather than doing this manually, Excel 2016 allows you to automatically format particular data that meets defined criteria. This kind of functionality can transform enormous sets of seemingly random bits of data into useful organizational intelligence that you can use to make sound decisions.

Conditional Formatting

Using *conditional formatting*, Excel displays data that meets specified criteria with the specified formatting applied. Essentially, data that meets certain conditions you define can stand out from the rest of your data. For example, on a budget worksheet, you may want all line items that are still under budget to appear in green text and line items that are over budget to appear in red text. Or perhaps you want to highlight in yellow all product lines on a sales summary that have increased in sales by more than five percent. Conditional formatting can perform these, and many other, tasks for you.

C	D	E	F	G	H	I	J	K

Sales Ledger

Qtr. 1	Qtr. 2	Qtr. 3	Qtr. 4	Total	Average	Highest	Lowest	Commission
$115,500	$65,500	$84,000	$187,110	$452,110	$113,027.50	$187,110.00	$65,500.00	$18,084.40
$113,500	$120,550	$243,760	$197,830	$675,640	$168,910.00	$243,760.00	$113,500.00	$27,025.60
$104,500	$113,000	$100,700	$110,925	$429,125	$107,281.25	$113,000.00	$100,700.00	$17,165.00
$79,500	$113,500	$88,000	$61,670	$342,670	$85,667.50	$113,500.00	$61,670.00	$13,706.80
$125,000	$170,000	$105,000	$192,215	$592,215	$148,053.75	$192,215.00	$105,000.00	$23,688.60
$120,550	$274,060	$76,000	$142,320	$612,930	$153,232.50	$274,060.00	$76,000.00	$24,517.20
$128,000	$243,760	$151,500	$92,215	$615,475	$153,868.75	$243,760.00	$92,215.00	$24,619.00
$113,000	$292,225	$84,000	$102,270	$591,495	$147,873.75	$292,225.00	$84,000.00	$23,659.80
$113,500	$243,240	$184,275	$147,150	$688,165	$172,041.25	$243,240.00	$113,500.00	$27,526.60
$119,000	$138,500	$63,000	$88,950	$409,450	$102,362.50	$138,500.00	$63,000.00	$16,378.00
$274,130	$296,120	$120,500	$118,335	$809,085	$202,271.25	$296,120.00	$118,335.00	$32,363.40
$156,000	$115,500	$88,500	$171,050	$531,050	$132,762.50	$171,050.00	$88,500.00	$21,242.00
$251,120	$86,500	$76,000	$136,650	$550,270	$137,567.50	$251,120.00	$76,000.00	$22,010.80

Figure 4-22: Various conditional formats applied to a worksheet.

Note: Excel Online App

Any conditional formatting that has been applied to workbooks will be visible in Excel Online; however, you must open the workbook in Excel 2016 if you want to apply or modify conditional formatting rules and styles. Everything in this topic applies to Excel 2016 only.

The Conditional Formatting Dialog Boxes

Each of the conditional formatting options covered in this topic has its own dialog box. These are all basically the same dialog box with a few minor exceptions for option-specific considerations. For example, the **Between** dialog box has two fields for values, whereas the **Greater Than** and **Less Than** dialog boxes have only a single value field. And, each of the dialog boxes is labeled with its corresponding conditional formatting option as the name.

The conditional formatting dialog boxes enable you to select both the criteria by which Excel analyzes the selected data and the formatting it will apply. You can select from among a small array of preconfigured formatting options or access the **Format Cells** dialog box to configure more specific formatting.

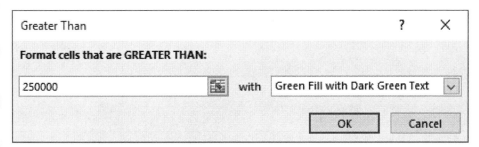

Figure 4-23: The Greater Than dialog box.

The Highlight Cells Rules

One of the most common types of conditional formatting that Excel users perform is highlighting cells that contain data meeting specific numeric criteria. To do this, you can select one of the options from the **Highlight Cells Rules** menu. These options enable you to select the criteria by which you wish to format your cell data and the specific formatting options you wish to apply to the data that meets the criteria. You can access the **Highlight Cells Rules** menu by selecting **Home→Styles→Conditional Formatting→Highlight Cells Rules**.

In the following example, the applied conditional format highlights cells in green when the data is greater than 250,000. In other words, the worksheet is drawing attention to sales reps who have made more than $250,000 in sales for a single quarter.

Employee Name	Region	Qtr. 1	Qtr. 2	Qtr. 3	Qtr. 4
Silva	Northeast	$115,500	$65,500	$84,000	$187,110
Maddox	Northeast	$113,500	$120,550	$243,760	$197,830
Koval	Southwest	$104,500	$113,000	$100,700	$110,925
Lindgren	South	$79,500	$113,500	$88,000	$61,670
Sykes	North	$125,000	$170,000	$105,000	$192,215
Lee	Southwest	$120,550	$274,060	$76,000	$142,320
Gilgamos	Southwest	$128,000	$243,760	$151,500	$92,215
Matthews	South	$113,000	$292,225	$84,000	$102,270
Anderson	North	$113,500	$243,240	$184,275	$147,150
Wagner	Northeast	$119,000	$138,500	$63,000	$88,950
Roberts	South	$274,130	$296,120	$120,500	$118,335

Figure 4-24: In this conditional format, cells are colored green when their data is greater than 250,000.

There are seven conditional formatting options in the **Highlight Cells Rules** menu.

Highlight Cells Rules Option	Applies the Selected Conditional Formatting To
Greater Than	Cells with values greater than the specified value.
Less Than	Cells with values less than the specified value.

Highlight Cells Rules Option	Applies the Selected Conditional Formatting To
Between	Cells with values between two specified values.
Equal To	Cells with values equal to the specified value.
Text that Contains	Cells that contain the exact text or value specified.
A Date Occurring	Cells that contain a date that falls within the specified time range.
Duplicate Values	Cells in a range that contain the same value as other cells in the selected range.

The Top/Bottom Rules

Another common use of conditional formatting involves highlighting cells that contain either the highest or the lowest values in a particular range or cells that are above or below average for the selected cells. The options in the **Top/Bottom Rules** menu can help you do just that. You can access the **Top/Bottom Rules** menu by selecting **Home→Styles→Conditional Formatting→Top/Bottom Rules**.

There are six conditional formatting options in the **Top/Bottom Rules** menu.

Top/Bottom Rules Option	Applies the Selected Conditional Formatting To
Top 10 Items	The cells in the selected range containing the 10 largest values.
Top 10%	The 10 percent of cells in the selected range containing the largest values.
Bottom 10 Items	The cells in the selected range containing the 10 smallest values.
Bottom 10%	The 10 percent of cells in the selected range containing the smallest values.
Above Average	All cells in the selected range with values that are greater than the average of all values in the selected range.
Below Average	All cells in the selected range with values that are less than the average of all values in the selected range.

 Note: The top and bottom 10 and the top and bottom 10-percent criteria are default settings that you can modify when applying conditional formatting to cells. For example, you can conditionally format the top 20 values or the bottom 33 percent of values.

Data Bars

Data bars are graphical representations of the relative value of data in a range of cells. Data bars appear in worksheet cells behind displayed values, giving worksheet viewers an instant picture of where particular cell values lie when compared to other cell data. The larger the value is in a particular cell, the longer the data bar will be. Excel includes a variety of pre-formatted data-bar styles and provides you with several options for customizing their appearance and behavior. You can access the data bars commands and options by selecting **Home→Styles→Conditional Formatting→Data Bars**.

Highest	Lowest	Commission
$187,110.00	$65,500.00	$18,084.40
$243,760.00	$113,500.00	$27,025.60
$113,000.00	$100,700.00	$17,165.00
$113,500.00	$61,670.00	$13,706.80
$192,215.00	$105,000.00	$23,688.60
$274,060.00	$76,000.00	$24,517.20
$243,760.00	$92,215.00	$24,619.00
$292,225.00	$84,000.00	$23,659.80
$243,240.00	$113,500.00	$27,526.60
$138,500.00	$63,000.00	$16,378.00
$296,120.00	$118,335.00	$32,363.40
$171,050.00	$88,500.00	$21,242.00
$251,120.00	$76,000.00	$22,010.80
$172,410.00	$77,500.00	$19,856.40
$154,500.00	$84,000.00	$20,388.60

Figure 4-25: Data bars comparing each salesperson's commission to their colleagues' commissions.

Color Scales

Like data bars, *color scales* give worksheet viewers a graphical representation of the relative values of cell data. Instead of appearing as bars of various lengths, however, color scales use various shades of either two or three colors to represent relative values. In a two-color scale, Excel displays high and low values in various shades of the two colors; the darker the color, the closer the value is to either the very highest or the very lowest values. You can use a three-color scale to represent low-, middle-, and high-range values. Excel includes a number of pre-formatted color scales and provides you with various options for customizing these to suit your needs. You can access the color scales commands and options by selecting **Home→Styles→Conditional Formatting→Color Scales**.

 Note: It is possible to apply more than one type of conditional formatting to the same range of cells.

Highest	Lowest	Commission
$187,110.00	$65,500.00	$18,084.40
$243,760.00	$113,500.00	$27,025.60
$113,000.00	$100,700.00	$17,165.00
$113,500.00	$61,670.00	$13,706.80
$192,215.00	$105,000.00	$23,688.60
$274,060.00	$76,000.00	$24,517.20
$243,760.00	$92,215.00	$24,619.00
$292,225.00	$84,000.00	$23,659.80
$243,240.00	$113,500.00	$27,526.60
$138,500.00	$63,000.00	$16,378.00
$296,120.00	$118,335.00	$32,363.40
$171,050.00	$88,500.00	$21,242.00
$251,120.00	$76,000.00	$22,010.80
$172,410.00	$77,500.00	$19,856.40
$154,500.00	$84,000.00	$20,388.60

Figure 4-26: A three-color scale comparing each salesperson's commission to their colleagues' commissions.

Icon Sets

Icon sets function in much the same way as data bars and color scales, but they use sets of icons to represent relative values. For example, you can use icon sets to identify relative values using a star-rating system: one star could represent very low values, three stars could represent mid-range values, and five stars could represent the highest values. Or, you might want to use a downward-facing red arrow to represent low values and an upward-facing green arrow to represent high values. Excel includes an extensive set of pre-formatted icon sets and provides you with further customization options. You can access the icon sets commands and options by selecting **Home→Styles→Conditional Formatting→Icon Sets**.

 Note: Data bars, color scales, and icon sets appear only in cells that contain some type of numeric data, such as values or dates. They do not work with text.

Highest	Lowest		Commission
$187,110.00	$65,500.00	⇨	$18,084.40
$243,760.00	$113,500.00	⬆	$27,025.60
$113,000.00	$100,700.00	⬇	$17,165.00
$113,500.00	$61,670.00	⬇	$13,706.80
$192,215.00	$105,000.00	⇨	$23,688.60
$274,060.00	$76,000.00	⇨	$24,517.20
$243,760.00	$92,215.00	⇨	$24,619.00
$292,225.00	$84,000.00	⇨	$23,659.80
$243,240.00	$113,500.00	⬆	$27,526.60
$138,500.00	$63,000.00	⬇	$16,378.00
$296,120.00	$118,335.00	⬆	$32,363.40
$171,050.00	$88,500.00	⇨	$21,242.00
$251,120.00	$76,000.00	⇨	$22,010.80
$172,410.00	$77,500.00	⇨	$19,856.40
$154,500.00	$84,000.00	⇨	$20,388.60

Figure 4-27: A colored arrow icon set comparing each salesperson's commission to their colleagues' commissions.

Note: You may have noticed that the primary conditional format options are divided into two groups in the **Conditional Formatting** menu. The **Highlight Cells Rules** and **Top/Bottom Rules** options both compare each individual cell to a condition; the **Data Bars**, **Color Scales**, and **Icon Sets** options compare values in cells to each other. This is an important distinction between these two groups.

Access the Checklist tile on your CHOICE Course screen for reference information and job aids on How to Apply Basic Conditional Formatting.

ACTIVITY 4-5
Applying Basic Conditional Formatting

Before You Begin

The **My Sales Data.xlsx** workbook file is open.

Scenario

Your supervisor had some suggestions after reviewing the sales data worksheet. He asked you to highlight all sales figures greater than $250,000 for each quarter, highlight the bottom 25 percent of sales reps based on sales totals for the year, and highlight the top 10 percent of sales reps based on average quarterly sales. Given how competitive your reps are, you also think it'll be helpful to visually compare each rep's commission earnings against the others. You decide that the easiest way to accomplish this is to apply conditional formatting to the worksheet columns.

1. Highlight all quarterly sales figures of $250,000 or more.
   a) Select the range **C5:F27**.
   b) Select **Home→Styles→Conditional Formatting→Highlight Cells Rules→Greater Than**.
   c) In the **Greater Than** dialog box, in the **Format cells that are GREATER THAN** field, type *250000*
   d) From the **with** drop-down menu, select **Green Fill with Dark Green Text**.
   e) Select **OK**.
   f) Deselect the range to verify that Excel applied the formatting as expected.

2. Highlight the lowest 25 percent of performers in total sales and the highest 10 percent of performers in average quarterly sales.
   a) Select the range **G5:G27**.
   b) Select **Home→Styles→Conditional Formatting→Top/Bottom Rules→Bottom 10%**.
   c) In the **Bottom 10%** dialog box, in the **Format cells that rank in the BOTTOM** spin box, set the value to **25**.
   d) From the **with** drop-down menu, select **Light Red Fill** and then select **OK**.
   e) Select all of the cells in the **Average** column, then select **Home→Styles→Conditional Formatting→Top/Bottom Rules→Top 10%**.
   f) Verify that **10** is the default value, then select **Green Fill with Dark Green Text** from the **with** drop-down menu. Select **OK** to apply the format.
   g) Deselect the **Average** column's cells to verify that Excel applied the formatting.

3. Add data bars for each rep's commission earnings.
   a) Select the range **K5:K27**.
   b) Select **Home→Styles→Conditional Formatting→Data Bars**.
   c) Under **Gradient Fill**, select **Blue Data Bar**.
   d) Deselect the **Commission** column's cells to verify that Excel applied the formatting.

4. Save the workbook.

TOPIC F

Create and Use Templates

For many Excel users, it's not uncommon to create and work with pretty much the same workbook over and over again with few, if any, significant changes. In these cases, it can be a waste of time to have to lay out the basic framework of your worksheets every time you create a new workbook. Fortunately, Excel enables you to leverage your existing workbooks to create similar new workbooks. By taking advantage of this functionality, you can essentially store all the time, effort, and research that went into creating your workbooks for future use.

Templates

An Excel *template* is a file that contains a number of preconfigured or pre-entered workbook elements, such as formatting, formulas, themes, and functions, that you can use to create and work with new workbooks. Essentially, templates are files that contain the desired structure for future workbook files. You can search for and download thousands of Excel template files from **Office.com** and a number of other websites, or you can create your own custom templates, either by building them from scratch or by modifying existing templates, to suit your needs.

The default file format for Excel 2016 template files is the XLTX file format. You can access your local Excel template files and search for others from **Office.com** from the **New** tab in the **Backstage** view. Excel template files are saved to a default folder on your computer, and custom templates will always be available to you if you use Excel on the same computer. You can transfer template files to other machines or simply re-download them from **Office.com** when you have to work with Excel on a different computer.

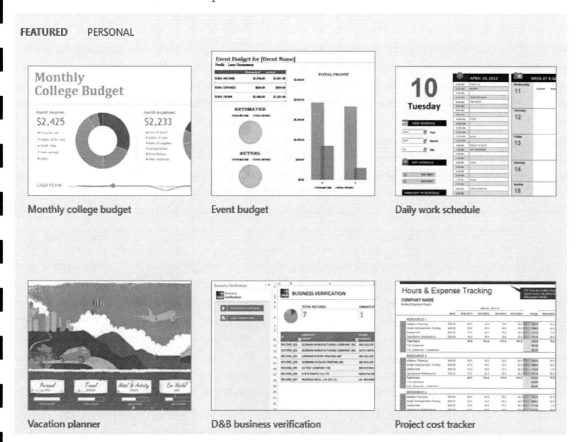

Figure 4–28: Office.com templates in the Backstage view.

Note: Excel Online App

Excel workbook templates are available in **Backstage** view by selecting **FILE→New**. If the template you are searching for is not listed, you can go directly to **office.com** and select **Templates** at the top of the page. The Office templates are organized by category and when you find the template you want to use, simply select it and then select **Open in Excel Online**.

Templates and the Backstage View

You can access both templates from **Office.com** and any templates you have saved locally to your computer from the **Backstage** view. You can access these either from the **Excel** screen, if you're just opening Excel, or from the **New** screen, if you already have Excel open. In either case, the **Excel** screen and the **New** screen are divided into two tabs: the **FEATURED** tab and the **PERSONAL** tab. The **FEATURED** tab displays a list of new and popular templates you can quickly choose from, and it presents you with the tools and commands necessary to search for and download templates for a wide variety of uses. When you download a template from the **FEATURED** tab, Excel opens the template as a standard Excel workbook. If you wish to keep a local copy of the template file, you must save it as a template file to your computer's hard drive.

The **PERSONAL** tab displays a list of all of the workbook template files you have saved to your computer. In order for your saved templates to appear on the **PERSONAL** tab, however, you must save them to the **C:\Users\<name>\Documents\Custom Office Templates** folder. If you save your Excel template files to any other location, you will not be able to directly access them from the **PERSONAL** tab.

Note: The **FEATURED** and **PERSONAL** tabs may appear only after you've saved a custom template to your computer.

FEATURED tab

PERSONAL tab

Figure 4-29: The FEATURED and PERSONAL tabs for viewing Excel templates.

 Access the Checklist tile on your CHOICE Course screen for reference information and job aids on How to Create and Use Templates.

ACTIVITY 4-6
Creating a Template

Before You Begin
The **My Sales Data.xlsx** workbook file is open.

Scenario
You're nearly done developing the worksheet you will present during the upcoming sales meeting. As you are likely to need the same sales data for future periods and other meetings, you decide to save the current workbook as an Excel template from which to create future workbooks. Because you don't want to include all of the current sales data in the template, you decide to delete most of the worksheet data before saving the file as a template.

1. Delete cell content not needed in the template file.
   a) Select the range **A5:F27** and press **Delete**.
   b) Delete the cell content in the following ranges and cells: **L5:L27**, **O1:O3**, **Q1**, and **Q3**.

    Note: Do not select cell **Q3** directly, as that will activate the link. Instead, select a cell near it and use the arrow keys to navigate to it.

2. Save the workbook as an Excel template file.
   a) Select **File→Save As**.
   b) From the **Save As** screen, select **Browse**.
   c) In the **Save As** dialog box, in the **File name** field, type *My Sales Data Template*
   d) From the **Save as type** drop-down menu, select **Excel Template (*.xltx)**.
   e) Ensure that Excel is saving the file to the **Custom Office Templates** folder, and then select **Save**.

    Note: If you don't save the template to this default folder, it won't appear in the list of personal templates in the **Backstage** view.

3. Verify that the template file name appears in the **Title bar** with the .xltx file extension and close the template file.

4. Verify that the template is available for future use.
   a) Select **File→New→PERSONAL**.
   b) Verify that the **My Sales Data Template** file appears, then select it.
   c) Verify that the template opens with all of your formatting intact. Enter data into any one of the cells, then close the template file without saving when you're done.

5. Leave Excel open.

Summary

In this lesson, you formatted worksheets in a variety of ways to enhance their readability. This robust set of formatting functionality will help you create highly functional, professional-looking workbooks without the need to waste time tweaking and adjusting numerous settings. Being able to quickly generate visually useful workbooks will allow you to focus on what's really important: what your data can tell you about your organization.

What are some of the ways you will use conditional formatting in your workbooks?

What are some of the reasons you'd create custom templates for use within your organization?

 Note: Check your CHOICE Course screen for opportunities to interact with your classmates, peers, and the larger CHOICE online community about the topics covered in this course or other topics you are interested in. From the Course screen you can also access available resources for a more continuous learning experience.

5 | Printing Workbooks

Lesson Time: 45 minutes

Lesson Introduction

You put a lot of work into creating, populating, and formatting your workbook. Now you may need to print hard copies of your workbooks to share with your colleagues, supervisor, or organizational leaders. Your workbooks may contain multiple worksheets, each of which could contain thousands of data entries, formulas, and results. Instead of printing all of this indiscriminately, you will need to print only what is necessary to deliver critical information to your audience. Microsoft® Office Excel® 2016 has a wide variety of printing options that can save your document recipients from having to sift through mounds of irrelevant data.

Lesson Objectives

In this lesson, you will:

- Preview and print a workbook.

- Set up the page layout.

- Configure headers and footers.

TOPIC A

Preview and Print a Workbook

Although most information these days exists digitally, you will likely still, on occasion, require hard copies of a document. But spreadsheets are not the same as most other documents. They can contain nearly any number of rows and columns, and the amount of data you can include on worksheets can be staggering. So, what defines a page for printed workbooks largely depends on your preferences. Excel 2016 includes a variety of printing options you can take advantage of—knowing what these are and how they work means you'll be able to generate hard copies of your data, exactly as you need to, quickly and easily.

The Print Tab

You can access the commands and settings you will need to print your workbooks by selecting the **Print** tab in the **Backstage** view. Selecting this tab displays the **Print** screen. From here you can select a printer, adjust numerous print settings, and view a preview of what your printed pages will look like based on the current settings.

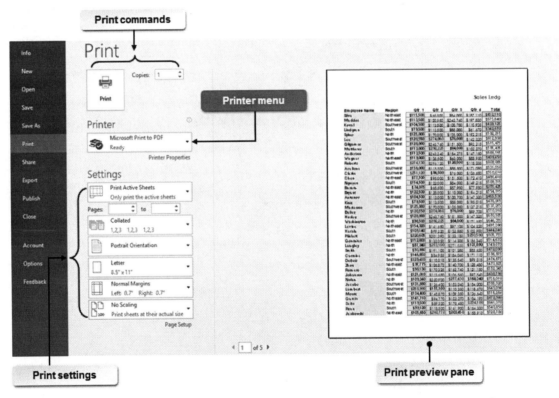

Figure 5-1: The Print tab in the Backstage view provides you with numerous options for determining how your workbooks will print.

The following table describes the functions of the various elements on the **Print** tab.

Print Tab Element	Allows You To
Print section	Access commands for selecting the number of copies you wish to print and for executing a print job.
Printer menu	Select the printer, device, or printer driver you wish to use.

Print Tab Element	Allows You To
Printer Properties link	Access the **Properties** dialog box for your selected printer, device, or printer driver.
Settings section	Configure general print settings, such as which worksheets to print, how to orient the printed pages, and what magnification level to use.
Page Setup link	Access the **Page Setup** dialog box, which enables you to configure the page layout of your worksheets.
Print preview pane	View a preview of how your workbook pages will look once printed.

> **Note: Excel Online App**
>
> When you print in Excel Online, the required steps vary slightly from those used to print Excel 2016 files. You continue to have the ability to preview how the printout will look; however, because the settings are not readily visible on the **Print** tab in **Backstage** view, you will need to follow the prompts to access the **Print** and **Page Setup** options.

The Print Settings

To ensure that your printed pages look exactly as you want them to, you'll likely need to adjust some of the print settings before you print. The **Settings** section of the **Print** screen contains all of the commands you will use to configure general print settings for your workbook. It is important to keep in mind that the print settings buttons appear with different text depending on your current selection, so the command buttons will not always match the following figure.

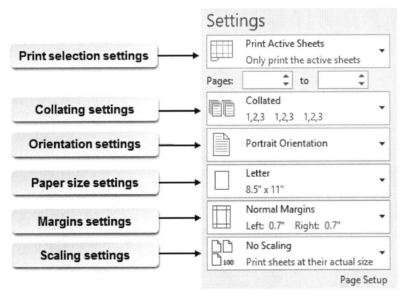

Figure 5-2: Settings commands.

The **Settings** commands give you control over the final printed copies of your workbooks.

Print Settings Command	Allows You To
Print selection settings	Decide among printing all worksheets in a workbook, printing the currently selected worksheet, or printing the currently selected cell or range. If you have defined a print area, you can also choose to ignore that in favor of whatever setting you select from this command.

Print Settings Command	Allows You To
Pages and **to** spin boxes	Select which range of pages to print. The content that appears on each page and the number of printable pages for a workbook depend on your other print settings.
Collating settings	Decide between collating and not collating your pages. Collated print jobs print each copy of a multiple-page document in sequential order, so each copy is in the correct page order. Non-collated print jobs print all copies of the first page and then all copies of the second page, and so on.
Orientation settings	Decide between the portrait and landscape orientations for your printed pages.
Paper size settings	Decide what size paper to print on. These settings depend on your printer's capabilities.
Margins settings	Set the margin size for your printed pages.
Scaling settings	Determine whether or not Excel changes the magnification level of your printed data and how it applies magnification to printed pages.

Page Orientation

Page orientation is a page layout setting that determines the general, overall layout of each printed page. This setting specifies whether pages should print in portrait orientation or landscape orientation. In portrait orientation, page height is greater than page width; this enables you to fit more rows of data, but fewer columns, than landscape orientation. Landscape orientation is just the opposite; the page width is greater than the page height, allowing for more columns, but fewer rows, than portrait orientation.

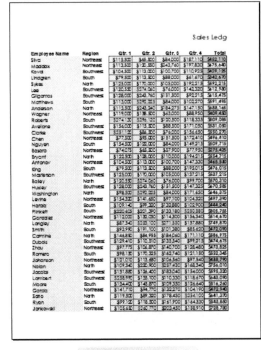
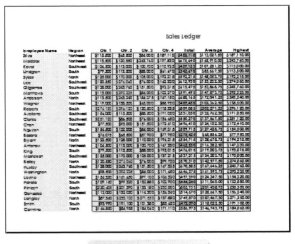

Portrait orientation   **Landscape orientation**

Figure 5-3: The same worksheet printed in both the portrait and landscape orientations.

Margins

Page margins are invisible boundaries that define where particular content is located on printed worksheets. Margins determine how much space there is between the worksheet content and the edge of the paper. Excel provides you with a set of common margin configurations to choose from, and it allows you to customize margin sizes to suit your needs. Margins can define where worksheet data, headers, and footers are arranged on printed pages. The **Margins** tab on the **Page Setup** dialog box also provides you with options for centering your content vertically or horizontally on the page.

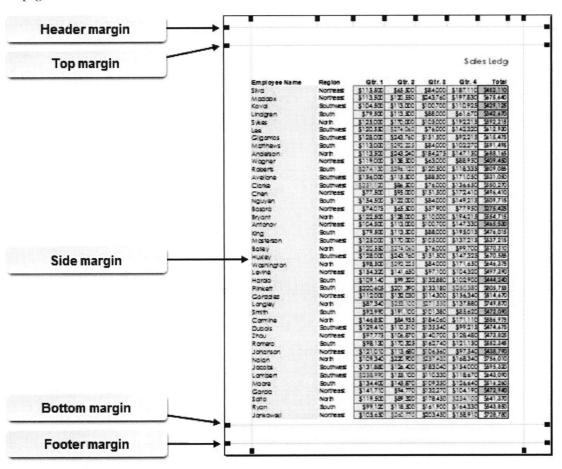

Figure 5-4: Page margins displayed on a worksheet page in print preview.

Print Preview

With so many options when it comes to printing your workbooks, you'll want to be sure you have configured your print settings properly before you print. Excel 2016 provides you with the ability to view a preview of your workbook print jobs. The print preview is displayed in the right pane of the **Print** screen in the **Backstage** view. You can access this by selecting **File→Print** or by selecting either the **Print** or the **Print Preview** button in the **Page Setup** dialog box.

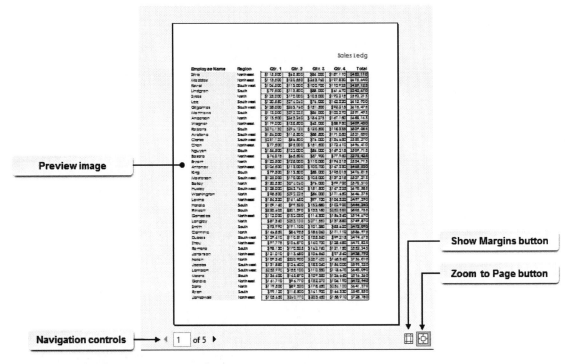

Figure 5-5: A workbook document displayed in print preview.

The commands in the print preview pane enable you to inspect each page of a print job before printing.

Print Preview Element	Description
Preview image	Displays how the currently selected page will print on paper.
Navigation controls	Enables you to navigate through and inspect each page in the current print job.
Show Margins button	Toggles the display of page margins on and off.
Zoom to Page button	Toggles between two magnification levels for viewing the print preview.

 Access the Checklist tile on your CHOICE Course screen for reference information and job aids on How to Preview and Print a Workbook.

ACTIVITY 5-1
Configuring and Previewing a Print Job

Data File

C:\091055Data\Printing Workbooks\Sales Data Final.xlsx

Before You Begin

Excel 2016 is open.

You have a printer driver installed and available.

Scenario

Due to a request from senior managers, you've included a number of other sales teams' data in your workbook. Your workbook is now complete and you're ready to print copies for attendees at the upcoming sales meeting. Before you do, you want to make sure the content will print correctly. You decide to configure and preview the print settings before you print actual hard copies.

---

1. Open the **Sales Data Final.xlsx** workbook file.

2. Select **File→Print**.

3. Preview the print job.
   a) In the right pane, review the first page of the print preview.
   b) Use the navigation controls to view the remaining pages of the preview and then navigate back to page 1.

4. Configure print settings.
   a) Set the collating settings to **Uncollated**.
   b) Set the orientation to **Landscape Orientation**.
   c) Set the scaling settings to **Fit All Columns on One Page**.
   d) Select the **Show Margins** button ⊞ to view the page content in reference to the margins.

e) Drag the top margin down slightly, and drag the bottom margin up slightly. Refer to the following screenshot for an approximate end result.

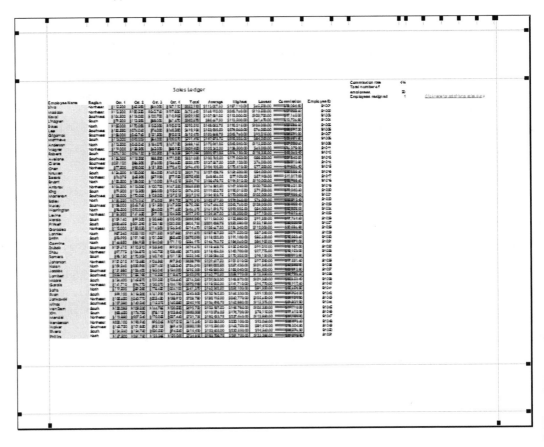

f) Select the **Show Margins** button again to toggle the margin view off.

5. Preview the print job to view the changes made by adjusting the print settings.

6. Save the workbook to the **C:\091055Data\Printing Workbooks** folder as *My Sales Data Final.xlsx*

TOPIC B

Set Up the Page Layout

Although the general print settings provide you with a solid base to print your workbooks, there's much more you can do when printing with Excel. As mentioned, workbook printing can be highly complex for a large number of reasons. You will, from time to time, need to be able to fine-tune how to print your workbook pages. Luckily, Excel 2016 has many options for just this purpose. Knowing what configurations are available and how to set them will allow you to create more visually helpful and appealing printouts.

The Page Setup Dialog Box

The **Page Setup** dialog box provides you with more options for configuring your workbooks for printing than the print settings in the **Backstage** view. The **Page Setup** dialog box is organized into four tabs that contain task-related commands and settings for configuring your workbooks to print. You can access the **Page Setup** dialog box either by selecting the **Page Setup** link at the bottom of the **Settings** section of the **Print** screen in the **Backstage** view, or by selecting any of the dialog box launchers on the **Page Layout** ribbon tab.

 Note: The **Print** and **Print Preview** buttons are displayed on the **Page Setup** dialog box only if you open it from the dialog box launchers on the **Page Layout** tab. You can also access most of Excel's print settings in the command groups on the **Page Layout** tab.

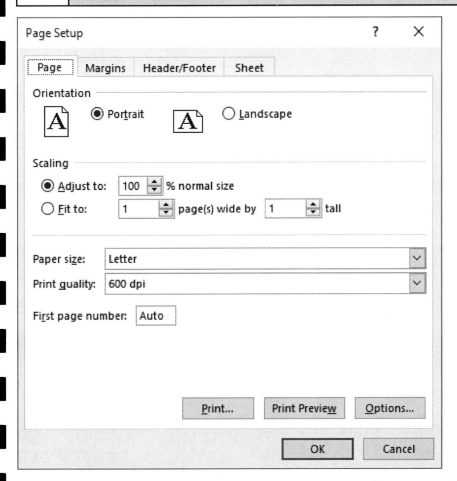

Figure 5–6: The Page Setup dialog box displaying the Print and Print Preview buttons.

The following table identifies the commands you will find on the various **Page Setup** dialog box tabs.

Page Setup Dialog Box Element	Provides You with Access To
Page tab	Commands to set page orientation and magnification level, the paper size, the print quality, and which page to start printing from.
Margins tab	Commands to adjust page, header, and footer margins and to determine how to center content on printed pages.
Header/Footer tab	Commands for inserting, modifying, and deleting headers and footers.
Sheet tab	Commands for defining a print area, determining which rows and columns print on every page, determining which page elements print on paper, and defining the order in which pages print.
Options button	The **Properties** dialog box for the currently selected printer, device, or printer driver. This command appears on all of the **Page Setup** dialog box tabs.

The Print Area

The *Print Area* feature enables you to select specific cells and ranges to print from your workbooks. Once you've set a print area, only those cells within the print area will print. Cells within the print area appear surrounded by a thin, gray border. You can expand the print area by adding cells to it, and you can clear the print area to print the entire workbook or any other areas you designate via other methods. You cannot add objects, such as graphs, to print areas. Once you've set a print area, it is saved along with the workbook; it won't affect other workbook files.

Print areas are also worksheet-specific, so you have to configure them for each worksheet individually. If you select the **Print Entire Workbook** option from the print settings, any worksheets on which you have set print areas will print only those areas, while worksheets without print areas will print in their entirety. You can access the **Print Area** options by selecting **Page Layout→Page Setup→Print Area**.

▲	A	B	C	D	E	F	G
1							
2						Sales Ledg	
3							
4	**Employee Name**	**Region**	**Qtr. 1**	**Qtr. 2**	**Qtr. 3**	**Qtr. 4**	**Total**
5	Silva	Northeast	$115,500	$65,500	$84,000	$187,110	**$452,110**
6	Maddox	Northeast	$113,500	$120,550	$243,760	$197,830	**$675,640**
7	Koval	Southwest	$104,500	$113,000	$100,700	$110,925	**$429,125**
8	Lindgren	South	$79,500	$113,500	$88,000	$61,670	**$342,670**
9	Sykes	North	$125,000	$170,000	$105,000	$192,215	**$592,215**
10	Lee	Southwest	$120,550	$274,060	$76,000	$142,320	**$612,930**
11	Gilgamos	Southwest	$128,000	$243,760	$151,500	$92,215	**$615,475**
12	Matthews	South	$113,000	$292,225	$84,000	$102,270	**$591,495**
13	Anderson	North	$113,500	$243,240	$184,275	$147,150	**$688,165**
14	Wagner	Northeast	$119,000	$138,500	$63,000	$88,950	**$409,450**
15	Roberts	South	$274,130	$296,120	$120,500	$118,335	**$809,085**

Print area border

Figure 5-7: The print area is set from A7:G12 in this example.

The Ignore Print Area Option

Excel 2016 gives you the option of temporarily ignoring a defined print area if you wish to print content outside the print area. You can toggle this option on and off from the print selection settings on the **Print** screen in the **Backstage** view.

The Print Titles Command

Because Excel worksheets can contain thousands of columns' and rows' worth of data, it can be difficult for people to interpret printed worksheets if column and row labels don't print on all pages. Excel 2016 includes a feature that enables you to determine which rows and columns will print on every page: the **Print Titles** command. By using this feature, you can save your worksheet viewers from having to flip back to the first page to understand the data they're looking at. Selecting **Page Layout→Page Setup→Print Titles** opens the **Page Setup** dialog box with the **Sheet** tab automatically selected. This is where you can enter row and column references to determine which cells appear on all printed pages.

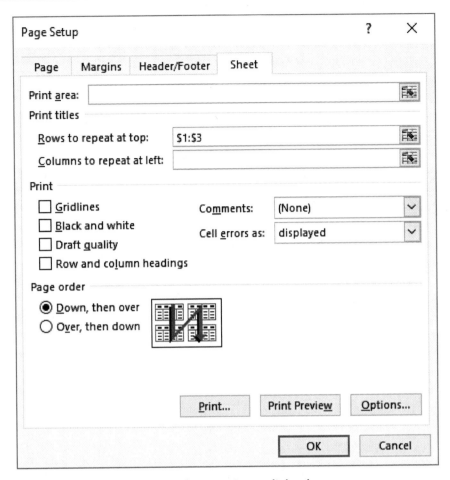

Figure 5-8: The Sheet tab in the Page Setup dialog box.

Note: Excel Online App

You must open your workbook in Excel 2016 to define print titles and set page breaks because these advanced printing features are not currently available in Excel Online.

Page Breaks

Sometimes scaling your worksheets up or down to fit on the desired number of pages doesn't quite give you the results you're looking for in terms of what content prints on which page. In these cases, you may want to manually tell Excel where one printed page ends and another one begins. To do this, you can insert *page breaks*. Page breaks are, essentially, boundaries that divide worksheet pages for printing purposes only. Excel 2016 enables you to insert and delete specific page breaks and to remove all page breaks on a given worksheet. Default page breaks appear as dashed lines on Excel worksheets, whereas manual page breaks appear as solid lines. They are worksheet-specific, so you need to set them for each worksheet in a workbook individually. When you insert page breaks, Excel divides the pages by creating page breaks above and to the left of the selected cell. You can access the page break commands by selecting **Page Layout→Page Setup→Breaks**, or by using the Page Break Preview view.

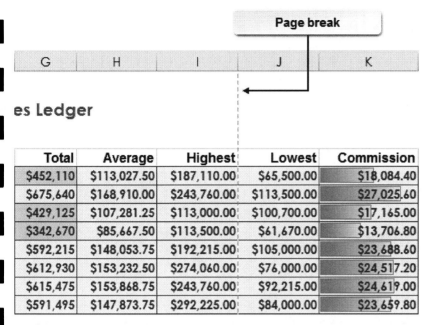

Figure 5-9: A default page break on an Excel worksheet.

Workbook Views

You may not have even realized it, but you've probably been viewing your Excel workbooks in the Normal view, which is the default workbook view in Excel 2016. There are other preconfigured *workbook views* that display the Excel user interface (UI) and your worksheets in vastly different configurations. A workbook view is, simply, the way Excel displays an open workbook. Workbook views can affect the placement and layout of worksheets and the Excel UI, and can affect whether or not particular elements, such as page breaks, appear. They are meant to configure the Excel environment to be easier to work with for a number of different tasks. Aside from including several preconfigured views, Excel 2016 provides you with the ability to create custom workbook views. You can access the commands you will use to change your workbook views in the **Workbook Views** group on the **View** tab.

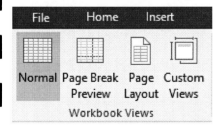

Figure 5-10: The commands in the Workbook Views group.

 Note: The Normal view is the default because it is designed to be the best all-around view for most workbook tasks.

The Page Break Preview View

The Page Break Preview view is ideal for inserting, deleting, and arranging page breaks on your Excel worksheets and for defining print areas. In this view, default page breaks appear as blue dashed lines, whereas manual page breaks appear as solid blue lines. To arrange page breaks when in this view, simply drag them to the desired location. Once you move a default page break, it becomes a manual page break.

When you set a print area in the Page Break Preview view, only cells within the print area will appear in full color. Cells outside the print area appear grayed-out. You can manually adjust the boundaries of print areas in this view just as you can manually adjust page breaks. When you right-click any cell in the Page Break Preview view, the context menu that appears contains commands for working with page breaks and print areas.

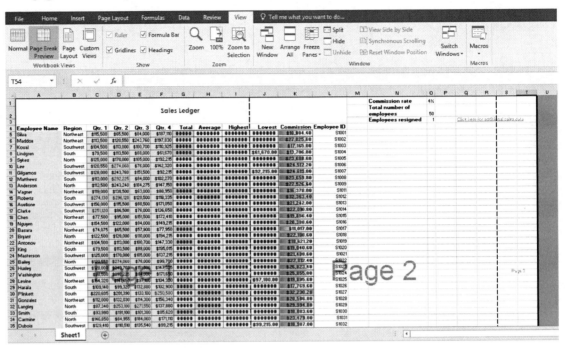

Figure 5-11: The Page Break Preview view.

 Access the Checklist tile on your CHOICE Course screen for reference information and job aids on How to Set Up the Page Layout.

ACTIVITY 5-2
Setting Up the Page Layout

Before You Begin
The **My Sales Data Final.xlsx** workbook file is open.

Scenario
Having previewed the sales data worksheet, you now have a better idea of the precise page layout you would like to define before printing the pages. You decide to make the column labels print on each page so it's easier to read the data no matter what page you're looking at. You also think that the supplementary information (commission rate, number of employees, etc.) isn't relevant to your audience, so you'll define a print area to exclude that part of the worksheet. Lastly, you want each page to divide more evenly, so you'll adjust where the pages break.

1. Set the column labels to print on each page.
   a) Select **Page Layout→Page Setup→Print Titles**.
   b) In the **Page Setup** dialog box, ensure that the **Sheet** tab is selected.
   c) In the **Print titles** section, to the right of the **Rows to repeat at top** field, select the **Collapse Dialog** button.
   d) Select row **4** and press **Enter**.
   e) Select **OK**.

2. Define a print area to exclude the supplementary information.
   a) Select the range **A1:L54**.
   b) Select **Page Layout→Page Setup→Print Area→Set Print Area**.
   c) Deselect the range.

3. Adjust where the pages break.
   a) Select **View→Workbook Views→Page Break Preview**.
   b) In the preview, drag the horizontal dotted blue line to the half-way point of the sheet, around row **26**.

c) Verify that the blue line becomes solid, indicating that you have manually set the page break.

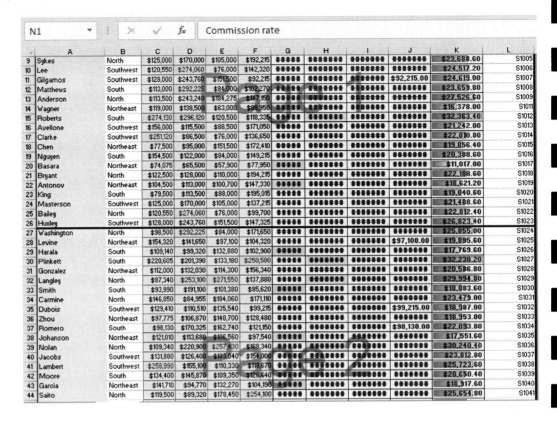

4. Preview the page layout.

   a) Select **File→Print**.
   b) Verify the following:
      - All columns fit on the page.
      - The supplementary information (commission rate, total employees, etc.) doesn't appear.
      - Only about half of the rows appear on the first page.
   c) Navigate to page 2 and verify that the worksheet title and the column headers all appear on the second page, and that the other half of the rows also appear.

5. Save the workbook.

TOPIC C

Configure Headers and Footers

Although you've set up the page layout to your liking, you may still want to enhance your printed worksheets by adding supplementary information. For example, numbering each individual page can make it much easier for your readers to navigate your printed workbooks. There's also plenty of other identifying information you might want to include on all or most of your printed pages—like your company's name, the date the workbook was printed, and so on. Excel 2016 makes adding these print-only elements quick and easy through the use of headers and footers.

Headers and Footers

Headers and *footers* are small content placeholders that display additional information or images in certain Excel views and on printed pages. Headers appear along the top of the page, whereas footers appear along the bottom. They are not considered part of the worksheets themselves and cannot be referenced by formulas and functions. Headers and footers are worksheet-specific, so you have to configure them for each worksheet in a workbook individually.

Excel 2016 includes a number of preconfigured headers and footers, and you also have the option of creating custom headers and footers. Headers and footers can contain text or images, and can be placed to the left or right, or centered, along the top or the bottom of the page. You can also create different headers and footers for odd and even pages, and exclude them from the first printed page or create unique headers and footers for the first page. Common items included in headers and footers include page numbers, the date, the name of the person who created the worksheet, the name of your organization, and organizational logos.

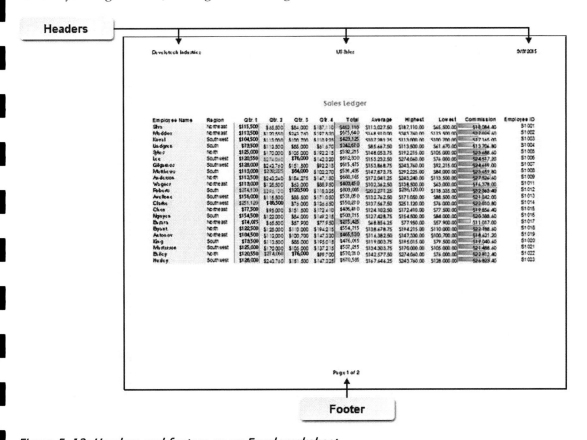

Figure 5-12: Headers and footers on an Excel worksheet.

Note: Excel Online App

Headers and footers must be defined in Excel 2016. When you print a workbook in Excel Online, you have the ability to turn the printing of headers and footers on or off.

The Page Layout View

The Page Layout view displays worksheets as they would print on separate pages based on the current print settings. When you select the Page Layout view, Excel also automatically displays rulers along the top and left sides of the UI to assist with the placement of on-screen objects. Page Layout view displays all header and footer placeholders, which enables you to graphically create, edit, and delete headers and footers. When you select a header or a footer placeholder while in the Page Layout view, Excel displays the **Header & Footer Tools** tab, providing you with access to the various commands you can use to create and customize headers and footers.

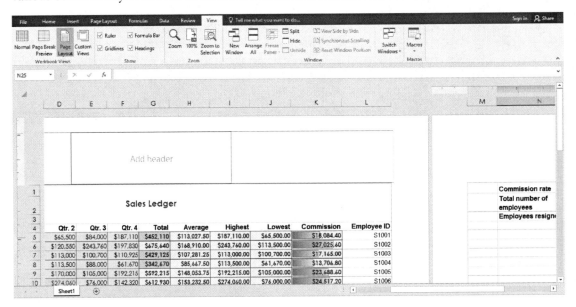

Figure 5-13: A worksheet in Page Layout view.

Contextual Tabs

The **Header & Footer Tools** tab is one example of a contextual tab. *Contextual tabs* are specialized, temporary ribbon tabs that display commands for working with a particular type of worksheet content. Contextual tabs appear when you select the associated content type, such as a graph or an image, and they close when you change your selection. Contextual tabs can contain one or multiple other tabs that contain command groups like any of the other ribbon tabs.

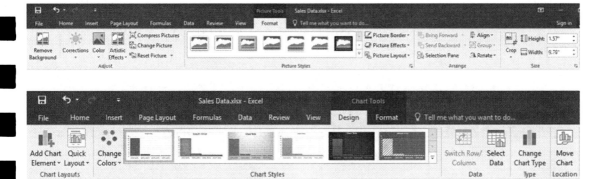

Figure 5-14: The Picture Tools contextual tab contains only one tab, whereas the Chart Tools contextual tab contains two.

The Header & Footer Tools Contextual Tab

When you select a header or footer placeholder in Page Layout view, Excel displays the **Header & Footer Tools** contextual tab. From here, you have access to the commands you can use to work with headers and footers in the ribbon environment. These enable you to enter specific text or images to create unique customized headers and footers.

 Note: You can also immediately switch to Page Layout view and activate the **Header & Footer Tools** contextual tab by selecting **Insert→Text→Header & Footer**.

Figure 5-15: The Header & Footer Tools contextual tab.

The Header and Footer Dialog Boxes

The **Header** and **Footer** dialog boxes are an alternative to using the **Header & Footer Tools** contextual tab in Page Layout view. You can access the **Header** and **Footer** dialog boxes by selecting the **Custom Header** or **Custom Footer** buttons from the **Header/Footer** tab in the **Page Layout** dialog box.

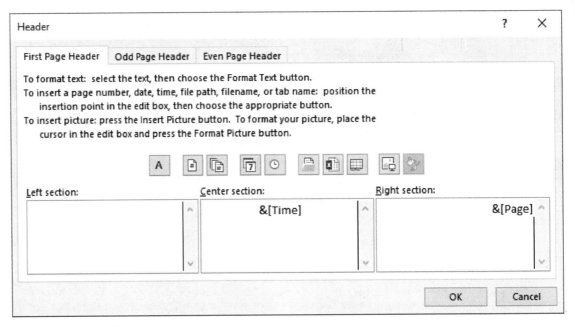

Figure 5-16: The Header dialog box.

Header and Footer Options

There are several header and footer options that warrant covering in a bit more detail. These options provide you with a greater level of control over configuring your worksheet headers and footers. You can access these settings either from the **Header & Footer Tools** contextual tab or on the **Header/Footer** tab of the **Page Setup** dialog box.

Header and Footer Option	Description
Different First Page	Tells Excel that you want to configure unique headers and footers for the first page of your document. This is useful, for example, if you want to include a document title.
Different Odd & Even Pages	Tells Excel that you want to configure your headers and footers differently for odd and even pages.
Scale with Document	Selecting this option tells Excel to scale header and footer text up or down when scaling other worksheet content.
Align with Page Margins	Selecting this option automatically aligns headers and footers with the left and right page margins.

 Access the Checklist tile on your CHOICE Course screen for reference information and job aids on How to Configure Headers and Footers.

ACTIVITY 5-3
Configuring Headers and Footers

Before You Begin

The **My Sales Data Final.xlsx** workbook file is open.

Scenario

You also decide to add headers and footers to the workbook to include the date of the sales meeting, a title for the workbook, and page numbers. Adding this information will make printed copies easier to read, while not using up any actual cells in the worksheet.

1. Add headers to the worksheet.
   a) Select **View→Workbook Views→Page Layout**.
   b) Select the box to the left of the **Add header** box.

    Note: You may need to scroll to see the correct box.

   c) Type *Develetech Industries*
   d) Select the next header box to the right.
   e) Type *US Sales*
   f) Select the next header box to the right.
   g) Select **Header & Footer Tools Design→Header & Footer Elements→Current Date**.

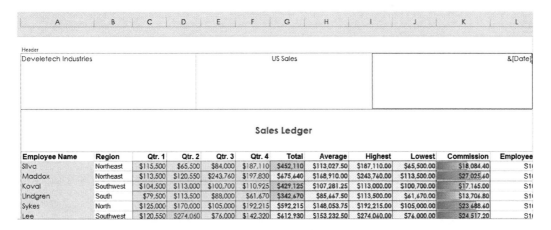

2. Add a page numbering footer to the worksheet.
   a) Select **Header & Footer Tools Design→Navigation→Go to Footer**.
   b) Verify that Excel activated the rightmost footer box.

    Note: You may need to scroll to see the correct box.

   c) Select **Header & Footer Tools Design→Header & Footer→Footer→Page 1 of ?**.

3. Preview the worksheet and verify that your headers and footer will print.

4. (Optional) Print the worksheet.

a) Select the **Print** button.

b) If you're printing to a file, save it to **C:\091055Data\Printing Workbooks** as *Sales Data Print*

c) Navigate to the file with File Explorer and open it. If you printed a physical copy, retrieve it.

d) Verify that the printed copy appears correctly.

e) Close any open files and folders and return to your workbook in Excel.

5. Save and close the workbook.

Summary

In this lesson, you configured, previewed, and printed a workbook. You also defined the worksheet page layout to print only the desired content. Taking advantage of all of the print functionality available in Excel will enable you to create hard copies of your workbook content for nearly any situation. By limiting what content you print to only what is necessary, you will save on printer resources and prevent your document viewers from having to sift through irrelevant or unimportant data.

Which page layout options do you expect to use most frequently? Why?

What do you see as being the main benefit of using the Print Area option?

 Note: Check your CHOICE Course screen for opportunities to interact with your classmates, peers, and the larger CHOICE online community about the topics covered in this course or other topics you are interested in. From the Course screen you can also access available resources for a more continuous learning experience.

6 Managing Workbooks

Lesson Time: 45 minutes

Lesson Introduction

So far, you have largely worked within workbooks and worksheets to enter, view, analyze, format, and present your organizational data. But there's more to being proficient in Microsoft® Office Excel® 2016 than simply working within your workbooks. Managing the overall structure of your workbooks, manipulating how you view your workbooks, and knowing how to find the workbook you need, when you need it, are all critical tasks you'll need to perform from time to time. Understanding what functionality is available and knowing how to use it will ensure you're able to get the most out of the workbooks, worksheets, and data you've already worked so hard to create.

Lesson Objectives

In this lesson, you will:

- Manage worksheets.
- Manage workbook and worksheet views.
- Manage workbook properties.

TOPIC A

Manage Worksheets

Workbooks with just a few worksheets are fairly easy to manage without much effort. But what if you're developing a workbook with dozens of worksheets or more? You want to be able to clearly and easily recognize your worksheets, arrange them in the proper order, and, possibly, remove some from view to display or work with only particular worksheets at any given time. Fortunately, Excel 2016 can save you from having to navigate through a disorganized or unwieldy workbook.

Tab Formatting Options

By default, worksheet tabs in Excel 2016 appear with generic sheet names, such as **Sheet1**, **Sheet2**, **Sheet3**, and in the default gray user interface (UI) color scheme. As you add more and more worksheets to a workbook, it's easy to see how this could become difficult to navigate. You may wonder if your critical sales data is on **Sheet11** or **Sheet12** and, if you don't format your worksheet tabs, you'll have no visual cues to help you out. This is why Excel 2016 provides you with a number of options for formatting your worksheet tabs. The most basic of these are the options to rename your worksheets and to change the color of worksheet tabs. You can access the commands for doing either of these by right-clicking the desired worksheet tab.

Figure 6-1: Renamed worksheet tabs with color formatting.

 Note: Excel Online App

You can rename, move, insert, delete, and hide worksheet tabs in Excel Online; however, changing the color of the worksheet tab is not available.

 Access the Checklist tile on your CHOICE Course screen for reference information and job aids on How to Format Worksheet Tabs.

Methods of Repositioning Worksheets

Excel 2016 provides you with two methods for repositioning your worksheets. The first method is to simply drag the desired worksheet tab or tabs to the desired new location. When you use this method, the tabs you're moving appear as small file icons and Excel displays a black location marker that indicates where the tabs will be located when you drop them in place. To use this method to move more than one worksheet simultaneously, you must first group the worksheets. You can drag worksheets to a different location in the same workbook or into any other open Excel workbook.

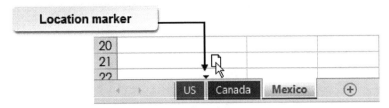

Figure 6-2: The location marker indicates where the worksheets will land when dropped.

The second method for repositioning worksheets is to use the **Move or Copy** dialog box. You can use the **Move or Copy** dialog box to reposition worksheets within the same workbook, move worksheets to another open workbook, or create a new workbook into which you can place existing worksheets. You also have the option of making a copy of a worksheet to paste to another location, an option not available when you drag worksheets into place. However, you can move only one worksheet at a time when using the **Move or Copy** dialog box. You can access the **Move or Copy** dialog box either by right-clicking any worksheet tab and then selecting **Move or Copy**, or by selecting **Home→Cells→Format→Move or Copy Sheet**.

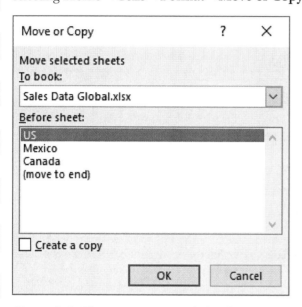

Figure 6-3: The Move or Copy dialog box.

The following table describes the various elements of the **Move or Copy** dialog box.

Move or Copy Dialog Box Element	Description
To book drop-down menu	Use this to select the workbook you want to move the selected worksheet to. By default, this is set to the currently selected workbook. You can also choose to create a new workbook as the destination for the existing worksheet.
Before sheet list	Select where to position the worksheet you're moving. Excel will place the relocated worksheet to the left of the worksheet you select here.
Create a copy check box	Check this check box to copy and paste the worksheet instead of moving it from one location to another.

Note: Excel Online App

While a **Copy** command is not available when you right-click the **Sheet** tab, you can achieve the same result by selecting all of the data on the sheet, pressing **Ctrl+C**, and then pressing **Ctrl+V** to paste it to another worksheet or workbook.

Methods of Inserting and Deleting Worksheets

By default, new blank Excel 2016 workbooks contain one worksheet. But you can add up to as many worksheets as your system's RAM (memory) will support. Likewise, if you don't need all of the worksheets you've added to a workbook, you can delete any you aren't using. You can also change the default number of worksheets Excel will include in new, blank workbooks.

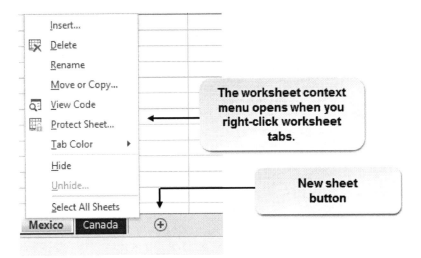

Figure 6–4: Some of the Insert and Delete commands for Excel 2016 worksheets.

Excel 2016 provides you with three options for inserting worksheets in your workbooks, and two for deleting them.

Insert/Delete Option	Description
Selecting the **New sheet** button	This inserts a new worksheet to the right of the selected worksheet in a workbook. Alternatively, you can use the **Shift +F11** keyboard shortcut to insert a new worksheet to the left of the selected worksheet.
Right-clicking any worksheet tab and then selecting **Insert**	This opens the **Insert** dialog box with **Worksheet** automatically selected. From here, you can simply select **OK** to insert a new worksheet to the left of the worksheet you right-clicked.
Using the **Insert** ribbon command	Select **Home→Cells→Insert down arrow→Insert Sheet** to insert a worksheet immediately to the left of the currently selected worksheet.
Right-clicking a worksheet tab, and then selecting **Delete**	This deletes the worksheet tab you right-clicked.
Using the **Delete** ribbon command	Selecting **Home→Cells→Delete down arrow→Delete Sheet** deletes the currently selected worksheet.

The Hide and Unhide Worksheets Options

If you need to work with or display only some of the worksheets in your workbooks, you can choose to hide the worksheets you don't want to see. This can be especially helpful when working in workbooks that contain numerous worksheets or when you need to display a workbook that contains sensitive information not meant for all audiences. Like hidden columns and rows, hidden worksheets retain their data, and formulas and functions can still reference their cells.

You can access the commands for hiding and unhiding Excel worksheets either by right-clicking the worksheet tabs or by selecting **Home→Cells→Format→Hide & Unhide**. Selecting the **Hide** or **Hide Sheet** command, respectively, will hide all currently selected worksheets. Selecting the **Unhide** or the **Unhide Sheet** command opens the **Unhide** dialog box, which enables you to unhide only one worksheet at a time.

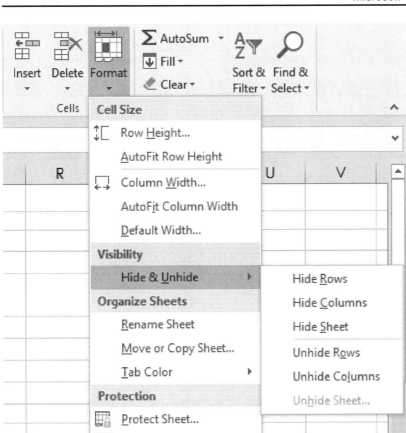

Figure 6–5: The Hide & Unhide Sheet ribbon commands. The Unhide Sheet command is inactive until you hide a worksheet.

Access the Checklist tile on your **CHOICE** Course screen for reference information and job aids on **How to Manage Worksheets.**

ACTIVITY 6-1
Managing Worksheets

Data File

C:\091055Data\Managing Workbooks\Sales Data Global.xlsx

Before You Begin

Excel 2016 is open.

Scenario

Develetech's management is pleased with the report you gave at the sales meeting. Now they'd like you to present information about sales in several key global regions at several more meetings. You have already created a global sales workbook with separate tabs for each of the regions, but it's difficult to navigate the workbook because the worksheet tabs still have the default names and there is no other formatting applied to them to help you tell them apart. You decide to rename and format the worksheet tabs to make the workbook easier to navigate.

Management has hinted that they'll be expecting more sales data from a number of other regions in the upcoming weeks. You decide to proactively add more worksheets to accommodate the additional data. You also feel it's a good idea to sequence the worksheets according to your needs and to hide the blank worksheets until you are able to populate them with data.

---

1. Open the **Sales Data Global.xlsx** workbook.

2. Rename the tabs to better reflect the data on each worksheet.
   a) Right-click the **Sheet1** tab and select **Rename**.
   b) Type *US* and press **Enter**.
   c) Double-click the **Sheet2** tab, type *Canada* and press **Enter**.
   d) Rename the **Sheet3** tab *Mexico*

3. Add color to the worksheet tabs to help further distinguish them from each other.
   a) Right-click the **US** tab and select **Tab Color**.
   b) In the **Standard Colors** section, select **Blue**.
   c) Select the **Canada** tab and select **Home→Cells→Format**.
   d) In the **Format** menu, in the **Organize Sheets** section, select **Tab Color**.
   e) In the **Standard Colors** section, select **Dark Red**.
   f) Color the **Mexico** worksheet tab green.

4. Move the **Mexico** tab so that it is displayed between the **US** tab and the **Canada** tab.
   a) Drag the **Mexico** tab to the left until the black location marker points to the spot in between the **US** and the **Canada** tabs.
   b) Drop the tab in place.
   c) Verify that the **Mexico** tab appears between the **US** and **Canada** tabs.

5. Make a copy of the **Canada** worksheet to reuse for the European region.
   a) Right-click the **Canada** tab and select **Move or Copy**.

b) In the **Move or Copy** dialog box, in the **To book** drop-down menu, ensure that **Sales Data Global.xlsx** appears.

c) In the **Before sheet** list, select **(move to end)**.

d) Check the **Create a copy** check box and select **OK**.

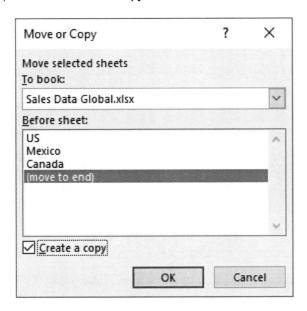

e) Verify that the **Canada (2)** worksheet tab appears at the end of the other worksheet tabs.

6. Modify the new worksheet.

a) Rename the **Canada (2)** tab *Europe*

b) Change the color of the **Europe** tab to orange.

c) Select cell **A1**, type *European Sales Ledger* and press **Enter**.

d) Change the color of the title text to orange.

e) Select the range **A5:F15** and press **Delete**.

7. Add a new worksheet you can use as a master employee list for all regions.

a) To the right of the worksheet tabs, select the **New sheet** button.

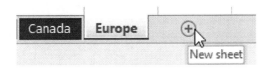

b) Rename the new tab *Employee Summary*

8. Hide the newly added worksheet tabs.

a) With the **Employee Summary** tab selected, press and hold down **Shift**, then select the **Europe** tab. This groups both worksheet tabs together.

b) Right-click either tab in the group, and then select **Hide**.

9. Save the workbook to the **C:\091055Data\Managing Workbooks** folder as *My Sales Data Global.xlsx*

TOPIC B

Manage Workbook and Worksheet Views

You've likely already noticed that large worksheets can be difficult to read. You may have to scroll quite a bit vertically or horizontally to view cell data and, when you do, you can't always see row and column labels. Also, you may want to compare data that exists in cells that are nowhere near each other or that are entered into completely different workbooks. By leveraging Excel's different view options, you'll be able to easily review data from different sources simultaneously, copy and paste data to the correct location without risking error, and save yourself time and headaches by avoiding scrolling through endless rows and columns of data.

 Note: Excel Online App

All of the features covered in this topic are only available in Excel 2016. The **VIEW** tab in Excel Online enables switching between **Editing** and **Reading** views.

Custom Views

You've already encountered Excel's preconfigured workbook views: Normal, Page Break Preview, and Page Layout. But if none of these quite suits your needs, you can create a *custom view*. Custom views save all of your print settings along with any display settings you have currently applied to a worksheet. Custom views are worksheet-specific, so you'll have to create them for each worksheet in a workbook. You can create multiple custom views for each worksheet. Custom views retain the following display and print settings: cell and column dimensions, hidden rows and columns, cell and range selections, page layout, print areas, margins, and headers and footers.

All custom views you have saved for a particular worksheet will be displayed in the **Custom Views** dialog box. From here, you can opt to create new custom views, delete existing custom views, or apply a custom view to the currently selected worksheet. You can access the **Custom Views** dialog box by selecting **View→Workbook Views→Custom Views**.

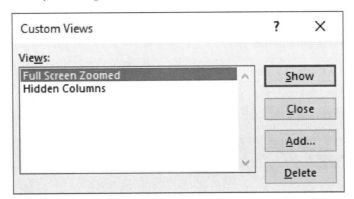

Figure 6-6: The Custom Views dialog box.

The Add View Dialog Box

When you select the **Add** button in the **Custom Views** dialog box, Excel displays the **Add View** dialog box, which you can use to create and save new custom views. The **Add View** dialog box enables you to name your custom views and to decide whether or not to include print settings or hidden rows, columns, and filter settings in your custom views.

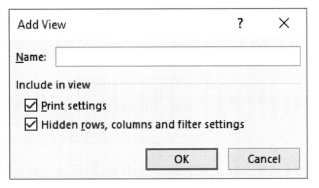

Figure 6-7: The Add View dialog box.

The Split Command

If you need to view various sections of the same worksheet simultaneously, you can use the **Split** command to do so. The **Split** command divides your worksheet view into either two separate panes, vertically or horizontally, or into four separate panes to enable you to view up to four different places in a worksheet at the same time. Excel displays separate scroll bars on either side of the split bars that divide the view, so you can independently scroll to view any area of the worksheet in the various panes. You can also drag the split bars to adjust how much space is dedicated to each of the panes. You can access the **Split** command by selecting **View→Window→Split**.

Selecting either a column or a row header before selecting the **Split** command will split the view in half either vertically or horizontally. Selecting a cell before selecting the **Split** command will split the view into four panes above and to the left of the selected cell.

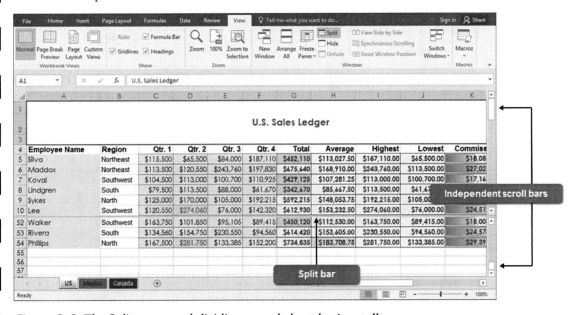

Figure 6-8: The Split command dividing a worksheet horizontally.

The Freeze Panes Options

You've already seen with the print settings how helpful it can be to ensure column and row labels print on each page. Likewise, Excel 2016 enables you to "freeze" particular cells so they always appear on screen regardless of how far you scroll down or to the right. This way, you can always reference column and row labels so you can more clearly read and interpret your worksheets and enter and analyze data accurately.

You use the **Freeze Panes** command to freeze the cells you wish to always have in view. The **Freeze Panes** command provides you with several options for freezing cells, enabling you to customize precisely how your worksheet cells scroll. You can access the **Freeze Panes** options by selecting **View→Window→Freeze Panes**. The **Freeze Panes** command is worksheet-specific, so you can set different **Freeze Panes** options for each worksheet in your workbooks.

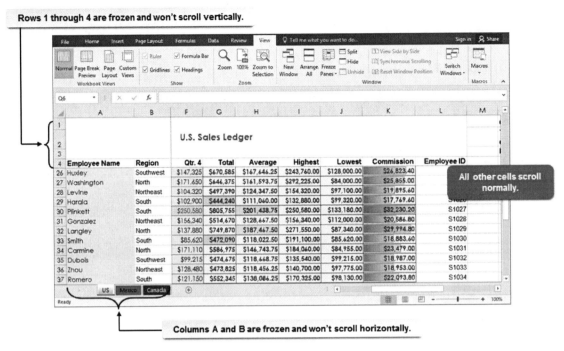

Figure 6-9: Cells that have been "frozen" in a workbook.

The following table details what each of the **Freeze Panes** options will freeze.

Freeze Panes Option	Description
Freeze Panes	Freezes all rows above and all columns to the left of the currently selected cell. Use this option to keep both row and column labels in view at all times.
Freeze Top Row	Freezes the top row of the currently selected worksheet.
Freeze First Column	Freezes the first column of the currently selected worksheet.
Unfreeze Panes	Unfreezes all cells on the currently selected worksheet. This option appears only once you've frozen panes on the worksheet.

The Arrange All Command

By default, all open workbooks in Excel 2016 appear within their own instance of the Excel UI. And, although you can manually resize and arrange each of the windows individually to view them all on screen at once, Excel 2016 gives you an easier method of doing so: the **Arrange All** command. The **Arrange All** command provides you with a number of options for arranging multiple workbooks on screen simultaneously, depending on your particular needs. You can access the **Arrange All** command by selecting **View→Window→Arrange All**.

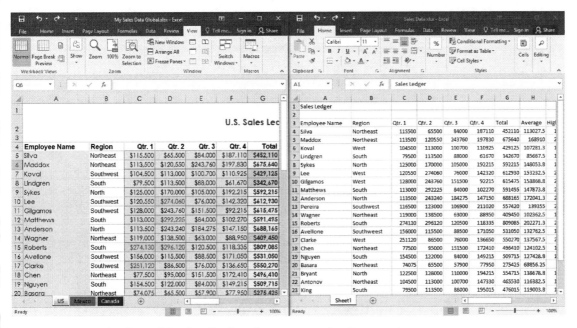

Figure 6-10: Multiple workbooks displayed on screen simultaneously.

The Arrange Windows Dialog Box

You can select the desired view option for the **Arrange All** command in the **Arrange Windows** dialog box. Selecting the **Arrange All** command automatically displays the **Arrange Windows** dialog box, which provides you with four display options.

 Note: Some of the display options affect your ability to immediately access particular UI elements, such as the ribbon.

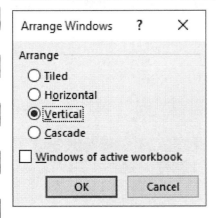

Figure 6-11: The Arrange Windows dialog box.

The following table describes each of the display options for the **Arrange All** command.

Option	Displays Open Workbook Windows
Tiled	In rows and columns, with an even amount of space allotted to each workbook window, depending on the number of open workbooks.
Horizontal	One on top of the other, with each window taking up the full amount of horizontal space. Excel divides the vertical space evenly depending on the number of open workbooks.

Option	Displays Open Workbook Windows
Vertical	Side by side, with each window taking up the full amount of vertical space. Excel divides the horizontal space evenly, depending on the number of open workbooks.
Cascade	In an offset stack, with just enough of the title bar for each workbook window in view so you can select the workbook you'd like to bring to the front. In this view, the workbook windows do not automatically adjust when you select windows from the back. So, you may need to rearrange the windows manually to view subsequent workbooks.

The View Side by Side Command

The **View Side by Side** command is sort of a cross between the **Split** command and the **Arrange All** command. It enables you to view worksheets from two different workbooks side by side for easy comparison. By default, the **View Side by Side** command synchronizes the scrolling of both worksheets so you can review them simultaneously with ease. You have the option of toggling that functionality on or off by using the **Synchronous Scrolling** command. Both the **View Side by Side** command and the **Synchronous Scrolling** command are available in the **Window** group on the **View** tab.

 Note: If you have more than two workbooks open, Excel prompts you to select which workbook you want to compare to the actively selected workbook in the **Compare Side by Side** dialog box.

 Note: By default, the **View Side by Side** command positions workbooks horizontally. You can use the **Arrange All** command to position them vertically while retaining the **View Side by Side** functionality.

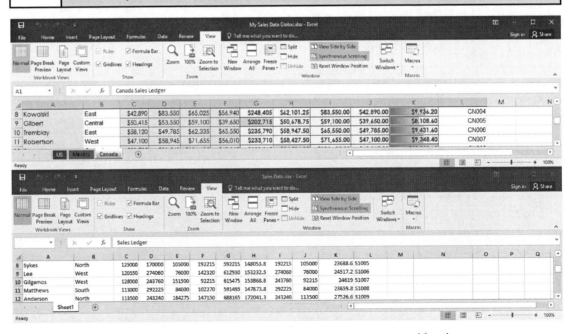

Figure 6-12: The View Side by Side command positioning two open workbooks.

The Switch Windows Command

The **Switch Windows** command enables you to easily switch among multiple open workbooks. This way, you can change which open workbook you want to view without having to minimize or manually arrange your workbook windows. This feature can be helpful when you select the **Cascade** option in the **Arrange Windows** dialog box, but works with any Excel view. You can access the **Switch Windows** command in the **Window** group on the **View** tab.

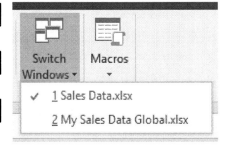

Figure 6-13: The Switch Windows command.

The New Window Command

The **New Window** command enables you to open another instance of any workbook so you can view and work in different parts of the same workbook simultaneously. You can use the **New Window** command in conjunction with the **Arrange All** or **View Side by Side** command to arrange all instances of the workbook to suit your needs. You can open multiple new instances of the same workbook; Excel appends the workbook file name with a colon and a sequential number, indicating which copy of the workbook is contained in each window. Changes made in any subsequent workbook instance affect all instances of the workbook and become part of the original file when saved. You can access the **New Window** command in the **Window** group on the **View** tab.

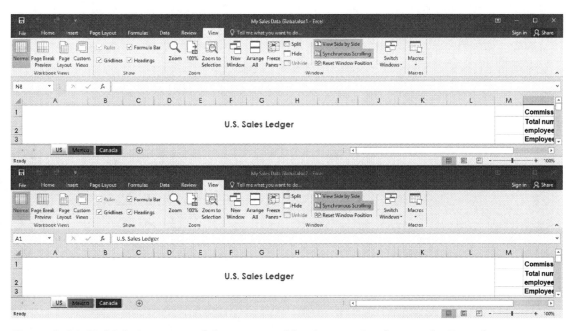

Figure 6-14: Multiple instances of the same workbook open simultaneously. Note the sequentially numbered file names.

Workspaces

In prior versions of Excel, because separate workbooks all opened within the same instance of the Excel UI, users were able to save multiple workbook arrangements as a workspace. Workspaces enabled users to save a particular configuration or arrangement of workbook windows as a workspace file. Although you can no longer save a workspace file in Excel 2016, you can open workspace files created in previous versions of Excel. When you open a workspace file, Excel automatically opens all workbooks saved in the workspace and arranges the workbook windows exactly as they were configured. This saves you the time and effort of opening multiple files and then rearranging them to be able to work as you need to. Workspaces can include multiple workbook files and they can contain multiple instances of the same workbook window opened by using the **New Window** command. The file format for Excel workspaces is the XLW format.

Note: You must have access to the original workbook files that are included in a workspace file in order to open and view the workspace.

Access the Checklist tile on your CHOICE Course screen for reference information and job aids on How to Manage Workbook and Worksheet Views.

ACTIVITY 6-2
Managing Workbook and Worksheet Views

Data File

C:\091055Data\Managing Workbooks\Sales Data.xlsx

Before You Begin

The **My Sales Data Global.xlsx** workbook file is open.

Scenario

You'd like to verify that you have copied all of your sales data into the sales data and global sales workbooks correctly, so you decide to open both workbooks at the same time and compare some of the entries. As the sales data worksheet has grown well beyond what can easily be viewed on one screen, and you need to review data from two different workbooks, you realize you will want to change your workbook views to be able to compare some of the data side by side. You also want your column headings, employee names, and regions to always be visible no matter where you've scrolled to in the spreadsheet, so you'll freeze the appropriate cells.

1. Open the **Sales Data.xlsx** workbook.

2. Split the workbook window to view different parts of the sales data worksheet simultaneously.
   a) Select all of row **16**.
   b) Select **View→Window→Split**.
   c) In the bottom pane, scroll to the bottom of the worksheet so you can compare the data in row **50** with the data in row **15**.
   d) Select **View→Window→Split** again to return to the Normal view.

3. View the **My Sales Data Global.xlsx** and the **Sales Data.xlsx** workbooks side by side.
   a) Select **View→Window→View Side by Side**.
   b) Verify that the two workbooks are displayed one above the other, in two separate windows.
   c) In the **My Sales Data Global.xlsx** workbook window, select the **US** worksheet tab.

    Note: You may need to select the tab twice to activate it.

   d) Scroll down and up through either of the workbooks and verify that both scroll simultaneously.
   e) Select **View→Window→Synchronous Scrolling** and verify that the workbooks scroll independently.

4. Close the **Sales Data.xlsx** workbook without saving changes.

5. Verify that the **My Sales Data Global.xlsx** workbook file is now displayed fully maximized.

6. Freeze panes so rows **1:4** don't scroll vertically and columns **A** and **B** don't scroll horizontally.
   a) Select cell **C5**.

b) Select **View→Window→Freeze Panes→Freeze Panes**.

c) Scroll vertically to verify that Excel froze the first four rows, and scroll horizontally to verify that Excel froze the first two columns.

7. Leave the workbook open.

TOPIC C

Manage Workbook Properties

You and your colleagues may end up generating a large number of Excel workbook files in your day-to-day tasks. Because many people often provide input or collaborate on the same projects, there are likely numerous versions of the same workbook files on your network shares and on people's computers. With all of these workbook files floating around, and with so many of them having similar titles and content, how can you find the exact file you're looking for? Fortunately, Excel 2016 provides you with a way to include identifying information about your workbooks within the workbook files themselves. This type of information can help you search through numerous workbook files to find precisely the one you need.

Note: Excel Online App

All of the features covered in this topic are only available in Excel 2016. When you select the **Info** tab on the **Backstage** view, Excel Online instructs you to open the file in Excel 2016 to work with the file properties.

Workbook Properties

A workbook property is, quite simply, a bit of information about a workbook file. This kind of "data about your data" is also known as metadata. *Workbook properties* can help identify key pieces of information such as who created a particular file, when it was created, when it was last modified, and what its current status is. Workbook properties even enable you to include *tags* about a workbook file, similar to the tags web developers use to help people search for particular websites. Tags are short descriptions, or keywords, that help identify the kind of content you will find within a file. For example, a sales workbook might be tagged with the territories it covers, the department it's associated with, and terms such as *sales*, *quarter*, and *commission*. When a user searches for any of these terms on a network or within a directory, the relevant sales workbook is more likely to show up in search results.

Excel generates some workbook properties automatically, such as the dates the file was created and last modified, the size of the file, and its current location. There are other workbook properties, such as tags and the workbook category, that are user-specified. Excel 2016 also provides you with the ability to create custom properties to better suit your organization's particular needs.

Workbook Properties in the Backstage View

Perhaps the simplest and most direct way to view and modify your workbook properties is on the **Info** tab of the **Backstage** view. When you select the **Info** tab, some of the most common document properties appear in the right pane. Some of these are automatically created, saved, and updated by Excel, and others can be modified. Properties that you can change here appear as text boxes when you place your pointer over the property value.

The **Show All Properties** link at the bottom of the right pane expands the view of workbook properties in the **Backstage** view so you can view and modify more of them. Once expanded, you can select the **Show Fewer Properties** link to collapse the view back to its default state.

Properties ▾

Size	32.1KB
Title	Add a title
Tags	Add a tag
Categories	Add a category

Related Dates

Last Modified	Today, 3:25 PM
Created	8/16/2011 9:28 AM
Last Printed	7/23/2015 11:04 AM

Related People

Author   Student

Add an author

Last Modified By   Instructor

Related Documents

☐ Open File Location

Show All Properties

Figure 6-15: Workbook properties displayed on the Info tab in the Backstage view.

The Properties Dialog Box

If you want to view all of the document properties for your workbook or create custom document properties, you can open the **Properties** dialog box. The **Properties** dialog box is divided into five tabs that enable you to work with all properties associated with the current workbook. To open the **Properties** dialog box, select **File→Info**, select the **Properties** drop-down arrow in the right pane, and then select **Advanced Properties**.

 Note: The **Properties** dialog box displays the file name of the currently selected workbook file before the word "Properties" in the title bar.

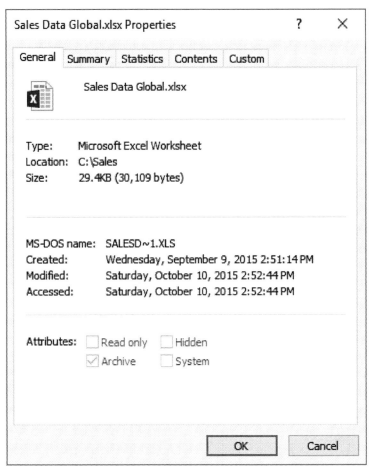

Figure 6-16: The Properties dialog box.

The following table identifies the workbook properties that are displayed on the various tabs in the **Properties** dialog box.

Properties Dialog Box Tab	Contains
General	General information about the workbook file, such as the file type, the file size, where the file is saved, and the dates when the file was created and last modified. Excel creates and updates these workbook properties automatically.
Summary	The default document properties that you can modify. Workbook properties on this tab include the document title, the author, keywords, and any included comments.
Statistics	System-level information about the workbook file, such as when it was created, last accessed, last modified, and last printed. Excel creates and updates these properties automatically.
Contents	The names of all worksheets in the document, and any named cell ranges. Excel creates and updates these properties automatically.
Custom	The commands you will use to create custom document properties.

Custom Workbook Properties

If you would like to create workbook properties that more specifically help you identify your files based on your organization's processes, departments, terminology, client list, or other standards, you can create *custom workbook properties*. Excel 2016 includes a number of preset categories of custom workbook properties, or you can create an entirely unique property. You can also restrict the values users can enter into custom property fields to ensure a large number of users will be able to successfully search for workbook files.

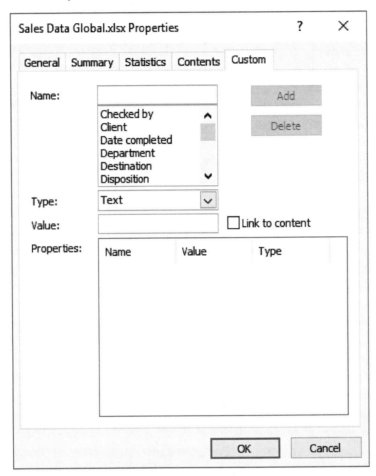

Figure 6-17: The Custom tab in the Properties dialog box.

The following table describes the various elements of the **Custom** tab.

Custom Tab Element	Description
Name field	If you select an existing name from the **Name** list, it will appear here. Or you can type a unique, new property name in this field.
Name list	Displays a list of the preset property categories. When you select a name from this list, it appears in the **Name** field.
Type drop-down menu	Allows you to select a content type to restrict what users can enter into your custom properties. You can select text, date, or number for values that can be typed into the property. Or you can select the **Yes or no** option to require users to select one of those two values. (This could be a useful option for properties such as "Approved" or "Review Complete.")
Value field	This is where you enter the value for the property.

Custom Tab Element	Description
Properties field	Displays all custom properties for the workbook.
Add button	Once you've configured a new custom property, the **Add** button adds it to the **Properties** field. When you select an existing custom property in the **Properties** field, the **Add** button becomes the **Modify** button, which enables you to save changes to existing custom properties.
Delete button	Deletes the selected custom property from the **Properties** field.

 Access the Checklist tile on your CHOICE Course screen for reference information and job aids on How to Manage Workbook Properties.

ACTIVITY 6-3
Managing Workbook Properties

Before You Begin
The **My Sales Data Global.xlsx** workbook file is open.

The **C** drive on your computer has been indexed.

Scenario
It has dawned on you that you will be creating a large number of workbook files that will contain similar types of data and have similar file names. You decide to include key information in your workbook file, in the form of workbook properties, to make it easier for you to search through these files. You also want to add a custom property so document recipients can easily tell if a file is the approved, final copy.

---

1. Select **File→Info**.

2. Add workbook properties to the file.

   a) In the right pane, below the **Properties** drop-down menu, next to **Title**, select **Add a title**.

Properties ▾	
Size	29.3KB
Title	Add a title
Ta...	Add a tag
Categories	Add a category

   b) Type *Global Sales Data*
   c) Next to **Tags**, select **Add a tag**.
   d) Type *sales data, global, regions, US, Mexico, Canada, Europe, employee list*
   e) Next to **Categories**, select **Add a category** and type *Sales*

3. Create a custom workbook property.

   a) Select the **Properties** drop-down arrow and then select **Advanced Properties**.
   b) In the **Properties** dialog box, select the **Custom** tab.
   c) In the **Name** field, type *Approved and Final*
   d) From the **Type** drop-down menu, select **Yes or no**.
   e) In the **Value** section, ensure that the **Yes** radio button is selected.
   f) Select **Add**.

g) Verify that the new custom workbook property appears in the **Properties** field and select **OK**.

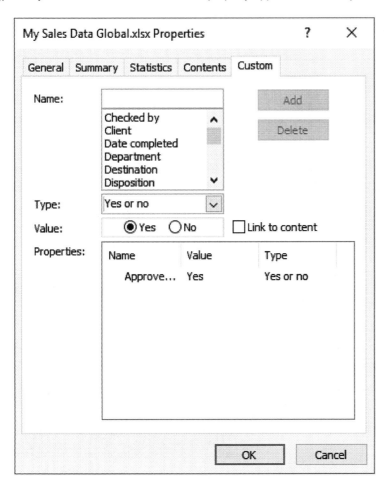

4. Save and close the workbook and then close Excel 2016.

5. Search for the workbook by using the modified workbook properties.

   a) Select the search box on the Windows 10 taskbar.
   b) Type *Europe*
   c) Select the **My stuff** link at the bottom.

d) Verify that the **C:\091055Data\Managing Workbooks\My Sales Data Global.xlsx** workbook file appears in the search results.

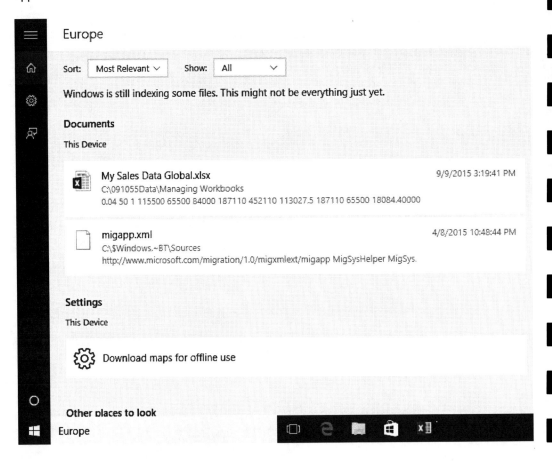

e) Select outside of the search pane to close it.

Summary

In this lesson, you managed worksheets, workbook and worksheet views, and workbook properties. By keeping your workbook files well-structured and organized, you'll save time, work more efficiently, and always know exactly where your critical data is. As you develop and work with a greater number of workbooks, these skills will be invaluable in helping you maintain control over the information that is critical to your organizational success.

Which of the worksheet or workbook management options do you think you'll use most often?

What are some creative ways you can use workbook properties to your advantage?

 Note: Check your CHOICE Course screen for opportunities to interact with your classmates, peers, and the larger CHOICE online community about the topics covered in this course or other topics you are interested in. From the Course screen you can also access available resources for a more continuous learning experience.

Course Follow-Up

Congratulations! You have completed the *Microsoft® Office Excel® 2016: Part 1 (Desktop/Office 365™)* course. You have successfully created and developed Excel workbooks to enter, modify, and present critical organizational data.

As technology progresses, organizational data will continue to grow to staggering levels. With that growth will come an increasing need for people like you to capture, organize, and make sense of that data. After all, data is useless unless someone can make sense of it, isolate issues, recognize opportunities, and communicate their findings to the people who make decisions. The more you can understand about your data, and the more insight you can glean from it, the better positioned your organizational leaders will be to make the decisions that will foster success.

What's Next?

Microsoft® Office Excel® 2016: Part 2 is the next course in this series. In that course, you will build upon the skills you have acquired by working with more advanced functions and formulas, using lists and tables to organize and analyze your data, and presenting your data visually using charts. You will also perform some higher-level analysis by using PivotTables, slicers, and PivotCharts.

Microsoft® 365™: Web Apps (with Skype® for Business) provides an introduction to using Office in a cloud-based environment. In this course, you will use Microsoft® Outlook® mail, Skype for Business instant messaging and online meetings, and Microsoft® SharePoint® Team Sites to work and collaborate on Office Online documents.

Additionally, you are encouraged to explore Excel further by actively participating in any of the social media forums set up by your instructor or training administrator through the **Social Media** tile on the CHOICE Course screen.

A | Microsoft Office Excel 2016 Exam 77-727

Selected Logical Operations courseware addresses Microsoft Office Specialist (MOS) certification skills for Microsoft® Office Excel® 2016. The following table indicates where Excel 2016 skills that are tested on Exam 77-727 are covered in the Logical Operations Excel 2016 series of courses.

Objective Domain	Covered In
1. Create and Manage Worksheets and Workbooks	
1.1 Create Worksheets and Workbooks	
1.1.1 Create a workbook	Part 1, Topics 1-C, 4-F
1.1.2 Import data from a delimited text file	Part 3
1.1.3 Add a worksheet to an existing workbook	Part 1, Topic 6-A
1.1.4 Copy and move a worksheet	Part 1, Topic 6-A
1.2 Navigate in Worksheets and Workbooks	
1.2.1 Search for data within a workbook	Part 1, Topic 3-B
1.2.2 Navigate to a named cell, range, or workbook element	Part 2
1.2.3 Insert and remove hyperlinks	Part 1, Topic 4-A
1.3 Format Worksheets and Workbooks	
1.3.1 Change worksheet tab color	Part 1, Topic 6-A
1.3.2 Rename a worksheet	Part 1, Topic 6-A
1.3.3 Change worksheet order	Part 1, Topic 6-A
1.3.4 Modify page setup	Part 1, Topics 3-A, 5-A-, 5-C
1.3.5 Insert and delete columns or rows	Part 1, Topic 3-A
1.3.6 Change workbook themes	Part 1, Topic 4-D
1.3.7 Adjust row height and column width	Part 1, Topic 3-A
1.3.8 Insert headers and footers	Part 1, Topic 5-C
1.4 Customize Options and Views for Worksheets and Workbooks	
1.4.1 Hide or unhide worksheets	Part 1, Topic 6-A
1.4.2 Hide or unhide columns and rows	Part 1, Topic 3-A
1.4.3 Customize the Quick Access Toolbar	Part 1, Appendix E

Objective Domain	Covered In
1.4.4 Change workbook views	Part 1, Topics 5-B, 5-C
1.4.5 Change window views	Part 1, Topic 6-B
1.4.6 Modify document properties	Part 1, Topic 6-C
1.4.7 Change magnification by using zoom tools	Part 1, Topic 1-A
1.4.8 Display formulas	Part 3
1.5 Configure Worksheets and Workbooks for Distribution	
1.5.1 Set a print area	Part 1, Topic 5-B
1.5.2 Save workbooks in alternative file formats	Part 1, Topic 1-C; Part 3
1.5.3 Print all or part of a workbook	Part 1, Topics 5-A, 5-C
1.5.4 Set print scaling	Part 1, Topic 5-A
1.5.5 Display repeating row and column titles on multipage worksheets	Part 1, Topic 5-B
1.5.6 Inspect a workbook for hidden properties or personal information	Part 3
1.5.7 Inspect a workbook for accessibility issues	Part 3
1.5.8 Inspect a workbook for compatibility issues	Part 1, Topic 1-C
2. Manage Data Cells and Ranges	
2.1 Insert Data in Cells and Ranges	
2.1.1 Replace data	Part 1, Topic 1-D
2.1.2 Cut, copy, or paste data	Part 1, Topic 1-D
2.1.3 Paste data by using special paste options	Part 1, Topic 2-C
2.1.4 Fill cells by using AutoFill	Part 1, Topics 1-D, 2-C
2.1.5 Insert and delete cells	Part 1, Topic 3-A
2.2 Format Cells and Ranges	
2.2.1 Merge cells	Part 1, Topic 4-C
2.2.2 Modify cell alignment and indentation	Part 1, Topic 4-C
2.2.3 Format cells by using Format Painter	Part 1, Topic 4-A
2.2.4 Wrap text within cells	Part 1, Topic 4-C
2.2.5 Apply number formats	Part 1, Topic 4-B
2.2.6 Apply cell formats	Part 1, Topic 4-A, Appendix D
2.2.7 Apply cell styles	Part 1, Topic 4-D
2.3 Summarize and Organize Data	
2.3.1 Insert sparklines	Part 3
2.3.2 Outline data	Part 2
2.3.3 Insert subtotals	Part 2
2.3.4 Apply conditional formatting	Part 1, Topic 4-E; Part 2

Objective Domain	Covered In
3. Create Tables	
3.1 Create and Manage Tables	
3.1.1 Create an Excel table from a cell range	Part 2
3.1.2 Convert a table to a cell range	Part 2
3.1.3 Add or remove table rows and columns	Part 2
3.2 Manage Table Styles and Options	
3.2.1 Apply styles to tables	Part 2
3.2.2 Configure table style options	Part 2
3.2.3 Insert total rows	Part 2
3.3 Filter and Sort a Table	
3.3.1 Filter records	Part 2
3.3.2 Sort data by multiple columns	Part 2
3.3.3 Change sort order	Part 2
3.3.4 Remove duplicate records	Part 2
4. Perform Operations with Formulas and Functions	
4.1 Summarize Data by Using Functions	
4.1.1 Insert references	Part 1, Topic 2-C
4.1.2 Perform calculations by using the SUM function	Part 1, Topic 2-B
4.1.3 Perform calculations by using MIN and MAX functions	Part 1, Topic 2-B
4.1.4 Perform calculations by using the COUNT function	Part 1, Topic 2-B
4.1.5 Perform calculations by using the AVERAGE function	Part 1, Topic 2-B
4.2 Perform Conditional Operations by Using Functions	
4.2.1 Perform logical operations by using the IF function	Part 2
4.2.2 Perform logical operations by using the SUMIF function	Part 2
4.2.3 Perform logical operations by using the AVERAGEIF function	Part 2
4.2.4 Perform statistical operations by using the COUNTIF function	Part 2
4.3 Format and Modify Text by Using Functions	
4.3.1 Format text by using the RIGHT, LEFT, and MID functions	Part 2
4.3.3 Format text by using the UPPER, LOWER, and PROPER functions	Part 2
4.3.4 Format text by using the CONCATENATE function	Part 2
5. Create Charts and Objects	

Objective Domain	Covered In
5.1 Create Charts	
5.1.1 Create a new chart	Part 2
5.1.2 Add additional data series	Part 2
5.1.3 Switch between rows and columns in source data	Part 2
5.1.4 Analyze data by using Quick Analysis	Part 2
5.2 Format Charts	
5.2.1 Resize charts	Part 2
5.2.2 Add and modify chart elements	Part 2
5.2.3 Apply chart layouts and styles	Part 2
5.2.4 Move charts to a chart sheet	Part 2
5.3 Insert and Format Objects	
5.3.1 Insert text boxes and shapes	Part 2
5.3.2 Insert images	Part 2
5.3.3 Modify object properties	Part 2
5.3.4 Add alternative text to objects for accessibility	Part 2

B | Microsoft Office Excel 2016 Expert Exam 77-728

Selected Logical Operations courseware addresses Microsoft Office Specialist (MOS) certification skills for Microsoft® Office Excel® 2016. The following table indicates where Excel 2016 skills that are tested on Exam 77–728 are covered in the Logical Operations Excel 2016 series of courses.

Objective Domain	Covered In
1. Manage Workbook Options and Settings	
1.1. Manage Workbooks	
1.1.1 Save a workbook as a template	Part 1, Topic 4-F
1.1.2 Copy macros between workbooks	Part 3
1.1.3 Reference data in another workbook	Part 3
1.1.4 Reference data by using structured references	Part 2
1.1.5 Enable macros in a workbook	Part 3
1.1.6 Display hidden ribbon tabs	Part 1, Appendix E
1.2 Manage Workbook Review	
1.2.1 Restrict editing	Part 3
1.2.2 Protect a worksheet	Part 3
1.2.3 Configure formula calculation options	Part 2
1.2.4 Protect workbook structure	Part 3
1.2.5 Manage workbook versions	Part 1, Topic 1-C
1.2.6 Encrypt a workbook with a password	Part 3
2. Apply Custom Data Formats and Layouts	
2.1 Apply Custom Data Formats	
2.1.1 Create custom number formats	Part 1, Topic 4-B
2.1.2 Populate cells by using advanced Fill Series options	Part 1, Topic 1-D
2.1.3 Configure data validation	Part 3
2.2 Apply Advanced Conditional Formatting and Filtering	

Objective Domain	Covered In
2.1.1 Create custom conditional formatting rules	Part 2
2.2.2 Create conditional formatting rules that use formulas	Part 2
2.2.3 Manage conditional formatting rules	Part 2
2.3 Create and Modify Custom Workbook Elements	
2.3.1 Create custom color formats	Part 1, Appendix D
2.3.2 Create and modify cell styles	Part 1, Topic 4-D
2.3.3 Create and modify custom themes	Part 1, Topic 4-D
2.3.4 Create and modify simple macros	Part 3
2.3.5 Insert and configure form controls	Part 3
2.4 Prepare a Workbook for Internationalization	
2.4.1 Display data in multiple international formats	Part 3
2.4.2 Apply international currency formats	Part 3
2.4.3 Manage multiple options for +Body and +Heading fonts	Part 3
3. Create Advanced Formulas	
3.1 Apply Functions in Formulas	
3.1.1 Perform logical operations by using AND, OR, and NOT functions	Part 2
3.1.2 Perform logical operations by using nested functions	Part 2
3.1.3 Perform statistical operations by using SUMIFS, AVERAGEIFS, and COUNTIFS functions	Part 2
3.2 Look Up Data by Using Functions	
3.2.1 Look up data by using the VLOOKUP function	Part 3
3.2.2 Look up data by using the HLOOKUP function	Part 3
3.2.3 Look up data by using the MATCH function	Part 3
3.2.4 Look up data by using the INDEX function	Part 3
3.3 Apply Advanced Date and Time Functions	
3.3.1 Reference the date and time by using the NOW and TODAY functions	Part 2
3.3.2 Serialize numbers by using date and time functions	Part 2
3.4 Perform Data Analysis and Business Intelligence	
3.4.1 Import, transform, combine, display, and connect to data	Part 3
3.4.2 Consolidate data	Part 3
3.4.3 Perform what-if analysis by using Goal Seek and Scenario Manager	Part 3
3.4.4 Use cube functions to get data out of the Excel data model	Part 3
3.4.5 Calculate data by using financial functions	Part 2

Objective Domain	Covered In
3.5 Troubleshoot Formulas	
3.5.1 Trace precedence and dependence	Part 3
3.5.2 Monitor cells and formulas by using the Watch Window	Part 3
3.5.3 Validate formulas by using error checking rules	Part 3
3.5.4 Evaluate formulas	Part 3
3.6 Define Named Ranges and Objects	
3.6.1 Name cells	Part 2
3.6.2 Name data ranges	Part 2
3.6.3 Name tables	Part 2
3.6.4 Manage named ranges and objects	Part 2
4. Create Advanced Charts and Tables	
4.1 Create Advanced Charts	
4.1.1 Add trendlines to charts	Part 2
4.1.2 Create dual-axis charts	Part 2
4.1.3 Save a chart as a template	Part 2
4.2 Create and Manage PivotTables	
4.2.1 Create PivotTables	Part 2
4.2.2 Modify field selections and options	Part 2
4.2.3 Create slicers	Part 2
4.2.4 Group PivotTable data	Part 2
4.2.5 Reference data in a PivotTable by using the GETPIVOTDATA function	Part 2
4.2.6 Add calculated fields	Part 3
4.2.7 Format data	Part 2
4.3 Create and Manage PivotCharts	
4.3.1 Create PivotCharts	Part 2
4.3.2 Manipulate options in existing PivotCharts	Part 2
4.3.3 Apply styles to PivotCharts	Part 2
4.3.4 Drill down into PivotChart details	Part 2

C | Microsoft Excel 2016 Common Keyboard Shortcuts

The follow table lists common keyboard shortcuts you can use in Microsoft® Office Excel® 2016.

Function	Shortcut
Switch between worksheet tabs, from left to right.	**Ctrl+PgDn**
Switch between worksheet tabs, from right to left.	**Ctrl+PgUp**
Select the region around the active cell (requires there to be content in the surrounding cells).	**Ctrl+Shift+*** or **Ctrl+*** (from the number pad)
Select the cell at the beginning of the worksheet or pane.	**Ctrl+Home**
Select the cell at the end of the worksheet.	**Ctrl+End**
Select the cell at an edge of the worksheet.	**Ctrl+Arrow keys**
Insert the current time.	**Ctrl+Shift+:**
Insert the current date.	**Ctrl+;**
Display the **Insert** dialog box.	**Ctrl+Shift++**
Display the **Delete** dialog box.	**Ctrl+-**
Display the **Format Cells** dialog box.	**Ctrl+1**
Select the entire worksheet.	**Ctrl+A**
Apply or remove bold formatting.	**Ctrl+B**
Apply or remove italic formatting.	**Ctrl+I**
Copy the selected cells.	**Ctrl+C**
Cut the selected cells.	**Ctrl+X**
Paste copied content.	**Ctrl+V**
Display the **Find and Replace** dialog box.	**Ctrl+F**
Display the **Insert Hyperlink** or **Edit Hyperlink** dialog box.	**Ctrl+K**

Function	Shortcut
Create a new workbook.	Ctrl+N
Close an open workbook.	Ctrl+W
Display the **Open** tab on the **Backstage** view.	Ctrl+O
Display the **Print** tab on the **Backstage** view.	Ctrl+P
Save the file.	Ctrl+S
Repeat the last command or action, if possible.	Ctrl+Y or F4 (when the insertion point is not in the **Formula Bar**)
Undo the last command or action.	Ctrl+Z
Redo the last undo.	Ctrl+Y
Enter data in a cell while keeping it the active cell.	Ctrl+Enter
Select all contiguously populated cells in a column from the selected cell to the end of the range.	Ctrl+Shift+Up Arrow or Ctrl+Shift+Down Arrow
Select all contiguously populated cells in a row from the selected cell to the end of the range.	Ctrl+Shift+Right Arrow or Ctrl+Shift+Left Arrow
Toggle among relative, absolute, and mixed references when the insertion point is in or next to a cell reference in the **Formula Bar**.	F4
Open the **Save As** dialog box.	F12
Activate the **Tell Me** text box.	Alt+Q

D Adding Borders and Colors to Worksheets

Appendix Introduction

In addition to the formatting options discussed in the course, Microsoft® Office Excel® 2016 also allows you to add borders and fill coloring to your worksheets.

TOPIC A

Add Borders and Colors to Worksheets

Advertisers know how to use a variety of colors and design layouts to catch your eye and get you to focus on key elements of their messages. In much the same way, you can apply particular types of formatting to your worksheet borders and cells to help draw your audience to the important information in your workbooks. By doing so, you can reduce clutter on your worksheets and organize your content visually, while maintaining a professional, polished look.

Border Options

It's easy to distinguish one cell from another on an Excel worksheet; by default, they are displayed with light grey gridlines that define them. You may wish to distinguish particular areas of your worksheets from others and you may not always want to have empty spaces between them to do so. Fortunately, Excel 2016 allows you to apply a variety of border formatting options to your worksheet cells to help highlight and define various sections of your data. Excel allows you to define the color and style of your cell borders. You can select from a number of quick-configuration border formatting options, manually draw borders on worksheets, or format a selection of cells by using the **Border** tab in the **Format Cells** dialog box.

Employee Name	Qtr. 1	Qtr. 2	Qtr. 3	Qtr. 4	Total
Silva	$115,500	$65,500	$84,000	$187,110	$452,110
Maddox	$113,500	$120,550	$243,760	$197,830	$675,640
Koval	$104,500	$113,000	$100,700	$110,925	$429,125
Lindgren	$79,500	$113,500	$88,000	$61,670	$342,670
Sykes	$125,000	$170,000	$105,000	$192,215	$592,215

Employee Name	Qtr. 1	Qtr. 2	Qtr. 3	Qtr. 4	Total
Silva	$115,500	$65,500	$84,000	$187,110	$452,110
Maddox	$113,500	$120,550	$243,760	$197,830	$675,640
Koval	$104,500	$113,000	$100,700	$110,925	$429,125
Lindgren	$79,500	$113,500	$88,000	$61,670	$342,670
Sykes	$125,000	$170,000	$105,000	$192,215	$592,215

Employee Name	Qtr. 1	Qtr. 2	Qtr. 3	Qtr. 4	Total
Silva	$115,500	$65,500	$84,000	$187,110	$452,110
Maddox	$113,500	$120,550	$243,760	$197,830	$675,640
Koval	$104,500	$113,000	$100,700	$110,925	$429,125
Lindgren	$79,500	$113,500	$88,000	$61,670	$342,670
Sykes	$125,000	$170,000	$105,000	$192,215	$592,215

Employee Name	Qtr. 1	Qtr. 2	Qtr. 3	Qtr. 4	Total
Silva	$115,500	$65,500	$84,000	$187,110	$452,110
Maddox	$113,500	$120,550	$243,760	$197,830	$675,640
Koval	$104,500	$113,000	$100,700	$110,925	$429,125
Lindgren	$79,500	$113,500	$88,000	$61,670	$342,670
Sykes	$125,000	$170,000	$105,000	$192,215	$592,215

Figure D-1: Various cell borders applied to a range of data.

The Borders Drop-Down Menu

To quickly apply border formatting to your worksheet cells, you can use the options in the **Borders** drop-down menu. It is important to note that selecting most of these options will apply border formatting to the selected cells based on the color and style options currently selected in the **Line Color** and **Line Style** menus, which are located near the bottom of the **Borders** drop-down menu. The only exception to this is the bottom group of border options in the **Borders** section of the **Borders** drop-down menu. These options apply predefined border formatting.

The command button for the **Borders** drop-down menu, which is located in the **Font** group on the **Home** tab, will be displayed as the last option you selected from the **Borders** drop-down menu. This makes it easy to quickly apply the same formatting to multiple sections of a worksheet.

The **Borders** drop-down menu also provides you with access to the commands you can use to manually draw borders on your worksheets. These are located in the **Draw Borders** section. The options selected in the **Line Color** and **Line Style** menus also apply to manually drawn borders.

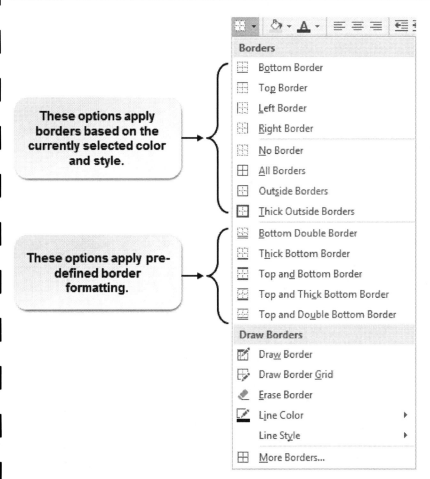

Figure D-2: The Borders drop-down menu.

The Border Tab

You can access a few more options for formatting your worksheet borders on the **Border** tab of the **Format Cells** dialog box. From here, you can apply all of the same formatting options you can access from the **Borders** drop-down menu, and you can add diagonal borders that split cells in half. It is important to remember, however, that diagonal borders do not actually create two separate cells. You need to format your text manually to display it properly, and Excel cannot distinguish between the two halves for calculating. The **Border** tab also displays a border preview, so you can configure and adjust your border formatting as necessary.

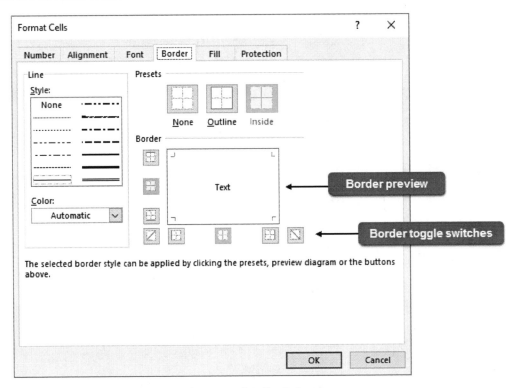

Figure D–3: The Border tab in the Formal Cells dialog box.

The commands on the **Border** tab allow you to customize and modify your worksheet borders.

Border Tab Element	Allows You To
Style menu	Select the desired border style.
Color drop-down menu	Select the desired border color. You can select from a set of common, predetermined colors or use the **Colors** dialog box to customize your border colors.
None button	Remove all borders from the currently selected cell or range.
Outline button	Apply a border around the outer edge of the currently selected cell or range.
Inside button	Apply a border to all internal cell borders in the currently selected range. Basically, this applies a border to any lines not along the outer edge of a range.
Border toggle switches	Apply formatting to or remove formatting from any of the particular lines within the currently selected cell or range.
Border preview	View the result of your currently selected border options.

Fill Options

Another, more colorful way to draw attention to particular sections of your worksheets is to apply a *fill*. A fill is a type of worksheet formatting that allows you to add colors, patterns, and gradient shading to the background of a cell or a range. Excel 2016 enables you to select from a predefined set of colors, create custom colors, and blend colors to create gradient effects for use as cell backgrounds. You can also select from a set of predefined pattern backgrounds and select a color to apply to the patterns. The **Fill Color** drop-down menu in the **Font** group on the **Home** tab provides you with quick access to solid color fill options, whereas the **Fill** tab in the **Format Cells** dialog box provides you with access to all of the commands you can use to format cell fills.

	A	B	C	D	E	F
1	**Employee Name**	**Qtr. 1**	**Qtr. 2**	**Qtr. 3**	**Qtr. 4**	**Total**
2	Silva	$115,500	$65,500	$84,000	$187,110	$452,110
3	Maddox	$113,500	$120,550	$243,760	$197,830	$675,640
4	Koval	$104,500	$113,000	$100,700	$110,925	$429,125
5	Lindgren	$79,500	$113,500	$88,000	$61,670	$342,670
6	Sykes	$125,000	$170,000	$105,000	$192,215	$592,215

Figure D–4: Fill colors applied to a range of cells.

The Fill Tab

Use the commands on the **Fill** tab of the **Format Cells** dialog box to customize your worksheet fills. From here, you can add pattern and gradient fills, which are not available from the **Fill Color** drop-down menu on the ribbon.

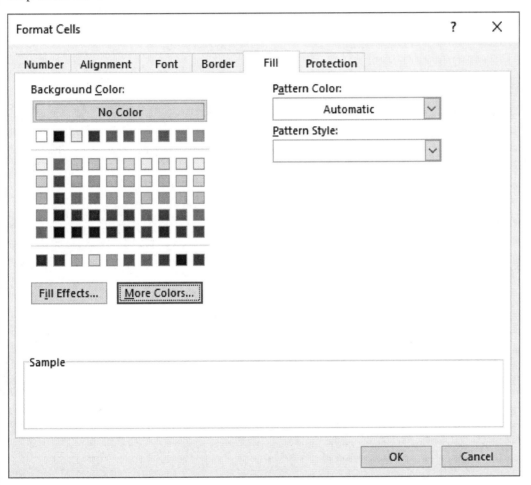

Figure D–5: The Fill tab in the Format Cells dialog box.

The following table describes the functions of the various elements on the **Fill** tab.

Fill Tab Element	Use This To
Background Color section	Select a solid color fill for worksheet cells.
Fill Effects button	Open the **Fill Effects** dialog box, which you can use to configure multi-color shading and gradient fill effects.

Fill Tab Element	Use This To
More Colors button	Open the **Colors** dialog box, which you can use to create custom fill colors.
Pattern Color drop-down menu	Select a color to apply to a pattern fill.
Pattern Style drop-down menu	Select a specific pattern to apply to cells as a fill.
Sample section	View the results of your currently selected fill options.

Sheet Backgrounds

Excel 2016 also provides you with the ability to add a picture to act as a worksheet background. Sheet backgrounds are background images that are not technically a part of your worksheets. Sheet backgrounds are for display purposes only, and will not print when you print your worksheets. You can use sheet backgrounds to enhance the visibility of your worksheets when presenting data in front of a live audience. You may need to toggle off the visibility of cell gridlines if you use these. If the image is not large enough to fill the entire sheet, Excel will repeat, or tile, the image until the entire worksheet is filled. You can add a sheet background by selecting **Page Layout→Page Setup→Background**.

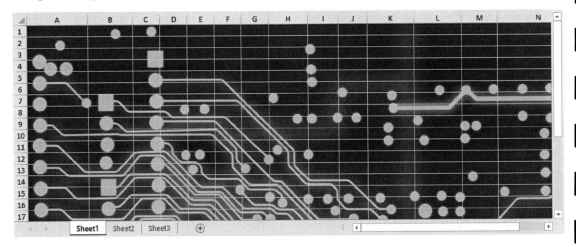

Figure D–6: An Excel worksheet with a sheet background.

 Note: To learn more about adding background images to your worksheets, view the LearnTO **Add a Non-Tiling Background to a Worksheet** presentation from the **LearnTO** tile on the CHOICE Course screen.

 Access the Checklist tile on your CHOICE Course screen for reference information and job aids on **How to Add Borders and Color to Worksheets**.

E | Basic Excel Customization

Appendix Introduction

Like other Microsoft® Office Excel® 2016 applications, Excel 2016 provides you with a variety of ways to customize the basics of your environment.

TOPIC A

Customize General Options and the Excel UI

Excel's user interface (UI) is designed to be as accessible as possible to a broad audience. But depending on what you use Excel for, you may regularly use whole sets of commands that most users barely touch. Or perhaps you simply want certain commands to be better categorized on the Excel UI based on your specific needs. Being able to customize the ribbon, the **Quick Access Toolbar**, and other basic options will help you create an experience that streamlines your workflow, leading to greater productivity and reduced frustration.

The Excel Options Dialog Box

You can adjust and configure global Excel 2016 system settings by using the **Excel Options** dialog box. It is divided into a series of 10 tabs, each of which contains a set of related system settings options. You can access the **Excel Options** dialog box by selecting **File→Options**.

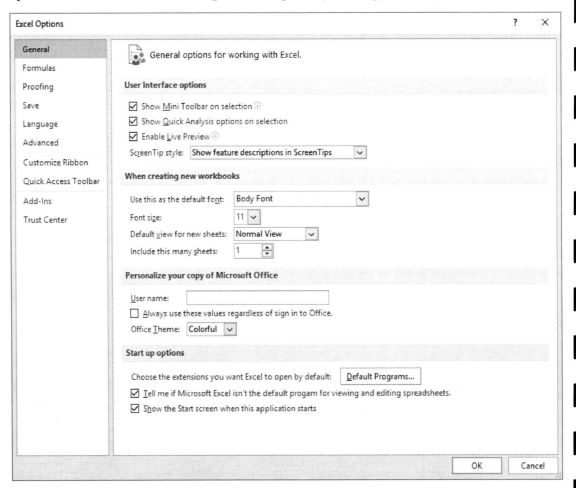

Figure E-1: The Excel Options dialog box.

The following table lists the types of system settings you will find on the various **Excel Options** dialog box tabs.

Excel Options Dialog Box Tab	Contains Options For
General	Adjusting the display of certain on-screen elements and toolbars, configuring the default settings for new workbooks, personalizing Excel for a particular user, and determining how Excel behaves when opened.
Formulas	Configuring formula, calculation, and error checking settings.
Proofing	Configuring AutoCorrect settings, configuring spelling check settings, and selecting the desired dictionary and language to use for proofing features.
Save	Selecting how often and to which directory Excel automatically saves workbook files, configuring offline editing settings, and preserving visual aspects of workbooks when opening workbook files in previous versions of Excel.
Language	Selecting the desired language for Excel editing, display, and help features.
Advanced	Adjusting settings that directly affect a variety of common Excel tasks.
Customize Ribbon	Customizing the tabs, groups, and commands on the ribbon.
Quick Access Toolbar	Customizing the **Quick Access Toolbar**.
Add-Ins	Installing, activating, and deactivating supplemental Excel features and functionality.
Trust Center	Configuring privacy and security settings that affect all Office 2016 applications.

General Options

The **General** tab in the **Excel Options** dialog box contains settings that affect some common Excel functionality.

General Tab Section	Contains Options For
User Interface options	Managing the display of the **Mini** toolbar, the Live Preview feature, ScreenTips, and Quick Analysis options.
When creating new workbooks	Managing default workbook settings, such as the font and font size, the view workbooks open in, and the number of worksheets in a new blank workbook.
Personalize your copy of Microsoft Office	Selecting the theme and modifying the default user name for all Office 2016 applications. This is the name that will be displayed as the author in Office file properties and in comments you add to documents.
Start up options	Choosing the file types that automatically open in Excel, toggling on or off the startup prompt for whether or not Excel is the default application for spreadsheet files, and determining whether Excel displays the **Start** screen or a new blank workbook when opened.

The Customize Ribbon Tab

The commands on the **Customize Ribbon** tab of the **Excel Options** dialog box enable you to modify the Excel ribbon so that all of the commands you use are right where you need them. You can rearrange the existing ribbon tabs and the groups within each tab. You can even move a group from one tab to another. Additionally, you can rename any tab or group, and you can remove any tab from the ribbon and any group from a tab.

Excel 2016 also enables you to create new custom tabs and groups if modifying the existing ones doesn't suit your needs. When you create a new custom tab, Excel automatically creates a group within that tab. You can add groups to existing tabs, and custom groups enable you to add *or* remove commands.

Customizing the ribbon does have some limitations. You cannot rearrange the default commands in any of the existing groups and you cannot remove the default commands. And, although you can rename tabs and groups, you cannot rename any of the commands, whether they are in custom or existing groups.

Once you have customized the ribbon, you can export your modified ribbon as a file and import it on another computer that has Excel 2016 installed on it. In this way, you can enjoy the same custom environment regardless of where you work. The default file extension for exported ribbon customizations is *.exportedUI*. These files also include any customizations you have made to the **Quick Access Toolbar**.

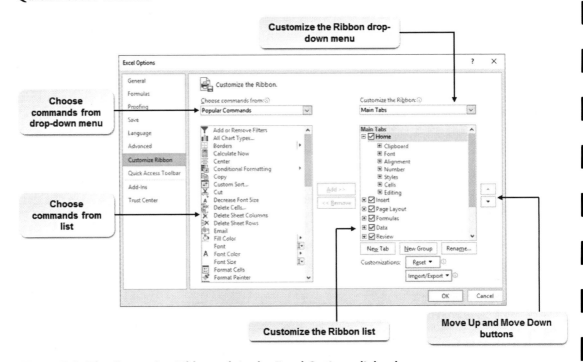

Figure E-2: The Customize Ribbon tab in the Excel Options dialog box.

The following table describes the various elements of the **Customize Ribbon** tab.

Customize Ribbon Tab Element	Description
Choose commands from drop-down menu	Selects which commands are displayed in the **Choose commands from** list.
Choose commands from list	Displays the commands you can add to custom ribbon groups.
Customize the Ribbon drop-down menu	Selects which tabs display in the **Customize the Ribbon** list. You can select all tabs, just the main tabs, or just the tool (contextual) tabs.
Customize the Ribbon list	Displays the tabs, groups, and commands in their current organizational structure.

Customize Ribbon Tab Element	Description
Add button	Adds commands selected in the **Choose commands from** list to the currently selected custom group.
Remove button	Removes the currently selected command, group, or tab from the ribbon. You cannot remove any of the default commands from their groups.
Move Up button	Moves the currently selected tab, group, or command up one place in the hierarchy. You cannot move default ribbon commands.
Move Down button	Moves the currently selected tab, group, or command down in the hierarchy. You cannot move default ribbon commands.
New Tab button	Adds a new custom tab after the currently selected tab. Excel automatically includes a new custom group on all new custom tabs.
New Group button	Add a new custom group after the currently selected group.
Rename button	Opens the **Rename** dialog box, enabling you to rename the currently selected tab or group. You cannot rename commands.
Reset button	Enables you to reset either the currently selected tab to its default state or the entire ribbon and the **Quick Access Toolbar** to their default states.
Import/Export button	Enables you to export your current ribbon customization configuration for use on other computers, or import a ribbon customization from another computer.

The Customize the Ribbon List Hierarchy

The **Customize the Ribbon** list is arranged in a tree hierarchy. The top level of the tree represents the ribbon tabs. The groups are contained within the tabs, one level down in the hierarchy. The commands are contained within the groups. Commands with a drop-down menu contain another sub-level, which displays the commands that are contained within the drop-down menu.

 Note: Custom tabs and groups appear with the text *(Custom)* next to their names.

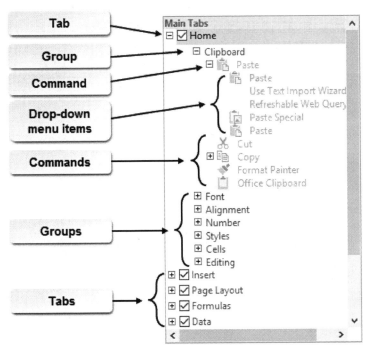

Figure E–3: The tree hierarchy within the Customize the Ribbon list.

The Quick Access Toolbar Tab

You can use the commands and other elements of the **Quick Access Toolbar** tab to customize the **Quick Access Toolbar**. This works in much the same fashion as the **Customize Ribbon** tab, with a few minor differences. As there is much less of an organizational structure to the **Quick Access Toolbar**, your options here are mainly limited simply to adding or removing commands and rearranging the order of commands. But you can also add sections to the **Quick Access Toolbar** for the purpose of organizing commands by using visual borders called separators.

 Note: When you add commands to either the ribbon or the **Quick Access Toolbar**, you can access those commands using the KeyTips Excel displays when you press the **Alt** key.

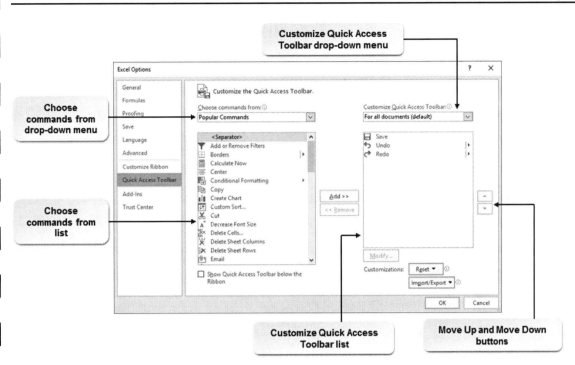

Figure E-4: The Quick Access Toolbar tab.

The following table describes the various elements of the **Quick Access Toolbar** tab.

Quick Access Toolbar Tab Element	Description
Choose commands from drop-down menu	Selects which commands are displayed in the **Choose commands from** list.
Choose commands from list	Displays the commands you can add to the **Quick Access Toolbar**.
Customize Quick Access Toolbar drop-down menu	Selects whether **Quick Access Toolbar** customizations apply to all workbooks or just the current workbook.
Customize Quick Access Toolbar list	Displays the current **Quick Access Toolbar** configuration.
Add button	Adds commands selected in the **Choose commands from** list to the **Quick Access Toolbar**.
Remove button	Removes the currently selected command from the **Quick Access Toolbar**.
Move Up button	Moves the currently selected command up one place in the **Customize Quick Access Toolbar** list.
Move Down button	Moves the currently selected command down one place in the **Customize Quick Access Toolbar** list.
Reset button	Enables you to reset either the **Quick Access Toolbar** or the **Quick Access Toolbar** and the ribbon to the default configuration.
Import/Export button	Enables you to export your current **Quick Access Toolbar** customization configuration for use on other computers or import a **Quick Access Toolbar** customization from another computer.

The Customize Quick Access Toolbar Menu

You can also add or remove commands from the **Quick Access Toolbar** by using the **Customize Quick Access Toolbar** menu, but your options here are a bit more limited. From the **Customize Quick Access Toolbar** menu, you can add or remove commands from a limited set of some of the most commonly used Excel commands. You cannot rearrange commands or add separators to the **Quick Access Toolbar** from here.

The **Customize Quick Access Toolbar** menu also provides you with the ability to move the **Quick Access Toolbar** so it is positioned below the ribbon. To access the **Customize Quick Access Toolbar** menu, select the **Customize Quick Access Toolbar** button ![icon] to the right of the **Quick Access Toolbar**.

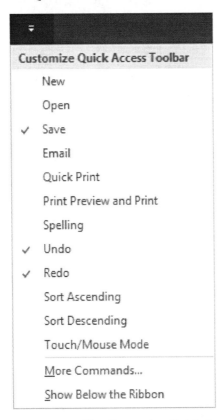

Figure E-5: The Customize Quick Access Toolbar menu.

 Access the Checklist tile on your **CHOICE** Course screen for reference information and job aids on **How to Customize the Excel User Interface**.

Mastery Builders

Mastery Builders are provided for certain lessons as additional learning resources for this course. Mastery Builders are developed for selected lessons within a course in cases when they seem most instructionally useful as well as technically feasible. In general, Mastery Builders are supplemental, optional unguided practice and may or may not be performed as part of the classroom activities. Your instructor will consider setup requirements, classroom timing, and instructional needs to determine which Mastery Builders are appropriate for you to perform, and at what point during the class. If you do not perform the Mastery Builders in class, your instructor can tell you if you can perform them independently as self-study, and if there are any special setup requirements.

Mastery Builder 1–1
Creating and Saving a Workbook

Activity Time: 10 minutes

Scenario

You're the sales manager for your organization and you've decided to create a workbook to track your sales reps by quarter. You want to determine who should be assigned to the most competitive regions and who should receive incentive rewards. As this year's first quarter sales figures are already in, you will add that data before saving the workbook.

Additionally, you're thinking of making the worksheet a bit more visually appealing. You decide to search for and find more information about SmartArt, a feature your colleagues have suggested to you.

1. Open Excel 2016 and create a new blank workbook.

2. Enter the following text labels and data on the **Sheet1** worksheet.

	A	B	C	D	E	F
1	Sales Rep	Qtr. 1	Qtr. 2	Qtr. 3	Qtr. 4	Total
2	Andy	32000				
3	Evan	47500				
4	Sara	53000				
5	Jose	28750				
6	Chan	37650				
7	Valerie	29995				
8	Kavitha	43275				
9	Raul	51200				
10	Daphne	48990				
11						

3. Use commands in the **Backstage** view to save the workbook to the **C:\091055Data\Getting Started with Microsoft Office Excel 2016** folder as *My Sales Tracker.xlsx*.

4. Use **Tell Me** to search for *SmartArt*.

5. From the search results, select the link to get help on SmartArt.

6. Use Excel Help to select a link that will provide you with more information on SmartArt.

7. Close Excel Help, save your workbook, then close Excel 2016.

Mastery Builder 2–1
Creating and Reusing Formulas and Functions

Activity Time: 10 minutes

Data File

C:\091055Data\Performing Calculations\Sales Tracker.xlsx

Scenario

You have just finished entering the past fiscal year's sales data into your sales tracker workbook. Now you wish to calculate the yearly total and the quarterly average sales for each of your reps, along with the overall total and average sales for your department. You decide to use Excel formulas and functions to do so. Additionally, you want to identify the highest and lowest quarterly sales figures out of all sales rep sales to get a sense of the range of sales your organization generates.

1. Open the **Sales Tracker.xlsx** workbook file in Excel 2016.

2. Enter a formula in cell **F2** that adds up the quarterly sales figures for Andy.

3. Enter a SUM function in cell **F3** to total the quarterly sales figures for Evan.

4. Use the AutoSum feature to total the quarterly sales figures for Sara in cell **F4**.

5. Copy the function in cell **F4** down the range **F5:F10**.

6. In cell **F12**, enter a function that calculates the overall sales total for the year.

7. Enter an AVERAGE function in cell **G2** to calculate the quarterly sales average for Andy.

8. AutoFill the function in cell **G2** down the range **G3:G10**.

9. In cell **G12**, enter a function to calculate the overall average quarterly sales for your entire team.

10. Enter a MAX function in cell **B12** that returns the highest single quarterly sales figure for all of the sales reps.

11. Enter a MIN function in cell **B13** that returns the lowest single quarterly sales figure for all of the sales reps.

12. In cell **B14**, use a simple formula to calculate the difference between the greatest and the smallest quarterly sales figures.

13. Save the workbook to the **C:\091055Data\Performing Calculations** folder as *My Sales Tracker.xlsx*.

14. Close Excel.

Mastery Builder 3-1
Modifying a Worksheet

Activity Time: 10 minutes

Data File

C:\091055Data\Modifying a Worksheet\Employee Roster.xlsx

Scenario

You are in charge of maintaining the employee master list for your organization. A colleague has already entered all of the raw information, so you'll need to go in and make some tweaks to how the worksheet is displayed. While looking over the worksheet, you realize there are several data entry errors that you need to correct. Some of the departmental entries for the Finance department are entered incorrectly, so you decide to use the **Replace** command to correct those as needed. Your colleague has also mistakenly entered ENF instead of ENG for all employees in the Engineering department. You realize you'll be able to correct those all at once. You also decide it would be a good idea to check the spelling of the entries for the employee position column to ensure that it contains no errors.

In addition to these corrections, you want to temporarily hide all rows containing employee information for the sales department. All other employees are eligible for an annual bonus (the sales reps are rewarded through commission payments), and you'd like to compile a list of only bonus-eligible employees to forward to the payroll department. Because you'd also like to track all employee bonuses, you decide to add a new column to the worksheet to accommodate that information.

1. Open the **Employee Roster.xlsx** workbook file in Excel 2016.

2. Adjust the width of all columns as needed to accommodate the employee information.

3. Use the **Find and Replace** dialog box to correct both instances of FIM to *FIN* in the **Department** column one at a time.

4. Correct all instances of **ENF** to *ENG* in the **Department** column simultaneously.

5. Check the spelling of entries in the **Position** column to verify they are all spelled correctly.

6. Hide rows **104:125**.

7. Insert a column between the **Pay Scale Code** column and the **Salary** column, and label it *Bonus*.

8. Save the workbook to the **C:\091055Data\Modifying a Worksheet** folder as *My Employee Roster.xlsx*.

9. Close Excel.

Mastery Builder 4–1
Formatting a Worksheet

Activity Time: 15 minutes

Data File

C:\091055Data\Formatting a Worksheet\Employee Roster.xlsx

Scenario

You've built out your employee master list and have asked a colleague in the payroll department to include bonus information and a calculation of total compensation for all employees. When you get the workbook back, you realize that your colleague removed all of the number formatting you had already applied to the various columns. You realize you'll need to reapply the appropriate formatting to the columns. You'd also like to make the worksheet generally easier to read, so you decide to format some of the text, apply cell styles to some of the cells, and realign some of the data.

You've also been asked to keep track of employee bonuses, specifically the largest ones, so you decide to conditionally format the cells in the **Bonus** column to highlight the top 20 percent of all bonuses paid. In addition, you'll likely need to create similar workbooks in the future, so you decide to create a template from the workbook for future use.

---

1. Open the **Employee Roster.xlsx** workbook file.

2. Reapply the number formatting your colleague removed.
   a) Apply the **Short Date** number format to the cells below the column label in the **Start Date** column.
   b) Format the cells below the column label in the **Years with Company** column to be displayed as numbers with only two decimal places showing.
   c) Apply the **Currency** number format to all cells below the column labels in the **Bonus**, **Salary**, and **Total Compensation** columns.

3. Apply other formatting to the worksheet to make it easier to read.
   a) Center the text in column I.
   b) Increase the font size to **12** and apply bold text formatting to the employee ID values.
   c) Apply the **Heading 3** cell style to the column labels.
   d) Apply the **Input** cell style to the values in the **Bonus** and **Salary** columns.
   e) Apply the **Calculation** cell style to the values in the **Total Compensation** column.

4. Apply the **Integral** theme to the workbook.

5. Conditionally format the cells in the **Bonus** column to highlight the top 20 percent of bonuses with a green fill with dark green text.

6. Save the workbook to the **C:\091055Data\Formatting a Worksheet** folder as *My Employee Roster.xlsx* and leave the workbook open.

7. Save the workbook as a template.

   a) Delete all data from columns **A:K** except the column labels.

   b) Save the workbook to the **Custom Office Templates** folder as a template file named *My Employee Roster.xltx*

 Note: There is a copy of the template file in the **solutions** folder for this lesson as a reference. Do not save your template to this folder; save it in the default **Custom Office Templates** folder.

8. Close Excel.

Mastery Builder 5–1
Printing Workbooks

Activity Time: 10 minutes

Data File

C:\091055Data\Printing Workbooks\Employee Roster.xlsx

Before You Begin

You have a printer driver installed.

Scenario

Your supervisor has asked you for printed copies of the employee master list to hand out to participants at an upcoming management meeting. You print a test copy and realize you will have to configure the print settings and define the page layout for the worksheet so document recipients can make sense of the data. Because the workbook will be presented to senior managers, you decide to add headers and footers to give it a more polished, official appearance.

---

1. Open the **Employee Roster.xlsx** workbook file in Excel 2016.

    Note: View the print preview for the workbook before configuring the print settings and defining the page layout to get a sense of what the printed document would look like if you didn't make the adjustments.

2. Configure the print settings for the worksheet.
   a) Ensure the print job is configured to collate the worksheet pages.
   b) Change the orientation from portrait to landscape.
   c) Scale the document so that all columns print on a single page.

3. Use the **Print Titles** command to ensure that row **1** prints on every page.

4. Add custom headers and footers to the document.
   a) Create a custom header that prints the document title in the top-middle of the first page only.
   b) Create customer headers that print the current date in the top-right corner of all pages.
   c) Create custom footers that print the page number in the bottom-right corner of all pages.

5. Use page breaks to force Excel to print a relatively even amount of data on each printed page.
   a) Set the workbook view to the Page Break Preview view.
   b) Manually drag the first page break up so that it falls between rows **35** and **36**.
   c) Manually drag the second page break up so that it falls between rows **70** and **71**.

6. View the print preview.

7. If you are connected to a printer, print one copy of the document.

8. Save the workbook to the **C:\091055Data\Printing Workbooks** folder as *My Employee Roster.xlsx*.

9. Close Excel.

Mastery Builder 6–1
Managing Workbooks

Activity Time: 15 minutes

Data Files

C:\091055Data\Managing Workbooks\Sales Tracker FY2014.xlsx

C:\091055Data\Managing Workbooks\Sales Tracker FY2015.xlsx

Scenario

You're looking over the net sales totals for your company for the past fiscal year. One of your staff members prepared the workbook for you, so you are reviewing the figures to give final approval. As you review the workbook, you notice the person who prepared it neglected to apply the proper worksheet tab formatting, has left the worksheets out of order, and has included two unnecessary worksheets. You decide to format the tabs and remove the unneeded worksheets. Because you have the worksheet open, you'd like to compare the annual figures to those from last year so you can begin preparing your annual report for senior managers. Also, because the workbook will be stored on a central network share and other users will likely need the data, you decide to configure the workbook's properties to ensure other users will be able to easily search for and find the document.

---

1. Open the **Sales Tracker FY2015.xlsx** workbook file in Excel 2016.

2. Place the worksheets in sequential order by worksheet tab name.

3. Delete the **Sheet6** and **Sheet7** worksheets.

4. Rename the worksheet tabs.
   a) Change the name of worksheet **Sheet1** to *Q1*.
   b) Change the name of worksheet **Sheet2** to *Q2*.
   c) Change the name of worksheet **Sheet3** to *Q3*.
   d) Change the name of worksheet **Sheet4** to *Q4*.
   e) Change the name of worksheet **Sheet5** to *FY 2015 Totals*.

5. Apply color formatting to the worksheet tabs.
   a) Group the following sheets together: **Q1**, **Q2**, **Q3**, and **Q4**.
   b) Apply a dark-blue background color to the grouped worksheet tabs.
   c) Apply a red background color to the **FY 2015 Totals** worksheet tab.

6. Save the workbook to the **C:\091055Data\Managing Workbooks** folder as *My Sales Tracker FY2015.xlsx*.

7. Compare the net sales figures for 2014 and 2015.
   a) Open the **Sales Tracker FY2014.xlsx** workbook file.
   b) Freeze the top row of the **Q1** worksheet in both workbooks.

   c) View both workbooks side by side to verify that the first quarter sales for 2015 were better than those for 2014.

   d) View the fiscal year totals tabs for both workbooks side by side and verify that overall 2015 sales were better than 2014.

   e) Close **Sales Tracker FY2014.xlsx** without saving.

8. Add properties to the **Sales Tracker FY2015.xlsx** file.

   a) Navigate to the document's properties.

   b) Give the document a title of *Sales Tracker for Fiscal Year 2015*

   c) Give the document the following tags: **net sales**, **sales summary**, **products**, **fiscal year**, and **2015**.

   d) Set *Sales* as the document category.

9. Save the workbook and close Excel.

Glossary

absolute references
Cell or range references that do not change when users move or copy a formula from one cell to another.

active cell
The currently selected cell a user can directly put data into.

application window
The outermost element of the Excel 2016 user interface. The application window contains the commands used to develop and work with Excel workbooks, and it displays particular information about workbook files.

arguments
Elements of Excel functions that define the values and references the function will use to perform a particular calculation.

AutoCorrect
A Microsoft Office feature that automatically corrects common misspellings as users enter them.

AutoFill
An Excel feature that recognizes data patterns in worksheets and fills in additional cells based on those patterns.

Backstage view
An element of Microsoft Office application windows that is displayed when users select the **File** tab. The **Backstage** view provides users with access to file-level commands and settings.

cell
A singular object on an Excel worksheet that you can use to input, store, and manipulate data.

cell references
Alphanumeric values used to identify particular cells on an Excel worksheet. Cell references consist of a row header and a column header, which identify the cell at the intersection of the row and the column.

cell styles
Unique sets of formatting options that users can apply to cells and ranges.

color scales
A type of conditional formatting that visually compares each cell in a range of data to the rest of the cells in that range. Color scales change the color of a cell based on its relative value.

column headers
Alphabetic labels that appear along the top of an Excel worksheet and are used to differentiate individual columns.

Compatibility Checker
A Microsoft Office feature that enables users to determine which elements of application files are not compatible with previous versions of the applications.

Compatibility mode
A feature of Microsoft Office applications that allows users to open and work with

files created in previous versions of the applications.

conditional formatting
Formatting that users can apply to worksheet cells or ranges based on particular criteria.

context menus
Small, floating menu windows that appear when users right-click particular worksheet or workbook objects. Context menus provide users with quick access to commonly used commands and options related to the selected object.

contextual tabs
Specialized, temporary ribbon tabs that display commands for working with a particular type of worksheet content.

Convert option
A Microsoft Office feature that enables users to convert files created in previous versions of Office applications to the newer file types.

custom views
User-defined workbook views that are specific to a particular worksheet.

custom workbook properties
User-defined workbook properties that can help users search for workbook files based on certain conditions.

data bars
A type of conditional formatting that visually compares each cell in a range of data to the rest of the cells in that range. Data bars change in size depending on the cell's relative value.

dialog box launcher
Downward-facing arrow command button that appears in the bottom-right corner of some ribbon groups. These commands open dialog boxes that provide users with access to complete sets of commands and options related to the functionality of the particular group's commands.

fill
A type of worksheet formatting that enables users to add colors, patterns, and gradient shading to the background of a cell or a range.

Flash Fill
A feature which automatically recognizes patterns across rows as data is entered, and then copies those patterns down a column of entries.

fonts
Unique collections of alphanumeric and other characters.

footers
Small content placeholders that display additional information or images in certain Excel views and on printed pages. Footers appear along the bottom of the page.

Formula Bar
Element of the Excel user interface that enables users to enter and edit data and formulas, view cell contents, and quickly insert any of Excel's built-in formulas.

formulas
Equations that perform simple or complex mathematical computations in Excel worksheets.

functions
Built-in, pre-existing formulas users can insert into Excel worksheets.

galleries
A type of Microsoft Office application menu that displays commands and options as thumbnail previews or icons, which provide visual clues as to how the commands or options will affect a document.

headers
Small content placeholders that display additional information or images in certain Excel views and on printed pages. Headers appear along the top of the page.

hyperlinks

Links within a document that, when selected, perform a particular action, such as navigating to a different location within the document, opening another document, creating a new document, navigating to a web page, or starting an email message.

icon sets

A type of conditional formatting that visually compares each cell in a range of data to the rest of the cells in that range. Icon sets change the icon in a cell based on its relative value.

KeyTips

An alternate method of executing Excel commands other than keyboard shortcuts and user interface commands. KeyTips appear when the user presses the **Alt** key and, when active, provide the user with single keystroke actions that they can use to navigate the Excel user interface and execute commands.

Live Preview

A Microsoft Office feature that enables users to view a temporary preview of particular formatting options before applying the formatting.

Microsoft Excel Help

An Excel feature that provides users with access to information, in a variety of formats, on a number of Excel topics.

Mini toolbar

A small, floating element of the Excel user interface that appears when users right-click certain worksheet objects. The Mini toolbar provides users with quick access to commonly used commands related to the selected object.

mixed references

A cell or range reference that includes both relative and absolute references.

number formats

Formatting options that enable users to control the display of such values as currency figures, dates and times, fractions, decimal places, and negative numbers.

page breaks

Boundaries that divide worksheet pages for printing purposes only.

page margins

Invisible boundaries that define where particular content can be displayed on printed worksheets.

page orientation

A page layout setting that determines the general, overall layout of each printed page. Pages can either print in the portrait orientation, where the page is taller than it is wide, or in the landscape orientation, where the page is wider than it is tall.

Print Area

An Excel feature that allows users to select specific cells and ranges to print from workbooks.

Quick Access Toolbar

A component of the Microsoft Office user interface that, by default, is displayed above the left side of the ribbon. The Quick Access Toolbar provides users with easy access to commonly used commands.

range

A contiguous group of cells that typically contains related data.

range references

Alphanumeric values used to identify particular ranges of data in Excel worksheets. Range references consist of two cell references, separated by a colon, that represent cells at the top-left and bottom-right in the range.

reference operators

Single characters that define how Excel deals with particular cell and range references in calculations performed by formulas and functions.

region

A group of contiguous, populated cells.

relative references

Cell or range references that change when users move or copy a formula from one cell to another.

ribbon

A component of the Microsoft Office user interface that contains all of the most commonly used commands for that application. The ribbon is divided into a series of tabs that contain functionally related groups of commands.

row headers

Numeric labels that appear along the left side of an Excel worksheet and are used to differentiate individual rows.

ScreenTips

Small pop-up windows that appear when users place the mouse pointer over commands and some other elements of the Excel user interface. ScreenTips provide information such as a command's name, a description of what the command or screen element does, and the keyboard shortcut that performs the same function.

spreadsheet

A paper or an electronic document, arranged in tabular form, that is used to store, manipulate, and analyze data.

syntax

The structure necessary to properly express Excel functions and to define their arguments.

tags

Short descriptions, or keywords, that help identify the kind of content users will find within a particular file.

Tell Me

A Microsoft Office 2016 feature that allows users to type into a search box to find particular ribbon commands.

templates

A file that contains pre-configured or pre-populated workbook elements that can be used to standardize new workbooks.

themes

Collections of formatting options that users can apply to an entire workbook, as opposed to a particular cell or range.

workbook

An Excel file that serves as a container to store related Excel worksheets.

workbook properties

Individual elements of information about workbook files that help users search for and identify particular workbook files. Workbook properties can provide information such as who created a file, when a file was created or last modified, and whether or not a file has been reviewed and approved.

workbook views

Specific configurations that affect the way Excel displays an open workbook. Workbook views are meant to configure the Excel environment to be easier to work with for a number of different tasks.

workbook window

The innermost element of the Excel 2016 user interface. The workbook window displays worksheets and their data, and provides users with access to common navigation features.

worksheet

An electronic spreadsheet that is used for entering, storing, and analyzing data in Excel.

Index